Practical Greenkeeping

Practical Greenkeeping

by
Jim Arthur B.Sc. (Agric.)

An invaluable guide for enthusiasts of
traditional golf, especially those whose
concern is the care, maintenance, management
and long-term welfare of golf courses

Compiled and edited by David White

First published in 1997 by The Royal and Ancient Golf Club of St. Andrews, St. Andrews, Fife. KY16 9JD Scotland.

© Jim Arthur 1997

The right of Jim Arthur to be identified as the author of this work has been asserted by him in accordance with the Copyright, Designs and Patents Act, 1988.

All rights reserved. No part of this book may be reproduced in any form or by any means without permission in writing from the publisher. Exception is granted to those within the media who wish to quote brief excerpts in connection with a review in magazine or newspaper produced traditionally or transmitted by electronic process.

Arthur, Jim
Practical Greenkeeping
British Library CIP Data: A catalogue record for this book is available from the British Library

Edited by David White

Design by Adrian Hodgkins Design, Oxford
Typeset by White Horse Graphics, Charlbury
Reproduction by MRM Graphics, Winslow
Produced by Book Packaging and Marketing, Silverstone

Printed and bound in Singapore by Kyodo Printing Co Pte. Ltd.

ISBN 0 907583 04 0

While all reasonable care has been taken to verify facts and methods described in this book, neither the publishers nor the author can accept liability for any loss or damage howsoever caused. The opinions expressed in this book are those of the author and the contributors and their publication in this form does not imply that they are unreservedly shared by the publishers.

Preface

For many years, Jim Arthur acted as consultant agronomist to the Championship Committee of the Royal and Ancient Golf Club, ensuring that courses for each Championship were played in the best possible condition.

However, Jim Arthur has never believed in compromising long term standards for short term presentation and thinks just as much about the ordinary golf club members' needs as he does about those required for players in the Open Championship.

Invariably controversial, but infuriatingly nearly always right, Jim Arthur's knowledge about courses and greenkeeping is probably second to none. For some time now, many people have tried to persuade him to give a wider audience the benefit of his expertise by setting out his well-tried advice in writing. He has now done so.

The Royal and Ancient Golf Club are delighted to support what we regard as the definitive book on golf course agronomy and management, which we are sure will be of invaluable help to green committees and course managers for many years to come.

MICHAEL F. BONALLACK, O.B.E.
Secretary
Royal and Ancient Golf Club of St. Andrews
Fife, Scotland
December 1996

Acknowledgements

Initially my thanks are due to the Royal and Ancient Golf Club of St. Andrews, whose financial underpinning has made production of this book possible.

However, without the encouragement, tolerance and patience of two people this project would never haven taken off. Initial enthusiasm soon was tempered by frustration and exasperation with all the problems that writing a text book induces and were it not for the understanding of my long suffering wife—to whom this book is dedicated—even my renowned obstinacy might have met its match. She has had to put up with all the explosions from my study while being incarcerated in the house and cut off from the world by my monopolising the telephone for the past year. How she has put up with me I do not know, but she has had 53 years experience and our life has never been uneventful!

The other sufferer is David White, whose input has been enormous, not only in respect of his editorial expertise and with providing and collecting all the illustrations, but in turning my typing into print by computer wizardry and by his expertise in publishing. He, too, has been a real friend in providing both encouragement when needed and constructive criticism, when this was called for!

The concept of this book goes back well over 25 years, when I have been repeatedly pressed to pass on some of the advice and experience of a life-time in greenkeeping agronomic advice. Since I was advising virtually single-handed a huge number—well over 500 at the peak—of golf clubs, working seven days a week for most of the year, there was not a lot of time to stop, let alone think. Credit must thus be given to Gordon Child (BIGGA south west administrator and educationalist) who nagged at me to start this work. Little did I know what he had talked me into, but he has given me constant help and encouragement.

The Book Committee chaired by Donald Steel, with whom I have worked on new courses for nearly 30 years, included David Golding (executive director of the Greenkeepers Training Committee) and he has happily tolerated almost daily assaults on the telephone from me and has encouraged me in many ways. Donald's chapter (2) on tradition epitomises my battle of 50 years to maintain the old traditions of golf and greenkeeping, not only producing the best playing conditions but at much lower cost and with no repercussions on the environment.

Many, many others have helped, both specifically and generally, and I hope that my inability to mention them by name will not diminish the sincerity of my thanks, especially to all those who kept exhorting me to stick to it and hang on in there! However, special acknowledgement is due to those who contributed to the contents of the book.

Acknowledgements

My son Richard contributed most of the chapter (4) on soils, carried out an enormous amount of research and provided geological advice on construction topics, as well as keeping me on the straight and narrow scientifically!

Jon Allbutt wrote the chapter (15) on Health and Safety, making a dull subject not only informative but entertaining. Nobody does it quite like he does and no one sleeps when he is at the lecture rostrum.

Neil Baldwin provided the chapter (11) on fungal diseases, along with the illustrations from his own field work. His reputation as the leading UK turf grass mycologist is undisputed. His speedy responses to queries has been invaluable.

Barry Cooper has advised my clients for well over 25 years and he has never in all that time let me or them down. He is a drainage wizard and has produced remarkably effective schemes for the most difficult of situations. He richly deserves his reputation as the best drainage consultant in the country.

Many helpful insertions and indeed constructive criticisms have been made by Watermation's Bill Hawthorn and Robin Sitwell, whose electro-engineering expertise and design skills are unrivalled—they should be, because they have been at it since pop-ups first came to Britain. I have used their skills and services from the very start and much of what is now accepted best practice in irrigation originated with them.

Brian Pierson and I go back a long way, more even in terms of friendship than business. I would not like to try to count the number of courses we have built together, way into three figures over 28 years and all built to the satisfaction of everyone, not least mine! His quiet and sensible encouragement when things were going wrong and at moments of extreme exasperation has probably prolonged my life. He is unquestionably the most experienced golf constructor in Europe and, like some of us, has seen it all before by having been there, done it, and worn the tee shirt!

My thanks are given to all the host of friends in the greenkeeping profession (and I use the term advisedly) who have contributed in so many ways, not just with photographs and opinions but by their encouragement. Perhaps the one thing that has distinguished this past decade in golf greenkeeping is the enormous strides made in education and the far better appreciation afforded to those looking after our courses, as well as better training for the young input—to which state of affairs full credit must go to David Golding. I have tried to return a little of what I owe to golf by being involved in this work and hope that this book will help. At least, in the words of some of my friends, they can understand what I mean and welcome the freedom from excessive technicalities—if you like, no techno-babble. We do not need it in a profession which is essentially an uncomplicated one based on common sense.

Jim Arthur, Budleigh Salterton, 1997

Picture Credits

The USGA Green Section Record—for reproduction of line drawings, etc.

Donald Steel—for the photograph of greenkeepers' scything at St. Andrews.

Watermation Sprinkler and Controls Ltd—for illustrations and photographs of irrigation parts and good practices.

Charterhouse Turf Machinery Ltd—for photographs of Verti-Drain model 7316.

The William Grandison Golf Gallery—for the glorious water-colour painting of Turnberry, used to illustrate the jacket cover.

Ransomes—for unlimited access to rare pictures from their photo library, and to Bob Rendle for his exceptional patience.

Michael Bird—for guidance and access to photographic sources.

Richard Arthur—for photographs used in his chapter on soils.

Neil Baldwin—for photographs used in his chapter on fungal diseases.

Sisis Limited—for unlimited access to their historic archives.

Walter Woods—for photographs of St. Andrews.

Lloyds & Co.—for the Paladin photograph.

Huxleys Limited—for the Huxtrux with topdresser model HX 10.

Hardi Limited—for state-of-the-art boom spraying machinery.

The Chart Hills Golf Club.

Danny Godfrey—for healthy roots illustration.

Barry Cooper—for access to his father's line drawings, plus many photographs.

Barenbrug U.K. Limited—for Barcrown fescue photographs.

Brian Pierson—for access to his splendid photo library.

Betty Hunt, publisher of *"On the Green,"*—for access to the photograph of Long Bay Club, Myrtle Beach, South Carolina.

Arne van Amerongen—for construction photographs.

M.A.F.F. York—for photographs used in the chapter Control of Pests.

To press officers and P.R.O's, too numerous to mention individually, who have contributed in their inimitable way.

Some of the more ancient photographs have been reproduced from scrap albums and cuttings and it has not always been possible to trace their source. Apologies then to anyone who, for that reason, is not included in this list. While every effort has been made to trace copyright holders, this has proved impossible in some cases. Owners of copyright are invited to contact the publishers. Other photographs and illustrations used are from the picture library of the editor, David White.

A NOTE ABOUT TRADE NAMES

Many of the terms used for the practices performed by certain types of machinery—or indeed the machines themselves—have become common in language and generic in title, even though makers distinguish and claim their products with trademarks. Throughout, where such designations appear and where author or editor are aware of a trademark, the designations are given full and proper title. It is, however, inevitable—like the ubiquitous and always abbreviated Frigidaire and old Mr Hoover's suction box—that some will have become part of the colloquial tongue peculiar to greenkeeping.

Contents

Chapter One: Introduction — 10

Chapter Two: Advancing the tradition of golf course architecture — 22

Chapter Three: Basic principles of greenkeeping — 34

Chapter Four: Soils and the golf course — 48

Chapter Five: Fertilisers and lime — 62

Chapter Six: Top dressing — 76

Chapter Seven: Aeration — 89

Chapter Eight: Mowing — 110

Chapter Nine: Irrigation — 124

Chapter Ten: Turf grasses — 142

Chapter Eleven: Turf grass diseases and the golf course — 159

Chapter Twelve: Control of pests — 177

Chapter Thirteen: Drainage — 189

Chapter Fourteen: Golf course construction — 200

Chapter Fifteen: Health and Safety in golf course management — 226

Chapter Sixteen: Golf course conservation — 241

Chapter Seventeen: All life goes in circles . . . — 261

Bibliography and further reading — 265

Index — 267

Chapter One
. . . . .
INTRODUCTION

Debate about the early days of golf must always be inconclusive, in the absence of any written evidence until 1457, but is both interesting and relevant, primarily because of the influence of natural golfing country on the evolution of the game.

Although the edict—the Black Act, of James II of Scotland, 1457—specifically banning golfe as it interfered with national service, to wit, archery

Variations of the Dutch game of kolve or kolven.

INTRODUCTION

On the ground again—an ancient teeing ground, circa 17th century.

practice, was the first written reference to the name of the game, clearly variations of a game based on hitting a small wooden ball with a club-shaped stick existed in the 13th century on a far wider scale than has been supposed. In the Netherlands het Kolven (Colf) was played, not solely on ice, but along roads, with holes of 1000–1500 m, the long game. It finally vanished in 1700, as much as anything because of the resultant damage to property, especially windows. There was also a quite different short game, Kolf, played on courts about 25 m long. Today, it is still played in the Netherlands on standard courts of 17.5 m.

Colf was played in the Netherlands, certainly from c.1300, possibly even at the end of the 13th century. A similar ball and club game existed in England. Fute-ball, club-ball, (like hockey) and cambuc, most closely related to golf, were all three banned by Edward III in an edict to English county shires in

June 1363, again due to them interfering with national service. There is also a stained glass window in Gloucester Cathedral dating from c.1350 depicting what is clearly an early golfer at the top of his swing.

Equally, in northern Germany there was a similar game called Kolbe. Even in America, when New York was New Amsterdam, Colf was banned in 1659 because of damage to property.

The debt that we owe to the Netherlands is, however, indisputable. Golf evolved on parallel lines along the east coast of Scotland, from Dornoch to Musselburgh, as a direct result of the impact of the very considerable trade across the North Sea with the Dutch. There were, of course, some inland courses, Perth for example, the royal seat of the Stuart kings of Scotland, but golf did not reach the west of Scotland until the 1850s.

As a result of the enthusiasm for the game, there was a simply enormous trade in wooden golf balls, a few Dutch villages living almost solely on the making of balls, first of wood and then of leather stuffed with cow hair. One sale alone was for 40,000 balls in the year 1500. Many barrels of golf balls were sold to Scotland but there was, however, a reciprocal trade in wooden clubs from Scotland in the 1650s, back to the Netherlands and France.

Colf was an autumn to spring game played not solely on ice, but feasible only where or when grass was short. For the same reason, golf was initially a winter game in Scotland. However, it was made possible over a longer season because of the existence of links; that very fine, wiry, slow growing turf found naturally on narrow strips of land linking the dunes with the more fertile soil inland. At least one could find the ball, even if putting surfaces left something to be desired by today's standards.

Golf evolved from the old ball and club games, widespread, though played in different ways in many European countries, to something approaching the traditional Scottish game, primarily because the short, wiry turf of links

Dating from the mid-14th century, this stained glass panel found in Gloucester Cathedral represents the earliest evidence that golf (or something closely akin to it), was being played in England at that time.

From a 16th century Flemish Book of Hours. A significant and historic picture; depicting the game being played on the ground, not on ice.

Introduction

Early links courses were created from wild though natural country, as this land adjacent to Royal Birkdale illustrates.

land grazed by sheep and rabbits in summer, provided a suitable surface on which to play an all-year-round sport. We can argue for ever on which came first; naturally occurring suitable playing conditions which permitted the evolution of the game, or the game seeking suitable playing conditions found naturally largely along the eastern seaboard of Scotland.

KINGS AND COMMONERS ALIKE

On such links land, it was a game played in Scotland by all, irrespective of class. Indeed it was as popular with the monarchy as it was with its subjects. Every reigning monarch from 1502 to 1688 played golf, two kings and one queen of Scotland and the four Stuart kings of the United Kingdom. The line was broken with the end of the Stuarts; William of Orange's "wee German Lairdies" soon putting a stop to golf south of the border.

It was, in fact, two centuries before golf became popular again in England and, for years there were more golf courses in the east of Scotland than in the whole of the rest of the United Kingdom.

Assessing the number of golf courses in Britain has always been fraught with problems. For one thing, there is always the confusion caused by so many golf clubs playing on the same course, akin to today's golfing societies. This situation still occurs, notably on municipal courses in Scotland. There is also a distinct lack of records, and, even if one takes the published

Golf balls through the ages—from feathery through gutta-percha to rubber core.

establishment dates of the senior clubs, there may well have been others, perhaps based on artisan membership playing over primitive courses, long before the official start of many of the older clubs. In fact, golf was played on many famous courses long before they had become officially established.

Early records indicate that, in 1857, there were only 17 courses in Scotland, but by 1888 there were 73, though only 57 in England, a mere six in Ireland and only two in Wales. Most, if not all, of these courses outside Scotland were started by Scottish garrison troops or expatriate Scottish professional men. Even that cradle of English golf, the oldest links course in England, Royal North Devon Golf Club at Westward Ho! which officially opened in 1864 (though golf was played on the Northam Burrows before that date), owed much to the support and advice given to its founder, the Revd. J. H. Gossett, by a visitor from St. Andrews, General Moncrieff. Even earlier, (Royal) Blackheath, dating from 1603, owed its existence to an insatiable demand from the largely Scottish Royal Court of King James the I and VI for a golf course.

Introduction

A boom in golf followed in the 1890s. It is interesting, if inconclusive, to speculate whether the demand, from especially English urban centres of population, stimulated the building of courses, often, but not always, in rather unsuitable environments, or whether the increased possibilities for preparing turf to a golfing standard made inland golf possible.

This phenomenal increase in the demand for new courses to meet the undoubted needs of urban golfers—especially in England—unquestionably stimulated the wider use of and improvements to reel-type mowers. These had been invented more than 50 years earlier, even if used only in rare instances, largely in maintaining the lawns of stately homes. Because it was possible now to mow grass and thus produce tolerable playing surfaces in less than ideal golfing country, the enormous expansion in golf course establishment was made possible.

We may speculate on other underlying reasons for this expansion in response to an undisputed demand and, possibly, never find the answer. Certainly, with the Open Championship coming south for the first time in 1894, to Sandwich (Royal St. George's) and then over the next two decades the Open being played over the Sandwich, Hoylake and Deal links no less than eight out of twenty years, there was no doubt about the interest.

Westward Ho! circa 1900. Nothing much has changed in over 90 years; indeed since its formation in 1864 the club has remained loyal to tradition.

PRACTICAL GREENKEEPING

THE FIRST GOLF BOOM

Whatever the reason, there was certainly a boom. From only 57 English courses in 1888, by 1890 there were 90 and by 1894 the total had doubled to 182, with a dramatic extension to no less than 655 by 1914. This means that no less than 473 new courses were built in England in those two decades alone, an average of nearly 25 a year. Similar expansion took place in Scotland with 223 new courses built between 1890 and 1909. Most of these clubs are still in existence, though not all are still playing on their original courses.

This expansion has never been equalled since. The boom of the 1980s

Sunningdale circa 1910. Note the extremely open outlook, with clear sight to the clubhouse, far right.

Sunningdale some 85 years later. Note in particular the encroaching trees, many of which are coniferous.

16

Introduction

may have seen many new courses started, but the actual establishment in England measured in terms of clubs affiliated to the E.G.U. is revealing. The increase from 1980 to 1990 was only from 1254 to 1371 clubs, and, in three successive years (1986–88), only one new club became a member of the E.G.U. each year. Bearing in mind the number of ventures planned, and indeed started, the deduction is that many failed even to complete construction and many others failed after starting.

The first pre-1914 major expansion resulted in many courses being built on unsuitable, poorly drained, heavy land with unsophisticated green construction, but this was of less significance than 60 years on, because golf, in those days, was largely a summer game in England, hence Bernard Darwin's comment that "no gentleman played golf before the first of May," but then he said that golf "was a game played by a few gentlemen and most Scotsmen."

The second boom, around the 1960s to 1970s, was based on urban courses being sold for development and the proceeds being used to build new courses in better environments. The third, between the 1980s and 1990s, was in response to a totally wrong belief that fortunes could be made by building courses round stately homes, or by moving half the countryside from A to B, based on charging golfers small fortunes to play golf. Most failed.

In these second and third big booms many courses were built to poor specifications and often with poor construction principles and materials. It was not that the correct fool-proof methods, with suspended water table green construction, were not being implemented by a few knowledgeable architects, but that the opportunity attracted a host of designers and constructors who did not know, or worse still did not know where to find, the facts, and many disasters followed; inflated and unjustified costs precipitating financial collapse. The problem was aggravated by the demand for improved all-year-round good playing conditions, enforced by the need to keep golfers on the course for as near 365 days a year as possible, if only to pay for the inflated costs of course construction and the extravagant provision of all the other facilities demanded by today's golfers.

It is a far cry from the days when all that golfers asked for was the provision of a level stance on the tee and good putting surfaces, playing the ball where it lay in between.

If courses have increased in numbers phenomenally, then golfers themselves have multiplied even more and the result is a huge pressure on greenkeeping staff to keep courses well presented and eminently playable, all-year-round. This, in turn, has stimulated enormous improvements in techniques, machinery, equipment and materials, if only to get the increased work load implemented, to keep ahead of play, not just to minimise interference to golfers, but simply to get the work done at all. It is, however,

PRACTICAL GREENKEEPING

important to note that the principles of sound golf course management have never changed in well over a century.

This, however interesting, is relevant only as background to this book, in which we are much more concerned with the evolution of golf courses rather than golf clubs, both in regard to their environment and ecology, as well as their management.

This brings us, briefly, to the question of the men behind the management. As we have seen, such management did not really become positive until it became possible to mow grass mechanically, as opposed to merely passively accepting conditions created by grazing animals, be they sheep or rabbits. Not until the mower became a feasible way of imposing the golfers' ideas of playing conditions on the turf, which today still is the most important factor in the game, was it possible to build and maintain courses away from naturally occurring fine turf areas, dominated then, as now, by the two main turf-

Willie Park, Jnr. Perhaps the first true golf course architect.

18

Introduction

forming grasses, namely fine fescues and bents, *Agrostis* spp., which produce natural good golfing conditions.

One notes, with some amusement and a sense of *déjà vu*, that the pundits of those pre-1914 days complained that, "since all greens were now uniformly like billiard tables with the use of the mowing machine, the skills needed to deal with a variety of different putting surfaces were no longer needed, making the game much easier and less of a challenge."

The earliest golf course architects were, generally, leading amateurs, or the best golf professionals. Old Willie Dunn laid out the London Scottish course in 1865 while he was a greenkeeper at Royal Blackheath. Even in those days there was a thriving export business in golf greenkeepers from Scotland. While it is perhaps invidious to single out one man, especially as course design is not the main concern of this book on managing courses, perhaps Willie Park, Jnr deserves the title of the first true golf course architect. He was a man of education and ambition, far more intelligent than the earlier type of golf professionals, who had risen from the ranks of caddies.

Willie was Open Champion in 1887 and 1889, but, more specifically, he was the first to decry the old method of designing courses by siting greens on "good looking" sites, often unrelated to the overall layout. He developed, if not invented, the concept of strategic, as opposed to penal, design, which obliged anyone with ambitions on winning to think out his tee shots with the view of placing his drives and second shots in positions from whence there was the best entrance to the green.

Certainly, this is not our concern, save only in its influence on course construction, but it is worth noting that one of Willie Park, Jnr's most famous memorials is the Old Course at Sunningdale, laid out in 1900. It seems extraordinary that, in those days when mechanisation meant the use of horse-drawn earth scoops and everything was done by hand compared with today, with massive investment in earth-moving equipment to ensure speedy construction, it took only a year for the course, which was seeded throughout, to be ready for play. Prior to its design and construction, there was universal criticism with experts jeering at the folly of imagining that grass could be made to grow on such sour thin heathland, but it is totally credible that a year later, those self-same critics were saying that any fool could lay out such a good course on such natural golfing country. Nothing changes!

THE EARLY GREENKEEPERS

More important than designers, in some eyes anyway, were the maintainers. The first record of the term greenkeeper that can be discovered was in 1888 when Willie Fernie was appointed at Troon (now Royal Troon) Golf Club "as greenkeeper, clubmaster and professional," in that order. In earlier years

Practical Greenkeeping

Introduction

courses were looked after by staff employed on general duties, which included "calling the members to dinner and changing the holes," again in this order, as with the Edinburgh Burgess' Society in 1774.

It is remarkable that early greenkeepers, often barely literate but who knew and loved their courses with an instinctive feeling for correct management, without the benefit of research, advice, precept or communication, could follow such very sound practices, but of course there were fewer siren voices—from wrongly motivated farmers to those selling the wrong materials—to divert them from practices which they knew gave the best golfing conditions. In those days too, the malign influence of the constantly changing green committee, well meaning but, sadly, so often wrong, had not started to dominate course management, but that is another story.

These old greenkeepers followed the soundest of all precepts, correct observations on which to base correct deductions. They used their courses as their own research stations and formulated treatments as sound today as they were a century or more ago. These treatments and basic principles may profitably be explored in more detail in chapter three.

Old Tom Morris. Four times the Open Champion. He is held also to be have been the first "Keeper of the Green".

Chapter Two
·····
ADVANCING THE TRADITION OF GOLF COURSE ARCHITECTURE

Transcribed from an address given in 1996 by architect Donald Steel, to members of the British Institute of Golf Course Architects.

Simple methods in the 1920s—the building of a green at the Berkshire Golf Club.

It is clearly initially important, in discussing tradition in golf course architecture, that we define what this means. This in itself is fraught with problems, if only because every golfer has his own ideas and standards—

The scoop at work. Without mechanisation, the architect was bound to work only with those contours which nature provided.

and they are nearly all different. We therefore must be clear from the start or else we shall not know whether we remain on the right track or whether we have erred and strayed from our ways like lost sheep.

Let me tell you the tradition which I think we should be advancing and you can see if it tallies with your version of events. I do not refer to the traditions started by the founding fathers of the Institute, if indeed one can build a tradition in 25 years. Rather it is the tradition forged by those men who influenced our founding fathers, celebrated architects like Harry Colt, Tom Simpson, Alister Mackenzie, Donald Ross, Hugh Alison, James Braid, Herbert Fowler, Fred Hawtree's father, Mackenzie Ross and A. W. Tillinghast.

Tillinghast represents the first great American-born architect, but America has tended to veer away from what I regard as the traditional style of golf course architecture, whose virtues Tillinghast extolled. I make an unashamed plea for the traditional style in general, and for British and Irish golf courses in particular, although much of the latter refers to most of northern Europe as well.

What happens in other parts of the world is, to a large extent, irrelevant. Britain gave golf and golf course architecture to the world and we have a duty to continue promoting and preserving the principles that make our courses the best, most varied and most enjoyable to play.

What then are these special characteristics of British golf? I pose the question because, without some sort of definition, we cannot judge ourselves fairly, while certainly the majority of golfers have an unhappy knack of applying the wrong interpretation.

The best of British golf is represented by links, heathland, moorland and downland courses, courses typified by their open and often exposed character, their firm, fast putting surfaces and wiry grasses, their firm and playable approaches and their style of bunkering. They represent the strategic, as opposed to penal, school of architecture; courses where the wind is the most effective hazard, where the bump and run approach shot is often the smart option.

They are generally quite simple courses which work entirely with the existing landform. Some of the best examples are those built before major earth movement was the fashion. They are invariably in wild settings, not courses manicured wall-to-wall, although the parkland landscapes, reflected by many of our other courses, act as a more orderly, sheltered contrast.

There is one other fundamental point upon which we should agree, and this concerns our interpretation of the good golf course, which must be the ambition of all of us. There are many definitions, but my favourite is that of Bobby Jones who, dare I say it, appreciated and loved our links courses best, for all his creation of the Augusta National, which was an architectural watershed.

Jones maintained that "the purpose of any golf course should be to give pleasure to the greatest number of golfers, offering problems a man or woman can attempt according to his or her ability. It will never become hopeless for the duffer, nor fail to challenge and interest the expert; and, like the Old

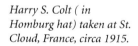

Harry S. Colt (in Homburg hat) taken at St. Cloud, France, circa 1915.

course at St. Andrews, it will become more delightful the more it is studied and played. A good course should attract players to play it again and again." Harry Colt put it a different way. He asked the pertinent question, WILL IT LIVE?

Jones's assessment is as true today as it was 65 years ago, but it is not always observed. The Americans swear allegiance to Donald Ross and Alister Mackenzie, their architectural patron saints, but it is not always reflected in their work. Many other foreign architects are at pains to state the influence which British links have on their thinking and design, but it is hard nowadays to see such influence translated in real life.

In the first line of Alister Mackenzie's book, *Golf Architecture*, he wrote "Economy in course construction consists in obtaining the best possible results at the minimum of cost." Well, you could have fooled me. I know course building is inevitably expensive in some parts of the world, but it is not as expensive as it often proves to be. I wonder how many of the recent courses in Britain, those costing many millions to build, have met their financial targets? Most have hardly been drowned by a flood of members, but British golf has always been accessible to every pocket and that has only been achieved by building sound, sensibly priced courses. Value for money should still be the operative watchword.

The Carnegie course at Skibo Castle. A modern classic design embracing the best use of natural terrain, with minimal earth moving.

Surely, one of the main reasons for building new courses is to allow more people to take up the game. We, in Britain, have long been spoiled by the variety and excellence of our courses. We do not seek five-star clubhouses. Those who have deemed otherwise seem to me to have misread the market.

There may be a demand for one or two multi-million pound ventures in Britain, but the more urgent need is for courses that everyone can play. The obsession for championship courses is horribly overdone. Of course, we make our courses as good as we possibly can. It is natural to be pleased if one is chosen for a championship event, and a number have been, but the best championship courses can be played and enjoyed by all and need not cost any more than those with more modest pretensions. It is a ridiculous notion that the more courses cost, the better they must be.

No new course in Britain is going to house the Open or Amateur championship, and the European Tour now plays only a small quota of events in Britain, several of which have permanent or semi-permanent homes. So what championships are all these so-called championship courses going to host? We are all well aware of publicity-seeking developers making claims to have a championship course, but it can only be so described if it has actually staged a championship.

Golf course design has inevitably changed, more in other parts of the world than here. It has been changed by the advent of the bulldozer and by architects who, in consequence, feel obliged to move hundreds of thousands of tons of dirt in order to achieve their expensive aims. Such methods have become the rule rather than the exception .

WORK WITH THE LAND YOU ARE GIVEN

Even if presented with the Garden of Eden, some architects never accept what they find. They are not happy until they have taken the land apart and put it back together in a different form. For what purpose? If courses cost 20 million pounds to build, then subscriptions, entry fees and green fees must of necessity be expressed in thousands and hundreds of pounds. That may be a fruitful formula in other countries, but it is not the recipe that has made the game as accessible to everyone as it is in, say, Scotland.

However, do not get me wrong, for I am not living in the past. Some wonderful modern courses have been built where large scale earth-moving has been the only option, and I enjoy playing these types of course from time to time. There are also occasions when dull or bad land can only be transformed by the bulldozer but, when it becomes a question of imposing a style regardless of the landscape and cost, that seems to me to be professionally indefensible. This form of architecture is the easiest, provided you have a bottomless pit of money. You can do what you like, but it breeds

The Long Bay Club in South Carolina— an exceptional modern design that required considerable earth moving.

a style which tends to make all courses look broadly the same. What is far harder, though infinitely more rewarding, is the production of a masterpiece from limited resources.

In this regard, it is heartening to learn that Ben Crenshaw has recently built a course in, I believe, Nebraska, for something just over half a million dollars, working entirely with what he was given. From all accounts, it is pretty good, but then Ben is a traditionalist who admires what we hold dear.

Another quote now, one I regard as important because it strikes a definite chord with me, but the source may surprise you. "Nature must precede the architect in laying out the course. The site of a golf course must be there, not be brought there. In this way, it will have its own character, distinct from any other course in the world." The author was an American, though admittedly, of Scottish descent. His name was Perry Maxwell, who died in 1952.

Maxwell's words are the antithesis of those proclaiming that reshaping the land is the only way. I must admit that, even today, working with nature involves some machine work to produce ideal results, but blending the course with the landscape and using the land form is more likely to please the environmentalists, while providing the habitats for flora and fauna which we all want to see. Not the least important aspect of golf courses is their aesthetic side and the haven for wild life that they can so easily provide.

The 12th hole at Rye— from a water-colour by J. M. Heathcote, 1899.

In sympathy with Maxwell's sentiments are those I found in the recently published lost commentaries of Donald Ross, *Golf Has Never Failed Me*, a book well worth acquiring. Ross contended, "the distinct charm of British golf courses lies in their environment and natural attractions. In the first particular, they possess something we in America cannot hope to rival: a certain sense of fitness, which harmonises with the ancient, Scottish game. From the latter, however, we can certainly learn much by making our courses less artificial, for the fascination of the most famous hazards in the world lies in the fact that they were not and could not have been constructed."

However, one other great attraction and advantage of what is called the British type of golf course is the variety of shots it allows. Bounce and run are vital dimensions of the traditional game. Not for us the computerised, automatic, stereotyped shotmaking called for elsewhere; with everything predictable and fair. Judgement, improvisation and vision are greater indicators of skill, and whatever happened to the phrase, rub of the green?

In his foreword to a book I wrote on links courses, Peter Thomson, who played them as expertly as anyone in history, wrote, "The thrill of squeezing a ball against the firm turf, trying to keep it low into a buffeting wind, is something that lingers in the mind forever. It reminds me that a great deal of golf is played along the ground, or at least it should be. Classic golf provides this. There is a lot of chipping and long putting to do. Approaches can be made with straight-faced irons, running the ball up little banks and through shallow hollows. It is an important part of the game, alas, little understood and appreciated, and now, in modern design, virtually ignored."

Therein lies our heritage. So what's to be done and where are our friends?

Tom Lehman, our worthy Open champion, said that he liked links courses because one needed to be more imaginative and inventive in order to flourish. What a compliment, and what an indictment of other types of course if the converse is true—that they require you to be unimaginative. When the US Open returned in 1986 to Shinnecock Hills, one of the oldest clubs and courses in America, there was a wave of enthusiasm for the change of diet, so to speak.

Lee Trevino saw the greatness of Shinnecock in the fact that it favoured nobody in particular. In his words, "you could go high, low, hook, fade, do what you want." Others expressed surprise that all the par 4 greens were open in front of the green. Of course, one of the principal reasons why courses have changed in America is the irrigation of fairways. In many parts of the world, irrigation is essential, while in hot climates it is simply a question of no irrigation, no golf course.

That is accepted, but in Britain there is a real danger that heavy-handed fairway irrigation will alter the character of the terrain and certainly limit the variety of shots you can play. I was intrigued a few months ago when the final round of a major tournament was played on an expensive modern course in gale force winds. Conditions cried out for the ball to be kept low but, with watered fairways and the fronts of some greens guarded heavily, that was virtually impossible.

I am sure you are all facing questions about the introduction of fairway irrigation, always assuming there is sufficient water available to make discussion worthwhile. I admit that dousing the fire of some fairways in high summer is not to be despised, but everyone must be aware of the dangers of overdoing fairway watering. Beautifully lush is a description that grates.

Colour is no measurement of quality, nor is heavy irrigation conducive to preserving traditional conditions or providing the salvation that many believe it does.

By eliminating the bounce and run, fairway watering can make courses play twice as long and that is not exactly a commendation for the average player. I noted with interest the recent comments of Bob Taylor, the S.T.R.I. ecologist, who wrote, "Heathlands, by their very nature, are held in a very sensitive balance; the grasses and plants are able to survive due to the very stressed nature of the environment and concomitant lack of competitive species. Irrigation can very quickly tip the balance."

Jim Arthur observes that, "if drought really did kill grass, most of southern England would be desert," but irrigation can also distort and destroy the strategic elements of the way in which architects intended a hole to play, as, indeed, can the over-watering of greens to pander to the poorer players. So, we architects need the help of greenkeepers and tournament committees to present our courses in the traditional manner. We must get away from the obsession, for instance, that tournament courses need rough like hayfields alongside fairways and around fringes of greens in order to bolster their defences.

If such conditions around greens were to become standard, the true art of chipping would become extinct. When hacking at a ball ten yards from the flag becomes more luck than judgement, one might wonder if the world hasn't gone crazy. Artful, modern green design is a more valid and valuable weapon in punishing error and rewarding good positional play than abnormal growth of rough. It also helps blunt the emphasis on power.

Speaking of which, we need help from the lawmakers in exerting tighter control on the manufacture of clubs and balls and I should like to think that the lawmakers would learn from closer consultation with architects on this vexed subject. The lawmakers must give a stronger lead, by shaping events rather than merely being carried along by them. I am going to give you another quote and, this time, ask you to guess the date it was said or written: "The game has been waging a battle against the inventor. The one aim of the inventor is to minimise the skill required for the game."

Those of you who identified John Low, in 1905, may take a bow, but the statement might have been written in 1935 or 1995. Nothing is new. We are forced to have to use our stealth and ingenuity to outwit and outfox the modern golfer without resorting to gimmickry, building replicas, or indulging in what I call preventative architecture. There is a very fine dividing line between what is challenging and fair and what is impossible, but that is where our skill and judgement come in.

Nevertheless, nothing seems to be done to control the manufacture of clubs and balls except more and more tolerance of the same problem. It might be possible to build new courses of 8,000 yards on 200 acres on some sites, although heaven forbid, but what about clubs which seek our help, existing in urban surroundings on 90 acres with not a hope of stretching their courses by another inch? Are they spared a thought by the lawmakers? Their welfare is just as relevant.

Gerald Micklem, the wisest of golfing administrators, once said that he thought the Royal and Ancient and the USGA made a mistake back in the 1930s in not limiting the width of the sole on iron clubs. It is no use crying over spilt milk, but think what a different game golf, and architecture, would be if a 9 iron or an old niblick were the most lofted club in our bags.

By allowing unlimited width of the sole, clubs have become laid back and lofted to the point where miraculous recoveries with a battery of wedges are commonplace. Had such freedom been curbed, golf courses would look very different. Golf has become very much a question of aerial bombardment,

Advancing the Tradition of Golf Course Architecture

with the modern golfer playing for the pin rather than just for the green, often seeking out landing areas no bigger than a tablecloth.

The game and the equipment have changed our courses dramatically and courses must adjust where they can, but to illustrate that nothing is new, I ask you to consider the two cartoons reproduced from Martin Sutton's *Book of the Links* published in 1912. Let me emphasise the date they appeared and ask you to consider especially the captions.

Chart Hills, Kent—The handicap golfer might view with some trepidation this design by Nick Faldo, though paying the price for inaccuracies is perhaps his intention.

"*the constant expense of re-arranging bunkers, necessitated by the ever increasing length of the modern golf ball, is causing something approaching anxiety to our green architects and secretaries. We can only see one way out of it. Have the bunkers on wheels. They can then be adjusted to the requirements of the latest balls, and with a little sand thrown around the base, are ready for use.*"

First player : "Did you hit yours well, old chap?"

Second player : "Not very, I cut it a bit; but I think it's on the green !"

"*the steadily increasing length derived from the continued improvements in the modern golf ball has already caused dismay to the designers of golf links, but when the length is enormously augmented by the baked state of the ground in hot summer, drastic reform in links architecture will be imperative.*"

They are, I think, both alarmingly prophetic. Sobering also, but it would be funny if the predictions weren't so accurate and the problem weren't so serious. You might well ask how the captions might be revised if we were putting the clock forward today by eighty years? The answer is, I don't know.

So, like the preacher, I return to my text, but it is a vital text if British golf courses are to retain their traditional values and not be hijacked. We architects have many responsibilities; to make the best of the land within the budget given to us; to realise that courses are as permanent in our landscapes or skylines as cathedrals. To blend our courses as naturally as possible into the landscape and to make our courses havens for wild life. That becomes more important, not less.

But, as I have mentioned, our greatest task is to provide challenge, fun and enjoyment for all golfers. Professional golf receives a prominence out of all proportion to its importance. We have heard a lot of bleating this year from the European Tour players about having courses set up in a way worthy of them, although there is a wide difference of opinion about how it should be done.

What we must remember is that shorter courses are far more suitable for the vast majority. Losing ten balls in a round, in lakes or deep rough, is hardly fun. We must encourage clubs to manage their courses vigorously and not allow habitats to be lost or altered by lack of management or the wrong management. We must build as much variety as possible into our layouts, because variety amongst 18 holes is as desirable as it is in a musical symphony or a box of chocolates.

However, nothing achieves this combination of virtues better than the traditional British course. It really doesn't matter what other people do in other countries, although there's nothing to stop us accepting lucrative commissions overseas to build a 30 million dollar extravaganza when it is the right and obvious way of tackling things. We can tackle these projects as well as the next man. It is quite wrong to believe that they are the prerogative of overseas architects, but our motto should be that British golf is for the people at a price the people can afford. I believe this applies to most parts of northern Europe as well.

Let Peter Thomson have the last word. "Our classic courses are treasures, sanctuaries of sanity, but, like any other items of long term value, they are under attack. It is our proud golfing heritage that is threatened. Such courses need to be preserved, like our historic buildings, for their aesthetic beauty and grand value; our new British courses must be forged on similar lines. If they are not, and we are guilty of slavishly following the fashions of others, the very essence of what we know and love about the game of golf will have been lost—perhaps forever."

Chapter Three

BASIC PRINCIPLES OF GREENKEEPING

The caddies of olden times, often young boys, would carry clubs without benefit of golf bags.

The course managers and agronomists of today should pay silent homage to that band of founding fathers of positive golf greenkeeping, who managed the relatively few golf courses, nearly all in Scotland, well over a century ago. The term—positive greenkeeping—relates to the change-over to the mowing machine from the grazing animal; rabbits, sheep and worse, which made it

Later, when bags were introduced, some caddies were called upon to tote two bags, one on each shoulder.

possible for the greenkeeper to control his environment, within reason, rather than react to the changes brought about by factors outside his control, not the least of these being the weather. At least, even with the primitive, heavy and clumsy, reel-type mowers of the day, one could produce playable surfaces even in periods of lush growth, when the resultant grass crop often defeated the four-legged mowers of the previous four centuries.

Those old greenkeepers were remarkable men. Many, though not quite all, graduated from being caddies and had only limited formal education. Their only contact with their peers was through golfing matches. In fact it was not all that long ago that greenkeeper associations were primarily just golfing societies. Those days have inevitably gone. With so much emphasis on education, rapid and inevitable change and steeply rising standards of presentation, no greenkeeper could survive on the basis of his own experiences alone. He needs to discuss common problems and consult not only with his peers, some of whom may have had those same problems and cured them, but also with specialists.

However, a century and more ago, almost the only contact with their fellow greenkeepers was at the time of rival competitions between district associations, such as those between Fife and the Lothians, or by friendly visits to neighbouring clubs. I doubt very much if secrets were shared on a wide basis and history does not relate about any greenkeeping education in those days, but there was enough common ground in the management of those few links, prior to the first golf boom, to suspect that there must have been some interchange of ideas and practices.

It is fascinating to consider how these relatively uneducated men, recruited from caddies who left school, if they ever attended one, before some, at least, could read or write, managed their courses on scientifically correct lines. Of courses their methods were different, but the principles on which they based their programmes have not altered in more than a century and are as true today as they were then.

How did they do it? The answer must lie in the fact that they were keen observers and also knew what they wanted, because they were, to a man, golfers. Indeed, many doubled as their club's professional. Correct observation is the first rule of natural science. The second is correct deduction. One is reminded of the young medical student who had been told by his tutor that if he were to make a good doctor he had to learn to observe the human race. He found himself, strictly of course in the line of medical training, at a nude review. He correctly observed that the first few rows were occupied by bald-headed old men. Less accurately he deduced that watching nudes induces baldness!

These observant stalwarts watched their turf. They saw for example that rabbit scalds, recovering from the initial scorch, showed lush stimulated growth, but of the wrong grass, especially annual meadow grass. Since they and their members wanted fine, wiry, fast-running turf, they concluded rightly that feeding was not the answer. Furthermore, they knew that if they fed, the resultant growth could easily get away from them, reliant as they were on hand-pushed mowers. Even in relatively recent times on a course that I helped to build just after the war, the links were looked after by one man who cut 18 greens with a hand-pushed machine. There was no way he has going to over-feed his greens, thus making a rod for his own back. All they got for years was a light ammonia, blood, hoof and horn and iron dressing once in spring.

The age-old greenkeeping adage "ask a farmer what to do and go and do exactly the opposite," was old-established 70 years ago. Certainly the sentiments are paraphrased at the end of the last century and must have originated in the reaction of long-suffering greenkeepers to the well-intentioned but wildly wrong pressures exerted by farmers on early management structures, even before green committees came into vogue.

Those early keepers of the green—the course as opposed to the house—were not called greenkeepers. Indeed in earlier times their tending of the turf took second place to other miscellaneous duties, more akin to a butler cum general factotum. It should be remembered that, in those days, golf clubs were really dining clubs with golf as an ancillary activity, hence the elaborate and formal uniforms of those days. Some clubs even had quite distinctly different uniforms for playing golf and for dining afterwards. The

Basic Principles of Greenkeeping

first recording of the term greenkeeper was, as we have noted, in 1888.

The basic principles of golf greenkeeping are thus enshrined by custom and use, going back well over a century. They apply in principle, modified by small differences in practice, to all courses in the temperate northern latitudes, where two fine-leaved grasses dominate natural turf, namely fine fescues (*Festuca rubra*) and the bents (*Agrostis* spp.).

They are simple, and based on the needs of these grasses. In other words they aim to copy those conditions which favour the desired grass species,

Typical links setting— Portmarnock, Ireland.

yet are unsuitable or unappreciated by coarser-leaved, more agricultural grasses.

These conditions have been described by many generations of botanists, advisers and practical greenkeepers. We need to remind ourselves constantly what these conditions are.

First and foremost, we must look at all the different ecologies and natural habitats where such fine wiry grasses dominate. They are many and varied. If we are looking for a common denominator in all such contrasting habitats, we need to think in depth. Where can the common ground lie between such different environments as alkaline (because of sea-shell content) dry arid links, downland and limestone heath and acid moorland; between areas dominated by light sandy soils or by heavy clays; or between tidally flooded salt marshes and dry as dust dune land?

It certainly cannot be soil type, nor can it be soil moisture content. It cannot be altitude, since the same grass species flourish at sea level and on moorland tops. It cannot even be soil acidity or alkalinity, but common ground there must be, since it is an undisputed environmental law that species dominate only where they find conditions which favour them and keep out competitors.

These old greenkeepers had found the answer by correct deduction. They knew rabbit and sheep scalds, after initial scorching, encouraged lush grasses, alien to links and which died in drought. They observed that paths across fine fescue turf changed first to annual meadow grass before compaction and abrasion scrubbed off even that ubiquitous weed grass. They noted that the best turf was found on the poorest soils, provided such soils were free draining. Even sea marshes dry out between high tides, while significantly on the wetter area and low slacks it is not fine fescues which dominate but a somewhat similar looking but useless species—sea meadow grass, *Pucinellia* (prev. *Glyceria*) *maritima*, which will survive neither close mowing nor removal from its maritime environment.

What they surmised a century and more ago has been proven by research and analysis countless times since. The secret of good golf greenkeeping is to copy basically infertile conditions—especially to avoid phosphatic fertilisers—and to ensure ideal conditions for deep-rooting by intensive deep aeration. In other words, for good greens use nitrogen only and aerate deeply. These same principles apply equally to every part of the golf course.

What did these rude forefathers of greenkeeping do which is still today the sound basis of greenkeeping? And what, one wonders, would they have made of the survival and, indeed, omnipotence of their thoughts and practices, despite all the modern aids and changes, wherever fine grasses are the object of desire.

SOOT AND SPIKING

The answer is surprisingly simple. They used nitrogen only, they deeply spiked (aerated) and they top dressed with sand, or sand and seaweed stacked and turned and screened to make a wonderful compost-like top dressing.

The nitrogenous dressing was soot. Soot was still being used in living memory. I have a note from a contributor about soot from Edinburgh chimneys being screened to remove all manner of bricks and rubble and sold to golf courses in the 1930s.

Scottish greenkeepers were great believers in the virtue of the graip or hand fork and I have seen a line of stalwarts slowly working their way backwards across a green, pushing forks (graips) in to the full depth of their tines, levering back, carefully removing them and re-starting the process every six inches. The process was called raise-forking and a skilled team could lift the turf without in the slightest disturbing the putting surface let alone leaving ripples. What was this but Verti-Draining, of which more anon? Nothing changes, only the need to do things better and quicker, to keep out of the way of the ever-present golfer. Gone are the days when one could walk a course in winter, from October to Easter, and never see a golfer during the week. Now greenkeepers have to rise early to get their work done before they are literally stopped by having constantly to let play through, and then some irascible complainant will snort that "one never sees a greenkeeper on the course, the lazy lot just hang about the sheds." What was the complainant doing at five a.m.? Certainly not up and about and working!

The truth was known to many. Dr C. M. Murray, working in the winter rainfall areas of South Africa from 1903, was one of the first to identify phosphatic fertilisers as the cause of annual meadow grass invasion of fine turf. Similar work in the United States came to the same conclusions and this formed the basis of the acid theory, first practised there in the 1920s and taken up so enthusiastically, but without discrimination, here in the 1930s. In itself, it achieved miraculous results on heavy land, at least for a period, but some links courses applying "ammonia and iron" as much as six or seven times a year, and especially in the absence of today's sophisticated irrigation, indeed often with none, rued the day, as such treatment destroyed the humus content and drought resistance of the root zones. Indeed, fine fescues do not like extreme acidity. A series of droughts in the mid-1930s, plus over-enthusiastic use, gave the theory a bad name, and, sadly, all too often fertiliser policies were reversed and that was the start of the dominance of annual meadow grass that so marred many of our courses. The old adage—the poorest clubs have the best courses—is based on the fact that they could not afford to over-feed.

Probably the first man to see the light in England was Norman Hackett

Norman Hackett.

(1882–1952), a West Riding industrialist, with a love not only of golf but of golfing grasses. He strongly condemned liming and the use of agricultural fertilisers, so common in the 1920s, with farmer-members advising clubs how to restore, or ruin, their courses after war-time neglect. Long before the Greenkeeping Station was set up in 1929 at Bingley, in the West Riding of Yorkshire, largely as a result of Hackett's enthusiasm, drive and initiative, he was carrying out hundreds of free advisory visits to golf courses every year, giving sound advice and criticism. He went overboard on the acid theory and never really became reconciled to the problems lurking behind the benefits.

It is a lasting disgrace that the Board of Greenkeeping Research, which owed its very existence to his influence, should have gone back on his principles, namely minimal fertiliser treatment, when a series of droughts in the late 1930s, coupled with a loss of humus and excessive acidity exacerbated drought damage. Their director swung back to advising heavy, complete (NPK) fertiliser treatments and we lost many years in the crusade for better bent/fescue greens before those with greater botanical knowledge made their influence felt. Norman Hackett never forgave the Board of Greenkeeping Research for this betrayal. I know, because he told me.

The main credit must go to a relatively unrecognised botanist, Richard Libbey, who taught on botanical, not chemical grounds, and was totally opposed to the policies of the then director, R. B. Dawson, and the heresies being propounded by his soil chemist. He taught me a great deal, and not just grass identification. When he and I left, Bingley reverted to type and advised heavy NPK fertiliser treatment based on using far too high levels of phosphate treatment. Eventually the S.T.R.I. saw the error of earlier ways and now advise what old greenkeepers did a century earlier, fundamentally to apply nitrogen only.

BASICS UNALTERED IN A CENTURY

Thus we come back to the basic principles which have never altered in more than a century, if only because neither have the basic needs of the grasses which make the best courses, and which we need to encourage. You cannot play golf on a football pitch is an old adage, yet we still have a constant running battle with those who cannot see the differences in the demands of two such opposing sports and who do all that is possible, wittingly and unwittingly, and I do not know which is worst, to convert our golf fairways

Basic Principles of Greenkeeping

and greens into passable imitations of a third division pitch, by following totally wrong advice.

Why should there be any disagreement on such basics, when they have been proven by a century and more of experience and practice and confirmed by research all over the temperate world? No one would deny that details are alterable, but they are details related to the different needs of different sites—details not principles.

It cannot be accepted that there are equally valid alternatives, nor can we accept the proposition that there are equal but opposite schools of golf greenkeeping. Essentially there is only good greenkeeping, based on encouraging bents and fescues; and bad greenkeeping, favouring agricultural grasses and pernicious weeds, the worst of which is annual meadow grass (*Poa annua*). This is one of the most common species throughout the world while remaining the source of 90% of greenkeeping problems.

The existence of opposed schools of thought can be explained. First, many of those pointed firmly in the wrong direction, and as often as not with at best only a rudimentary acquaintance with the game, rely all too often on agriculture, from which background so many came. Others may well know all about the specialist needs of other sports, but little or nothing about golf. Why is golf so special? First and foremost because in no other sport is the quality of turf so vitally and critically important to the game. Football can be, and sometimes is, played on mud. A cricket wicket has little or no grass, the roots of which serve to hold the wicket together in the short period before it is rested again. Many other sports are seasonal; bowls, tennis, croquet etc., but golf is played for as near 365 days a year as snow and frost permit.

A second cause of divergent opinions is because so many, including golfers, equate colour with quality. It needs stressing that golf is not played on colour, but on true surfaces and if grass is not green it is not necessarily dead. Few now remember golf courses without irrigation—a pale shade of khaki in a dry summer. They did not die, nor require wholesale reseeding. A few days of rain and they quickly greened up again. More to the point, even when droughted they provided good playing conditions. It has to be admitted, however, that they did not have to stand up to today's heavy play.

Third, many so-called advisers are often thinly-disguised salesmen, who are quite confused about the difference between coarser-leaved grasses useful in highly productive, agricultural grassland husbandry, and the management of those fine-leaved, wiry, non-productive species characteristic of the poorest soils, regarded by farmers as weeds to be removed by all means possible, notably manurial as well as mechanical. Converted farmers are rarities; the rest are a menace on any golf course.

There is nothing new about this. Greenkeeping seems to be caught in a

Applying lime to a fairway at Royal Mid-Surrey, circa 1920.

cyclical trap, with heresies propounded with vigour and enthusiasm until the dire results of such treatment become all too obvious. Then everything is thrown in reverse, only for the same process to be repeated in another decade. Failure to learn from the expensive mistakes of earlier generations is perhaps the most heinous sin of golf course advisory work.

Luckily for us, disasters can sometimes be overcome, albeit slowly, merely by stopping wrong treatments, or reversing ill-conceived management. If changes for the worst were always permanent, then greenkeepers would have a very hard time indeed. Certainly it is far quicker and easier to achieve bad results by misguided treatment than to reverse them. Such bad treatments, as liming and the use of phosphatic fertilisers, can, admittedly, quickly turn old, worn-out pastures into better, more productive grazing. If this were not true, then the only way to improve such old grassland would be to plough it out and reseed. However, we do not want productive pastures but fine wiry turf.

Sadly, the reverse is not so easy to achieve, for once the chemical status of a soil has been altered there is not much we can do, save rely on the normal leaching processes to impoverish it. Sometimes we can increase acidity with beneficial results, but high phosphates are another matter. This will be dealt with in a subsequent chapter.

Drought is often the catalyst that triggers off these disastrous, remedial measures. If the natural grass cover of any of our open moorlands, heathlands

Basic Principles of Greenkeeping

or dunes were liable to be killed off by drought, then half southern Britain would be an arid desert. Of course, it is not and these deep-rooting and fine-leaved native grasses become dormant, and with the first real rain the affected turf soon greens up again. There is an old greenkeeping proverb to the effect that "a good drought gets rid of a deal of rubbish." However, if these desirable grasses have been penalised or displaced by any number of factors, to be replaced by a more artificially maintained grass cover, then a severe drought without irrigation can well cause severe damage. To identify these factors, we must observe nature. Traffic creates wear, but it also compacts soils. If this compaction, which penalises deep-rooting grasses, is not corrected, our desired grass species will be replaced by those which are shallow-rooted. If fertility levels are increased in a senseless chase after colour, then more aggressive grasses are enabled to compete, whereas before such feeding they could not have gained a foothold.

There are many other reasons for undesirable changes and the loss of our natural fine turf, but, if we accept the premise that the ideal golfing turf is based on those tough, wiry, fine-leaved species, the bents (*Agrostis* spp.) and fine fescues *(Festuca rubra)*, then, logically, there can be only one broad set of basic greenkeeping principles, applying equally to all types of courses and to all parts of the world's temperate zones, wherever fescues and bents occur naturally.

While each aspect of these basic treatments will be dealt with in more detail later, it will clarify matters to summarise them briefly before doing so.

Aeration is almost certainly the most important operation on any course, if only because the vast increase in the intensity of play and extended seasonal use create more compaction and more need to counteract it.

Fertiliser treatment must be minimal and basically nitrogen only. While a case can be made for occasional applications of potash, the use of fertiliser phosphate can never be excused. This does not mean, of course, that even fine grass needs no phosphates at all. It has often been said that there is no such thing as phosphatic deficiency in soils supporting fine turf, primarily because the demand of such fine turf for phosphates is so low that it need never be added. The main rules are: never chase colour, minimal use (if in doubt, don't), no autumn fertilisers and keep them poor.

Top dressing is a third basic treatment. This is the only way to improve the accuracy and resilience of playing surfaces, increase drought resistance, and to provide a slowly available source of nutrition. There are two basic rules, both of which are inviolable.

- First, never chop and change. Select the correct top dressing, which must be compatible with the root zone, and stick with it. Avoid changes in physical composition as this can cause layering—the formation of defined strata—and associated severe root breaks at the change in the structure of the root zone. It is often so pronounced as to cause the turf to lift away from the root zone at the break.

- Second, match the top dressing and the root zone. Ideally the two should be the same and certainly never physically markedly different. With very sandy root zones use compatible, sandy, humus-enriched mixes. This does not mean that with very heavy, unimproved, root zones on old greens one uses heavy mixes. The aim is to build up a new and better root zone over the old one.

Mowing, of course, is the basis of producing good playing surfaces. Here again, there have been many abuses, the chief of which is to mow too closely (shaving) to speed up playing surfaces, with lethal results, hence the sobriquet "the quick and the dead."

In mowing we will discuss not just heights of cut and frequencies, but cutting in two planes—conventional horizontally but equally important vertically—and the differences between grooming, verticutting and scarification.

"GREEN IS NOT GREAT"

Typical parkland setting—Chateau des Vigiers, 13th green.

Irrigation is perhaps the second most abused aspect of turf management. "Over-watering is the cardinal sin of greenkeeping" is an immortal epitaph to the late Al Radko, past national director of the USGA Green Section. In what is clearly going to be a period when water supplies are going to be increasingly restricted and expensive, this may prove to be a blessing in disguise, if we learn how to use restricted resources properly.

The function of irrigation is merely to keep the grass alive, especially when it is stressed by other factors. It is emphatically not to make it green. "Green is not great" is another of Al Radko's truisms. It is also not to make grass grow, for this is limited by soil temperatures. It is worth remembering the basic rule, to the effect that in spring, cold wet greens start growth later than those which are cold and dry, as they take longer to warm up. Equally never use water to make greens more holding. Firm and dry is the motto, and learn to play the pitch and run-up game. Our golf is played along the ground, not in the air. Typically, target golf is played to soft, holding greens off lush fairways, rather than to more desirable firm, fast greens off tight lies, as in the traditional game.

These then are the five laws inscribed in blocks of stone. They never alter

Basic Principles of Greenkeeping

in principle, but do so very much in detail, since there are so many differing details, not only environmental, but even in the aim. No two golf courses are identical, nor indeed are the demands of golf club members, nor the aims and ambitions of course managers trying to meet those demands.

All the rest of greenkeeping is really detail. Partly it is concerned with the control of pests, diseases, weeds and other problems. Here again, perceptions are changing on the acceptability of what some see as toxic evils, capable of destroying life on earth, while others, who have seen most of it before, regard them as useful aids to good husbandry, if used sensibly. This means that we should think in terms of management control, rather than direct application of fungicides, insecticides and herbicides. All such pesticides are increasingly being banned or at least severely restricted in their use.

While few would deny that the problems of greenkeeping are much greater today than, say, fifty years ago, we should always relate this to other factors. The first, clearly, is the effect of more intensive use of all courses, expressed by the rather plaintive sentiments of one greenkeeper, yearning for earlier

Downland comparisons. Ninety years separate these two pictures of the Royal Eastbourne course. The trees are a little taller, a few bunkers and leylandii barriers have been added, while trees and scrub have invaded the skyline; the rest is timeless

45

and less complicated days. "I could always have my course in perfect order, if only I could banish the golfers."

A second one is that there is much more money about. Without money, the capacity to create disasters is very limited. With bigger budgets it is easier to spend unwisely, but remember the old adage about learning from the expensively acquired experience of one's predecessors. Not only are such self-inflicted wounds costly to make and even more costly to correct, but they can leave a legacy with a malign effect for many years on course condition.

One factor, linked with greater use for longer periods, is the fact that while there is a greater need for corrective measures there is less time available and more interference with routine management by play. Increasingly, greenkeeping management has found that the only feasible solution to avoid inefficient work programmes, and to keep ahead of play, is to start earlier and earlier and even to create special greenkeeping tracks to minimise greenkeeping traffic on fairways, unless actually working on them.

However, a final word may be helpful. Golf greenkeeping is not an exact science, if only because it is a study of living things. It is also not all that complicated. After all, we are dealing with only two species of grass—all the rest are weeds—which have fairly uncomplicated requirements.

All greenkeeping hinges on the precept that, if we copy the basic conditions found so widely in nature, where these fine fescue and bent grasses dominate, and therefore keep out competitors, then the grasses we want will thrive. Even where past mismanagement or inherently high fertility has resulted in annual meadow grass dominance, correcting the mistakes of management will slowly but surely achieve a swing back to better turf.

All these facets of sound basic greenkeeping will be covered individually and in more detail in subsequent chapters, but it is worth noting that they refer to every part of the course in play, though naturally at different intensities.

Today we really do have generally better and certainly larger greens; surrounds whose measure of quality is to permit a putter to be used with confidence from some distance off the actual putting surface (hazards permitting); approaches as extensive as greens and virtually fore-greens to favour good run-up conditions; large tees on which one can almost putt; fairways manicured for all year playability; and even the rough managed and controlled. This is done as much to conserve the ecology and natural character of the course as to aid disease control and weed invasion—and to speed up play.

All this makes for a vastly increased work load, higher and higher standards, the need for speedy corrective measures and the avoidance of

Basic Principles of Greenkeeping

Typical, well-managed heathland at Hankley Common.

avoidable crises. More men are obviously needed, but, even more important, more dedicated men, pointed firmly in the right direction, while enjoying the support of members as well as management in their never ending efforts to achieve perfection. The weather always has the last word, but hopefully the following chapters will help this aim and at least stop the cyclical pattern of repeated mistakes which has characterised greenkeeping all through its history.

It has been said, of another subject than greenkeeping, that those who ignore history are condemned to repeat it. In over five decades of golf advisory work it has never ceased to both amaze and sadden me that "they never learn."

Way back in 1934 that redoubtable pioneer of improved grasses, Professor Sir George Stapledon of Aberystwyth, stated that "greenkeeping suffered because of the chronic failure of greenkeepers to control farmers" and that "the history of greenkeeping is permanently bedevilled because so few of them could enforce their knowledge and skill on those controlling the management of their golf course."

The situation, though improved, is still not without its parallels today, but better education and better recognition of their profession has resulted in greenkeepers having more say and in courses improving. Hopefully these chapters may give all those pointed in the ideal direction more ammunition, especially in their fight against those whose idea of perfection is "nice and green" and who chase short-term solutions to problems, little realising their long-term repercussions. We must try to stop decisions being made by those who know nothing of the principles of greenkeeping, though they would always be entitled to define their aims. They must, however, leave the methods of achieving them to those better qualified to do so.

Chapter Four
· · · · ·
SOILS AND THE GOLF COURSE

THIS INTRODUCTION to the origins, structure and behaviour of soils is not intended to, and cannot be, either definitive, or exhaustive. It would take the entire book to do justice to the complexity and importance of soils. It is intended, primarily, to provide a background, in simplified form, for all those involved in golf course management and construction at all levels. The aim is to assist greenkeepers and students, course managers, employers or architects, in making a meaningful assessment of physical soil analyses and to help them to make decisions which avoid destroying the delicate balance of soils and their structure by bringing in poor materials, or inadvertently introducing problems which can sometimes create irreversible damage. Deliberately, it is restricted to the soils of temperate climates.

Chalk cliff formation at Seven Sisters.

Before dealing with soils and their management a brief, oversimplified description of geology may be helpful. It may be asked, what has this to do with golf? Despite popular misconceptions, geology is the scientific study of, not just rocks, but of all the processes which affect Planet Earth, including how soils are formed from rock.

To say that soil is just a pile of dirt, formed when the underlying rock becomes weathered, is basically correct, but is a gross oversimplification of the function of what is actually a highly complex, constantly changing, dynamic living system.

Western Europe has a very varied geology, with just about every age and type of rock represented. As soil is directly derived from rock, one might expect as much variation in soil types. Fortunately, weathering simplifies things, because as rocks are generally formed under immense pressure or temperature, or both, they are unstable at the Earth's surface and their minerals quickly, at least in geological terms, begin to disintegrate and decompose.

WEATHERING

Occasionally, by erosion and consequent removal of the weight of thousands of metres depth of overburden of overlying rock, which gave rise to the immense pressure responsible for turning sediment into stone, this is enough to cause the exposed rock to begin to fall apart. However, breakdown is more normally accomplished by physical and chemical changes, loosely referred to as weathering agents.

Climatic conditions on the planet vary a good deal, but most places experience rapid changes in temperature; from very hot to cold in deserts, or cold to very cold in high latitudes. Simple expansion and contraction provides enough mechanical stress to break up solid rock and the expansion of water, as it freezes and thaws in cracks and pores, exerts enormous force, easily splitting the rock.

Chemical reactions, mainly oxidation and hydration, at the surface result in decomposition or breakdown to new compounds or elements, of most common minerals with the exception of pure silica (quartz), which is largely inert. These reactions take place in water derived from rain and produce new minerals, mainly clay and soluble products. In passing, rain is always slightly acidic, because it absorbs atmospheric carbon dioxide to form weak carbonic acid. This aids the reactions and brings about the well-known solution of limestone. Worms and other soil organisms do much to help recycle fresh materials and their by-products increase acidity, which further assists chemical breakdown. Ultimately, all land deposits will end up washed, blown or dragged into the sea.

Weathering loosens bed rock so that the fragments and soluble products can be eroded. As soon as these fragments are carried by flowing water, wind or ice, they act much like dynamic, endless sandpaper, capable of wearing away completely unweathered rock. Indeed, glacial ice studded with rock fragments is capable of carving vast amounts of rock to create the classic, U-shaped valleys of mountainous regions. Much of this eroded rock ended up as a widespread thick blanket of "boulder clay" on the plains of northern England, which is now weathering to form heavy soil.

Other examples of loose deposits which give rise to soils are alluvium in river valleys and coastal sand dunes, but most soils come directly from underlying bedrock. This can often be clay strata, which confusingly is also the name of the fine-grained sedimentary rock, and, not surprisingly, produces clay soil. Britain has many areas of sandstone and these, equally unsurprisingly, produce sandy soil. Limestone mainly dissolves completely, but minute impurities are left behind to form thin, calcareous soils. Thin soils also tend to form on top of hard rocks, such as granite, usually coinciding with high moorland.

Peat deposits like sphagnum, sedge and fen are dealt with in another chapter. They consist of almost pure organic matter and occur in various stages of decomposition. They are not strictly speaking soils, though high levels of peat with small sand, silt and even clay fractions will act as soils.

THE MINERAL MAKE-UP OF SOIL

Almost all the rock of the Earth's crust is formed from previously existing rock. Minerals decomposed and were broken down at the surface only to be recombined by immense pressure and high temperatures as they become re-buried, before once again being uplifted and exposed at the surface to erosion, in a continuous cycle, lasting hundreds of millions of years. Clearly there were initial rocks to start this off and these crystalline rocks, like granite, formed from cooled magma (liquid rock). The minerals of crystalline rocks are the building blocks for all other rock and soils. There are only six silicate rock-forming minerals to consider and three of these decompose so rapidly at the surface they are not found in sediments or soils. Two more also decompose and are not important. Only the last, to form quartz (pure silica), survives. This is why quartz is such a common mineral and the principal component of sand. All the other minerals, on decomposition, become soluble products and clay minerals.

Only calcite (calcium carbonate), the mineral which forms limestone, has a different origin; owing its existence to life on earth. Plants and animals absorb atmospheric carbon dioxide and use this to form protective calcareous shells and these can accumulate to form a shell-rich limestone, or be

Soils and the Golf Course

The Bass Rock—the basalt core of an extinct volcano, an example of igneous rock.

incorporated into the structure of a reef. However, calcium carbonate can be precipitated inorganically from the solution of an earlier formed limestone.

Other minerals and elements are present in insignificant amounts, derived largely from the soluble products of weathering, and minor minerals such as metalliferous ores.

CHEMICAL CONTENT

We are not concerned in this context with the chemical constituents of soil. It is sufficient to say that most of the important nutritional substances namely nitrogen (N_2), phosphates (P_2O_5), potash (K_2O) and lime (CaO), are present in virtually all soils to a level well above the minimal needs of the poverty-tolerant, fine-turf forming grasses. Trace elements, similarly, while having a significant influence in very high intensity grassland farming, are irrelevant in fine turf management, save only in the case of sand-only greens where the grass has to be fed hydroponically, and is entirely dependent on what it receives from above, as there are no reserves nor retention of plants foods, nor indeed of water. It is with the physical components of soil that we are concerned. These constituents are discussed later.

We need not concern ourselves with debates about pH values (the concentration of hydrogen ions in solutions filtered from soils, and not truly of the soil or sand itself). Note that there is no direct relationship between pH values and lime requirement figures. In practice, the soils with which we are concerned range from the mid pH 3s to the mid pH 8s. Strictly pH 7 is neutral, lower figures being acid and higher alkaline. In greenkeeping we would regard anything over pH 6.0 as being insufficiently acid. In practice the ideal pH is the one you have, since trying to alter it is as unrewarding as it is impermanent. Working with the soil we have makes much more sense, a parallel being in course design, to make use of the contours with which we are presented, rather than trying to alter them by massive and destructive earth moving.

SOIL FORMATION

What distinguishes soil from a pile of weathered dirt is not just the addition of humus or other organic matter, but a distinct series of changes which produce structure and a characteristic layering or zonation. Humus is, of course, vital to water retention and to the health and growth of both plants and animals living in the soil. It is from such life that humus originates in the first place. Humus is a broad term used to describe everything organic, from almost recognisable leaves to completely decayed vegetable matter, well broken down by bacteria and joined by other nitrogenous waste in an acidic mix, best described as being like liquid manure. This colloidal humus forms chemical compounds with clay minerals, clumping together these tiny particles into larger masses, a process known as flocculation.

Occasionally thick accumulations of organic matter called peat are formed when bacterial decay is halted; usually by a mixture of water-logging, the exclusion of oxygen, and a build-up of acidic toxic conditions.

The zonation of soil, which is best developed in what are called podsols, is brought about when rainwater percolates down, carrying with it soluble minerals and minute clay minerals, produced from the weathering of minerals nearer the surface. This ground water eventually builds up and saturates all available pore spaces, forming a water table. In this saturated region, oxidising conditions, as found on the surface, change to reducing (anaerobic) conditions, and, as a result, many of the minerals and the colloidal clay become deposited, drastically reducing permeability and forming mineral pans or impermeable strata. Thus, the upper layers become depleted in some minerals and lower layers are enriched, as with iron pans. Below this lies weathered bedrock. Subtle changes in the development of this zonation gives rise to a soil classification, important to climatologists and farmers but of little real value to golf.

Soil profile. Lias clay overlying jurassic limestone.

Migration of fine clay particles forms a clay pan, a consolidated layer where clay accumulates. This can happen relatively quickly and can cause real problems with drainage, while also being difficult to break up. Such action and deposition is accelerated by over-watering.

Compaction by play or mechanical operations reduces pore space, compressing the particles closer together, breaking down crumb structure and forcing fine clay in suspension between the larger particles, reducing drainage and impeding root development.

THE PARTICULATE CONSTITUENTS OF SOIL

Soils, however derived, consist of varying proportions of gravel, sands, silts, clays and organic matter and, of course, air and water. In practical terms, the separation of the above constituents is determined by particle size analysis. This entails differentiating and separating the particle sizes into groups, in the case of the larger particles by vibratory sieve analysis and for the very small sizes by settlement in a column of water. Analysis results are percentages by weight and not by volume, which is not a problem when dealing with particles of similar density but it is a point to remember when comparing, say, peat with sand.

This breakdown into particle size groups, (shown in the diagram), has become standardised in a classification system devised very many years ago by the United States Department of Agriculture. Adopted by the USGA Green Section and used, in 1960, in their specification for the construction of golf greens, this system is today used virtually universally so far as greenkeeping and other sports turf management is concerned. There are slightly different classifications favoured by soil analysts dealing with road construction, building foundations and other civil engineering regimes, but this USDA/USGA classification has the merit of antiquity and is acceptable to all involved in the physical soil analyses of sports turf. It is, of course, essential that analysis techniques are standardised, so that, within reason, identical results are reported on the same soil analysed by different laboratories. It is quite unacceptable that materials, which have been used satisfactorily for decades, with proven performance records, should be rejected by one laboratory but passed by another, while unsatisfactory material is passed by the first and rejected by others. That this happens can be due to different methods, as well as standards, of analytical procedure being followed.

Soil Analysis Grading USDA/USGA	
Grading	Diameter mm
Stones	> 8
Coarse gravel	8 – 4
Fine gravel	4 – 2
Very coarse sand	2 – 1
Coarse sand	1 – 0.5
Medium sand	0.5 – 0.25
Fine sand	0.25 – 0.125
Very fine sand	0.125 – 0.05
Silt	0.05 – 0.002
Clay	< 0.002

By definition, soil particles do not exceed 2 mm in size. Anything larger is classified as stones or gravel and, although often present in soils, they are not part of them. Very fine sand, silt and clay are often lumped together as 'fines'.

Coarse sands and gravels

A very important constituent of soils, in greenkeeping especially, are these larger particles, in that the larger the average particle size, the better soils drain. Many of these large particles derive from rock fragments, remnants of incompletely weathered rock, that is from quartz, or pure silica. Excessive amounts of such particles in soils can cause some management problems in relation to mowing, e.g. damage to mowers, and in reduced drought resistance, but such problems pale into insignificance compared with those caused by having too many fines, which seal surfaces, create severe drainage problems and inhibit deep root development.

Medium sands

These are the greenkeepers' friend. They help, together with humus, to structure heavy soils and keep an open texture in the soil of root zones. This is true whether the root zones are manufactured, as in building suspended water table type greens, or are natural, as in heathland and linksland.

The narrower the range of particle size, the more effective is the drainage, because the nearer one achieves a single uniform particle size (though in practice this is impossible), the greater the volume of the interstitial spaces between the particles. It bears repetition that roots grow in the spaces between the soil particles and not in the soil itself. Such spaces should show a balance between being filled with air or water. If all spaces are filled with water, stagnation results and kills the grasses, while, if they are all air-filled, then drought problems are imminent.

There are, of course, sands formed from minerals other than silica, such as crushed shell. This is a common and often significant constituent of estuarine and sea sands, and a problem because of their alkalinity. The use of sea sands in bunkers all too often results in a muddy mess of worm casts around them, wherever the sand is blown or blasted out onto the surround, because alkalinity attracts earthworms.

Fine and very fine sands

These are the enemy of good greenkeeping. Fine sand particles infiltrate into the spaces between larger particles, block drainage and inhibit deep root development. The use of very fine top-dressings, based on such very fine sands and silts, is to be condemned because of this sealing effect, even if they are quickly absorbed and so less obvious to the golfers.

Silts and clays

Many advisers do not bother to separate silt and clay in analysis, because both act in the same unsatisfactory manner. By lumping the two together, analyses can be speeded up and cheapened, which is of some significance during construction work, when there must be no hold-ups and delays in getting needlessly complicated analyses completed cannot be accepted.

Although the essential difference between silts and clays is particle size, both are so very fine grained that it really makes little difference in the context of golf. While both exhibit cohesion, clays have characteristic plasticity. Clays, perhaps surprisingly, can have quite high porosity, but they are generally mainly or completely impermeable. Although there are many pores, these are very small and effectively do not interconnect, while surface tension forces are large enough to overpower water movement.

Many experienced advisers often anticipate laboratory analyses by relying

PRACTICAL GREENKEEPING

on the finger and thumb test. Well-documented standards describe coarse sands as when the particles are large enough to grate together, while in fine sands the particles can still be felt, but are less obvious. Silt, which sticks to the fingers, feels smooth and soapy and only slightly sticky; while clays are characteristically silky and plastic. Tasting soils is another way. Silts can be differentiated from clays by this means because they feel slightly gritty on the teeth, while clays are always plastic and smooth.

Loam soils

While these are regarded as the ideal for agriculture and horticulture, the term loam is not a subdivision in particle analysis as are sands, silts and clays. Loam and similar soil terms describe a mixture of sands, silts and clays in stated proportions. In other words they are descriptions of soil types, not headings for particle size analysis.

Particle shape

Particle shape is almost as important as size. Angular shapes tend to lock together, resulting in reduced pore spaces. The ideal shape is semi-rounded, (see diagram). The perfect soil will have a narrow range of particle sizes and semi-rounded shapes. Pure spherical shape, even if it could be found, lacks stability. This is illustrated in a case where a golf club used perfectly spherical plastic material, as used in filtration beds, in bunkers. Golfers went in over the tops of their shoes and golf balls disappeared out of sight, a great source of revenue to the bunker-rakers.

In theory, if one could find identically shaped particles, then a soil with only one particle size would have the same interstitial pore space as another of a different size. As an example, if three identical buckets were filled respectively with ball bearings, golf balls and cricket balls, one could pour the same volume of water into all three. However, if the ball bearings and golf balls were mixed, there would be a dramatic reduction in pore space, measured in terms of how much less water would be needed to fill the bucket.

It is difficult to imagine just how minute clay minerals are. They are frequently described as colloidal; to all intents dissolved but incapable of passing

USGA Green Section, examples of sand particles and shapes.

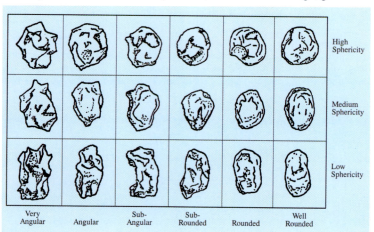

56

through filter paper, but it may help to provide a graphic illustration relating the diameter of a clay particle to that of a sand grain. If a bullet stop on the page (•), diameter one millimetre, represents the largest clay particle, the largest sand particle would be one thousand times larger, to the same scale, i.e. a ball one metre in diameter. Much smaller clays exist, consisting of only a few layers of silicate atoms, and these might be between a hundred and a thousand times smaller. If the same full stop is now used to represent these clay particles, then the sand grain has to be represented by a ball one kilometre in diameter. This may make it easier to visualise just how easily clays can migrate between larger particles, and how minute are the pore spaces between clay particles, and how efficient they are at clogging up micro, intergranular drainage channels. Clays are tiny, but they are also a pain and get everywhere, because their particles are so small.

Clays have another property which assists soil structure. The very fine particles can bunch together, a process known as flocculation, to give a better crumb structure. Without going into chemical reasons, clays (alumino-silicates) can link together with sodium, calcium or hydrogen ions. Sodium clays are very fine particled indeed and are de-flocculated, that is they do not form a crumb structure. Calcium clays are much more flocculated and structured, giving better drainage and being easier to work. Calcium ions will replace sodium, and this is the reason why farmers lime land. Unfortunately, the soil is made alkaline and this encourages earthworm casting and creates muddy weed-infested turf. Lime is therefore a very bad idea on a golf course. Fortunately, sodium ions can also be displaced by hydrogen ones and thus acidification has the same beneficial effect on soil structure as liming, without the disadvantages, since hydrogen clays show the same crumb-forming properties. This acidification has been achieved, since the 1930s, by applying sulphur at rates predetermined by trials (waiting six months for the oxidation of the sulphur to sulphuric acid to be completed), before assessing the optimum application rate. The resultant acidification creates an acid-tolerant bent (*Agrostis*) turf, with every earthworm departing in haste. As a result the turf becomes free draining, wiry and weed-free.

One of the reasons why sea water inundation does such lasting harm to heavy clay fields in low lying coastal areas, is that the calcium in such cases is displaced by sodium in massive excess and the de-flocculation is extreme. This leaves a sticky, plastic, unworkable soil. In this case gypsum (calcium sulphate) is more effective than liming, but it is a slow process.

Most natural soils contain some clay, which can represent almost any percentage of the make-up of soils, from 100% to as low as 5%, but at any level they have far more influence on the behaviour of soils than sands.

Humus

Without an organic fraction, soils would indeed be little more than the pile of dirt mentioned earlier. It is the humus content which creates satisfactory root zones and healthy soils, that is, those with thriving populations of soil macro- and micro-organisms, together with natural drought resistance, deep root development and a good quality turf. Alternative sources of humus are dealt with elsewhere in this book, but two aspects need stressing. The material must not be too rich in nutrients or it will encourage the wrong, fertility-demanding grasses. Second, it must be completely decomposed, otherwise it provides excellent food for earthworms. Undecomposed materials are bad in that they are difficult to incorporate in the soil complex.

It is worth examining why earthworms are attracted by alkaline soils and hate acid ones. There are two reasons. First, earthworms feed on partly decomposed organic matter. They drag leaves into their burrows to aid decomposition, as they cannot ingest them raw. In acid conditions, such a breakdown is minimal. Second, the acidity really does irritate them, as can be demonstrated, and they high-tail it to more congenial and less acidic living conditions.

GEOLOGICAL SURVEYS

It is not suggested that before every new construction is planned, let alone started, a detailed geological survey is essential, but, in most cases it is very well worthwhile and can prevent potentially enormous losses. It is, however, unfortunately still far from standard practice. Such surveys can determine problems with drainage and slope failure, as well as the construction of foundations.

Landslide at Mam Tor, Derbyshire—A major section of the highway has slithered downhill.

Slip-sliding away. Erosion at the sloping exit from 17th green Seaford Head golf course.

A check on geological profiles will sometimes dispose of the facile claim of irresponsible drilling companies, that water can be found a short distance from the surface, which, to say the least, is unlikely if the new construction is on a hill overlying, say, 300 feet of permeable strata with no impermeable layer to trap the water within economic reach.

When siting the club house or the greenkeeping complex, knowledge of the geological stability of the site is very important. There have been well documented cases where a well exposed, and apparently solid rock of limestone turned out to be honeycombed, at a very shallow depth, with large solution cavities, literally caverns where the limestone had been

Practical Greenkeeping

dissolved by groundwater, a foundation nightmare which can easily be overlooked, before construction exposes the problem.

Major disasters, potential or actual, have occurred where courses have been planned on contoured waterlogging clays. Here, permeable soils, overlying sloping, wet, heavy clays, maintain a precarious stability which can easily be de-stabilised, with disastrous results.

Even more spectacular landslides can occur if drainage water is unwittingly channelled into an existing clay shear-failure surface, instead of being intercepted and diverted, thus lubricating the interface and drastically reducing the stability of the slope so that landslides are inevitable. Once started, these are very hard to stop. In coastal areas, with the sea washing away the buttressing lower basal support, the slip will be very spectacular and will continue literally for centuries, until the strata responsible have been completed eroded away.

When constructing a golf course on potentially unstable land, slope failure can be triggered off during earth moving operations, as in levelling fairway sites laterally on a cut and fill system. This may well remove the buttressing lower slopes of the hill, across which the hole is planned. The same situation

There seems little doubt that the land here is "on the move".

can arise where the extra weight of the build up of a perched water table green construction proves just too much for the stability of a somewhat unstable landslide-prone clay. In such a way, whole hillsides, possibly carrying buildings and car parks with them, can slide down-hill, all for the want of a survey to assess potential problems. Even on stable land, a full geological survey is invaluable to gain insight into the whole character of a course. Furthermore, it will help in developing a sound, literally from the bottom up, planning strategy.

Where such surveys reveal potential problems, if carried out soon enough, the developer can decide whether to ask for a re-design to avoid the problem areas, or to abandon the project before wasting money. Such simple surveys can save huge costs and avoid disasters, but, needless to say, they must be carried out by experienced specialists. In this, as with all similar cases, experience relates to having done it before, combined with sound geological and engineering qualifications.

CONCLUSION

There is one clear message about soils and soil analyses, physical or chemical. That is to use common sense and instinct and to avoid extremes. Greenkeeping and golf course construction are not exact sciences. Extremes of soils, be they pure sand, pure peat, or pure clay, are equally bad for healthy root growth and thus healthy turf. Compromise and adjustment, based on sound knowledge of soils and their structure, is the secret of success, whether this is in the maintenance of existing soils or in copying them in the building of new courses. In analyses, set realistic and achievable parameters and tolerances and become concerned only with results which are well outside these limits.

Never become obsessed with soil analyses. They are not an end in themselves, only a confirmation or a guide. In early learning curves, it is helpful to link certain analysis results with certain soil properties. One then can associate observed physical conditions with analysis results and eventually anticipate the results themselves. This is called experience, for which there is no short-cut other than constant use and correct observation.

With this background, it is hoped that it will be easier to achieve good results, by avoiding the errors made by others before you and, above all, to prevent the destruction and destructuring of soils by preventable mistakes.

Chapter Five

Fertilisers and Lime

IF AERATION IS undoubtedly the most beneficial remedial, routine treatment of golf courses, and indeed all other sports turf, then the misuse of fertilisers and lime over more than a century has been responsible for more disasters, more expensive corrective measures and more deterioration of good golfing conditions, by a huge margin, than any other factor. Furthermore, there has been a cyclic pattern of disaster and recovery that is still going on.

This is, in my view, due to two related factors. One is the malign influence of farmers, who only rarely can be persuaded that they can contribute very little to the management of fine turf, because what they are expert in managing is coarse turf; namely broad-leaved, productive, agriculturally-valuable grasses. Just as those grasses which we seek to encourage are regarded by them as agricultural weeds, to our eyes their broad-leaved grasses are anathema. "You cannot play golf on a football pitch," summarises greenkeepers' views. There is a greenkeeping saying, to the effect "Ask a farmer (or agricultural adviser!) what to do, and go and do exactly the opposite". I certainly did not invent it, but I have certainly used it for 50 years and it goes back to the end of the last century

The second cause, in more recent times, was the vogue for chemical soil analyses. Soil chemists, backed by fertiliser salesmen with no knowledge of botany or golf, set up arbitrary standards and analysed soils as a commercial gimmick, blinding equally ignorant green committee members with pseudo-science. Perhaps, before developing the first aspect, we should demolish the need for chemical analyses. Note that this is not a condemnation of physical soil analysis, though frankly even in that sphere, an experienced eye and sensitive trained fingers can give a quick and accurate guide, thus avoiding the built-in problems of delays awaiting soil analysis results. One cannot hold back construction for days, even weeks, while materials are tested to

FERTILISERS AND LIME

Sedburgh's moorland course is sited within a designated National Parks area. This little par 3 nestles into the hillside and is barely visible except from the tee itself.

see if they comply with predetermined and often arbitrary standards.

To return, however, to chemical analyses. I am happy to note that some laboratories no longer carry out routine testing, as they freely admit the results tell them nothing. If the figures revealed show, as they almost always do, too high a figure, what are we do about it? It is revealing that in 1982, after the retirement of the then director and soil chemist of the Sports Turf Research Institute at Bingley, a survey was carried out of the analysis results of 1800 soil samples examined "chemically" in the previous year. To quote only one facet—phosphate (P_2O_5) levels—it was shown that less than 5% of the samples showed phosphate levels below 60 p.p.m. and that no less than 27% of all results showed levels in excess of 330 p.p.m., which was the upper limit of analytical measurement in those days. The significance of these figures, which indicated gross over-feeding with phosphatic fertilisers, is that anything lower than 60 p.p.m. was deemed to be deficient and the advice was to apply phosphates. Today few would suggest that levels even of 10 p.p.m. would warrant corrective treatment and indeed, we have figures from truly excellent fine turf (bent) greens of as low as 3 p.p.m. P_2O_5.

Equally, there are many examples of quite good greens where it is known for certain that no phosphatic fertilisers have been applied for 25 years, where figures of 30 p.p.m. and more are still found, indicating the persistence of phosphate in the soil. Whether such phosphates are readily available to plants is not so certain.

POA ANNUA LOVES PHOSPHATES

Those who are not ahead of me on this point may enquire what is so important about the precise level of phosphates. The significance lies in the fact that there is a commonly accepted link between annual meadow grass (*Poa annua*) invasion and phosphates in fertiliser form. This was known in the early 1900s, through the work of Dr C. M. Murray at Witwatersrand University in South Africa, who noted this undesirable invasion in the winter rainfall areas, as a direct result of the application of phosphatic fertilisers. The finding was repeated at the USGA research station at Rhode Island in the 1920s; by the Board of Greenkeeping Research at Bingley, Yorkshire in the 1930s and again, post-war, in an eight-year trial at Washington State University (Goss, Brauen & Orton) published in 1975.

The work was repeated continuously with the same proven link, yet—until a determined crusade to revert to nitrogen only was started in the late 1960s—fertiliser manufacturers still advised and sold complete NPK mixtures. Even convinced greenkeepers who used, and had used, nothing but nitrogen over the years, were hard to convince that 8:0:0 represented better value for money, quite apart from being what the fine grasses wanted, than, say, 10:15:10. Sadly, far too many academic and commercial bodies still use soil analysis to sell fertilisers. "Send us your soil for testing and we will tell you what it needs," including even trace elements!

In a fairly large sample in an R & A-sponsored S.T.R.I. investigation in 1995, no less than 61% of the clubs involved used not only no phosphates but an 8:0:0: mix. This mix is the classic one of equal parts of sulphates of ammonia and iron, with dried blood and fine hoof and horn meal. "Phosphatic fertiliser applications on the rest were very variable, and there was no relationship between the amount of phosphate applied and the measured level in the soil. This almost certainly reflects unnecessarily high levels of phosphate nutrition in the past" (Dr S. W. Baker).

At the other extreme, some of the worst greens I have ever had the

The links, Royal St. David's. An evocative overview from the Links Hotel balcony.

misfortune to advise on their treatment ("dig them up and start again from scratch" was not popular), had phosphate levels varying from 600 p.p.m. to well over 1000 p.p.m. Needless to say they were *Poa annua* dominated, while the best on a famous moorland course showed levels as low as 3 p.p.m. P_2O_5, with excellent healthy bent *(Agrostis)* greens.

This, then, is one very good reason why I have campaigned against chemical analysis on the basis of which over-feeding was encouraged. Soil laboratories are increasingly taking this criticism to heart, while unbiased ones will analyse only to back up problems diagnosed in the field, or to cover toxicity.

Most laboratories analyse on only three chemical criteria, the levels of pH (soil acidity), phosphate and potash. Some also give levels of magnesium (Mg) and so-called trace elements, which have absolutely no relevance, save perhaps on pure sand greens, an equal irrelevance save for desert areas, where phenomenal levels of irrigation are needed not just to keep the grass alive, but to cool the soil. The feeding by hydroponics of such sterile root zones is another matter entirely.

Let us look at these three nutritional elements. It should be noted that the pH level is not the same as lime requirement, but in any case, as we will see shortly, we do not want to make acid greens more alkaline and certainly we can do little about making alkaline greens more acid, even if we wanted to. In my view the pH level is of academic interest only and not for action.

This can be summed up by saying the ideal pH for a golf green is the one you have. If you really must know the pH value, a small amateur indicator kit or pH meter can give you quite as accurate a figure as you need to know.

Phosphates, as we have seen, are not needed. It again may be of academic interest to know that you have excessive P_2O_5 levels, but you cannot do much about it. You will certainly never have deficiencies on anything other than a pure sand green, and in the latter case, the green will have died long before deficiencies can be corrected. Such pure sand greens demand constant, regular feeds of NPK plus trace elements and indeed also lime. They, after all, are entirely dependent on what they are given, including water as well as nutrients, since they should be, although sometimes are not, top dressed with sand only, to be compatible with the root zone. They are, however, a tiny minority; officially disapproved of outside desert conditions. They are totally unnecessary outside those same desert areas and have no place whatever in northern temperate climatic zones.

I rejected the concept of the infallibility of chemical soil analyses fifty years ago, long before computers had been invented, or many of my critics had been born. It has taken some time for others to come to the same conclusion. It is certain that, despite claims to the contrary, there are no phosphate and potash deficient courses in the northern temperate European zone, indeed there are many with excesses. It has been claimed, with justification, that many of our greens could be dug up and quite legally sold as fertiliser.

Potash, being soluble, may need occasional topping up, compared with phosphates which are not only insoluble but fixed in the soil complex.

This leaves only nitrogen, the most important nutrient (in small doses) for fine turf. There is no satisfactory test for nitrogen. I rest my case.

So much for the chemical analyses—don't bother! The grass will soon tell you what you want to know.

WHAT SUITS FARMS SPOILS COURSES

To revert to farming influences. Over a century ago, wise heads were remarking that what suited farms was not necessarily the right treatment for golf courses. The problem was exacerbated by the fact that farmers learned the value of lime and tillage, i.e. fertilisers, in increasing crop yields under 1914–1918 war-time stress, and, as a result of their subsequent improved financial standing, some took up golf and, of course, were elected to the green committee. This never was the most sensible way to manage a golf course. Give me an amiable dictator, any day, though the problem is not only to keep him amiable but how to replace him when the time comes for him eventually to stand down.

Fertilisers and Lime

Even in the 1880s, criticism was being made of courses being dressed with bone ash and lime to improve the herbage for the benefit of the sheep, followed shortly afterwards with grumbles that the fairways were like meadows and polluted with worm casts. The connection was never seen by the culprits.

The history from club minutes of the repeated cycle of disaster and recovery in course condition from one famous northern club is worth recording.

1892	Course limed and given bone dust (despite being on a limestone heath).
1899	Tillage, i.e. fertiliser of the day, applied to the fairways, "to feed the sheep."
1906	One ton of worm-killer applied, followed by two truck loads of sea sand (full of shell and very alkaline)!
1909	More worm-killer (mercuric chloride) and more sea sand!
1910	More fertiliser—deduced to be basic slag.
1913–14	Limed again.
1920–21	Limed yet again.
1922	Course reported as going from bad to worse (blamed on the removal of the sheep).
1926	Consultation with the local university on the best type of lime to apply!
1927	Fairways very lush (blamed on the wet weather). (In passing, the club records show that in the annual reports the poor condition of the course over 21 years was blamed, in 18 of them, on *abnormal* weather conditions.)
1928	Dr Alister Mackenzie gave as his opinion that "the course which 25 years ago was the best inland course in Britain" showed sad deterioration and "due to feeding with alkaline fertilisers, its beautiful moorland turf has deteriorated into rich agricultural vegetation full of weeds, daisies, worms and mud." He stated that "what was right for agriculture is wrong for playing fields" (sic).
1929	Norman Hackett was advising the use of neutral not alkaline (sea) sand, "due to the use of lime and slag the fairways were losing their mat and finer grasses were being smothered by weeds and coarse grasses." He advised switching to the acid theory and de-worming.
1930	A year later following his advice, the finer grasses were returning and the daisies had gone. Fairways were being hand weeded against plantains!
1932	Two years later "visitors fees were at record levels."

1934	Tom Simpson noted that he was "particularly pleased to find that the greenkeeper favoured aeration."
1935	The fairways were de-wormed with lead arsenate, and the first Sisis aerator was purchased.
1938	The fairways were still worm free.
1944	War-time neglect had done no harm and there were independent reports that "the course compared favourably with any in the country."
1946	Fairways de-wormed again with lead arsenate, repeated in 1953.
1956	An abnormal drought left bare areas in fairways but all had recovered by December with spiking and no fertiliser.
1963	The rot started with a change of green committee. In January the whole course was heavily fed with a triple-concentrated complete NPK fertiliser and left looking as if light snow had fallen. By June, criticism of the lushness of the fairways was widespread.
1966	Poor conditions for a major tournament were blamed on the weather!
1967	Comments were made that "the course was in danger of becoming a water meadow," yet deterioration was still blamed on the weather. The greens were heavily sanded because they were so soft—and the resultant root break is still there to see today.
1969	A counter-revolution started with advocacy of mechanical rather than manurial remedial measures, and a reduction in irrigation of greens.
1970	Advice to slit the greens weekly was not carried out as the green committee felt it "to be neither desirable nor necessary."
1976	S.T.R.I. unbelievably advised high level phosphatic fertiliser for the greens and liming the fairways on the basis of soil analyses.
1977	Luckily this programme was abandoned.
1978	I returned to find thatchy *Poa annua* greens and increasing ryegrass in the fairways. An austere greenkeeping programme was faithfully followed.
1981	The AGM reported that "the new methods were paying off" and that green fee revenue had vastly increased.

In succeeding years, even fescues have returned to some greens, putting surfaces are excellent virtually all year round and fairways have been restored to their true heathland character.

One hopes that the club will have learned a lesson from this long history of wrongly conceived methods, creating unintended but inevitable disaster, with a long costly haul back on the road to recovery. It would be easier to

ensure that there is no repeat of such backsliding, if the green committee were disbanded and management based on an agreed written policy document. Meanwhile at least we do not have constantly changing chairmen trying to make their name in their short period of office, an infallible recipe for disaster.

To sum up on fertilisers, while there will always be a tiny minority of exceptions, all that mown fine turf requires, where the cuttings are collected, is a little nitrogen in spring, no phosphates and very little potash. When the grass cuttings are returned and there is consequently no depletion of nutritional reserves, no fertiliser is required at all. Grass which has suffered in drought or from wear is emphatically not suffering from the effects of manurial deficiencies—more frequently it is short of air and water. Prevention is better than cure. Improved drought resistance can be created by regular deep aeration, thus getting rain deep down instead of running off in winter or evaporating in summer. This applies especially if this is backed up, in the case of very thin soils (and indeed very heavy ones too), by working in humus-rich material, whatever is most easily and cheaply obtainable, from peat, fen peat, even rotted seaweed.

Parkland at Mill Ride. This fine course was built on the former stud farm of Sir William Waldren, later Crown property used for stabling and gallops. It became a golf course in 1990.

Even when disaster has struck, the same techniques will aid speedy recovery, sometimes to the extent that the need for expensive and relatively inefficient over-seeding is obviated. If grass died as a result of drought, half of southern England would long ago have become a desert. Anyone who has seen bleached and droughted fairways green over again after a few days of significant rainfall—and with the right grasses, if that is what you began with originally—will never worry about drought damage, but that is another story. There is indeed an old greenkeeping proverb that "a good drought gets rid of a deal of rubbish."

THE GREENKEEPERS' FRIEND

Discussion on fertilisers would not be complete if we did not mention sulphate of iron, the greenkeepers friend. "Ammonia and iron" has been used ever since the ingredients were available at the end of the last century, and were the basis of the acid theory propounded by Piper and Oakley in the United States in the early 1920s. Sulphate of ammonia was first produced in 1890 in Germany.

Sulphate of iron has many beneficial effects, though strictly speaking it is not a fertiliser. It acidifies soil, blackens moss, hardens soft turf, scorches and kills weeds, inhibits earthworms indirectly and acts as an effective mild fungicide. Over-used, it can scorch or create a thin turf, but it has one other benefit, it colours turf green without stimulating out-of-season vulnerable growth, therefore it is often used, with or without ammonia, as the first dressing of the year in the usual false spring, which is often followed by severe wintry weather in April. This pleases golfers and does no harm at all to the playing surface.

The management of pure sand root zone greens is another aspect on which I will barely touch, if only because informed opinion is totally against them in our temperate climate, so that there is no justification for building them, save where irrigation has to be at phenomenal levels to keep the grass alive, as in desert conditions. It is sufficient to say that in such cases we are dealing in hydroponics—a soil-less culture—and so in such sterile conditions, unless they are fed heavily and completely, including liming, the turf deteriorates and dies. Only intensive skilled management and very expensive budgets has kept some of the few examples here in reasonable condition. Most are disasters. We have enough problems without creating them.

While trace elements are completely unnecessary for all other types of greens and greenkeeping, there are products, again not strictly fertilisers, which are of value. These include natural products, extracted from sea weed, which have a useful if not dramatic effect in stimulating root growth and improving soil health, as well as having some beneficial effects on soil

Fertilisers and Lime

Heathland at West Sussex. The 6th green on a winter's day.

structure. While not essential for those on tight budgets, I have advised their use for 25 years and more. In support of their use, one must remember that greenkeepers more than a century ago were aware of the benefits of seaweed in several ways. There are records of links greens being smothered in rotted seaweed for a week, before it was removed, for later use, stacked with sand and turned to make top dressing.

It is a remarkable fact that what was common practice, both in fertiliser use and other aspects of management, a century and more ago, is still technically and scientifically soundly based today. Early links greenkeepers used soot and sand as the basis of their treatment of greens. The sand was local and often put through a heap with seaweed as mentioned, and what is that but exactly the same top dressing as we use today. Soot is a slow-acting nitrogenous fertiliser and still, a century and more later, slow release nitrogen is the best feed for fine grasses. There are many records of a big trade in soot with greenkeepers, with chimney soot being riddled to remove half bricks and bagged up. It must have been punishing work.

Today's sources of slow release nitrogen are less messy. They work in various ways, the organic ones being, still, the best. These are broken down slowly by soil micro-organisms, so that if the weather is adverse, activity of soil micro-organisms is slow and release minimal, thus there is no loss by leaching. Still the best formulation is an equal proportion mix of sulphates of ammonia and iron with dried blood and finely gristed hoof and horn meal. This has been the basis of golf green fertilisers for six decades and more. Despite the introduction of many alternatives it is still the best seller to discerning greenkeepers by knowledgeable manufacturers, though I fully admit it is not the easiest mix to spread on windy courses. I well remember a good number of years ago, on an advisory visit to a famous links, meeting the long-retired head greenkeeper and looking at the few bags of 8:0:0 organic fertiliser in the shed which were sparingly used. He asked me what was in it and on being informed he smiled, explaining that this was the same formulation he had laboriously hand-mixed way back in the 1930s. Let me emphasise, there is nothing new in greenkeeping!

Largely unsubstantiated claims have been made for other slow release sources of nitrogen, variations on urea, urea-form, IBDU and methylene urea, but all suffer from the release being less closely linked with soil conditions and weather. They work on the basis of low solubility. Another type is based on didin, a nitrification inhibitor, which delays the availability of the nitrogen source.

Even less useful are sulphur- or resin-coated pellets, not because they are inefficient but because the mini-pellets are picked up in the box at the first close mowing. They may have a place on less closely mown turf, but why use them when we have a perfectly satisfactory tried and tested alternative. This is perhaps why this "old-fashioned" mix is still the best seller.

We need not concern ourselves with the source of other nutrients, since we do not need fertiliser phosphate on any fine turf, and potash is best supplied as its sulphate salt.

It is claimed, by many so-called experts, that all plants need phosphates as well as nitrogen and potash. They well may, but in such minute quantities in the case of fine fescues and bents that the tiny quantities needed can be supplied in normal top dressings or from soil reserves. In practice, virtually all soils have sufficient phosphatic levels to supply the needs of fine turf, without extra being applied, for the next 50 years or more.

A typical fertiliser programme for a golf course, which does not really vary from course to course, while applying equally to links and heathland as to heavier land, is based on this presumption.

The first application, timed for what we know as the usual false spring—any time between late February and early April depending on latitude, altitude and the seasonal weather pattern—is a simple mix of sulphates of ammonia and iron (3:1), the old established lawn sand of by-gone years. If it is wasted by the weather deteriorating, no harm is done.

The next is delayed until growth shows signs of starting, which is usually no earlier than late April, since in most of northern temperate zones April is a winter month. This consists of a light application 25–50 g/m^2 of an 8:0:0 mix of ammonia, blood, hoof and horn and iron, plus carrier.

Repeat applications are discretionary; once generally, a second rarely, but as a rough guide nothing should be given after the end of July. With all fertiliser applications, the motto is "if in doubt, keep it in the bag."

No autumn fertilisers are needed and indeed are both wasteful and harmful. Growth is at a normal peak in autumn and needs no boosting, while late applications of nitrogen result inevitably in severe attacks of fusarium patch fungal disease (*Microdochicum nivale*), a self-inflicted wound which is costly to cure and whose scars remain until growth starts again. The more one spends on fertilisers, the more one will have to spend on fungicides. Chronic fusarium is always a sign of overfeeding—not necessarily currently but certainly a legacy from the past.

Tees may well receive one, or possibly two, dressings on the same pattern. Approaches, especially if they are managed as foregreens and mown with boxes to collect the clippings—the best way in my view to improve turf density and texture—need only one light dressing at the most.

Fairways need no fertilisers. Anything they need nutritionally can be given as a liquid, the commonest being a filtered and deodorised concentrated extract derived from farmyard manure. This again has been traditionally used for decades and has been commercially available since at least the 1960s. It originated from attempts to find an outlet for the slurry emanating from dairy cattle kept on slatted floors in south-west Scotland.

We must always copy nature when feeding fine turf. If the turf is not fine, then austere greenkeeping will make it finer. It is defeatist to feed more heavily if, say, *Poa annua* dominates, but it is a brave man who suddenly changes to restricted feeding with nitrogen-only from a high NPK diet. Softly, softly is the answer, to avoid the wrath of golfers being taken out on the greenkeeper.

I well remember one worried committee, recalling me after a year of such a switch in policy, saying they thought the greens were dying. Initially they were not amused to be told that the grass was not dying, but rather was being killed, deliberately. Within the next season a major change in grass type had been achieved and with no change in policy it has produced predominantly *Agrostis* bent greens — 25 years later!

The reason for applying fertiliser must always be remembered. It is merely to assist nature to stimulate growth to aid recovery from the winter's wear and tear. Colour is not the main reason, and though uniformity of colour is desirable it can be achieved without fertiliser. No fertiliser will work if the weather is cold or dry. The soluble side simply leaches to the drains.

The harm done by fertiliser companies in the era of over-feeding in the 1960s and 70s is now generally accepted. Too many agricultural fertiliser companies thought they could diversify into sports turf and golf especially. Frankly, the small amount of fertiliser needed by the average golf club would never warrant sending a salesman round to collect the order. Most of these firms have seen the light, while others are no longer in existence.

At this point, may I include a plea for accuracy in reportage. One reads,

A hand-pushed rotary spreader in action.

in the context of applying nutritional material, the word fertilisation used. This is wrong. Fertilisation refers to reproduction, while the correct term for nutrition is fertiliser treatment.

THE LASTING LEGACY OF LIME

We now come to the vexed question of lime, so beloved of farmers and the cause of so much harm to our golf courses. This is a direct result of farmers failing to realise that what they want and the methods of achieving those aims is the complete opposite of good greenkeeping. Within reason we want acidity, as liming acid land destroys the very turf which makes golf possible. Admittedly, there are cases of courses in good condition but with very alkaline soil, the chief of these being links, where the presence of crushed shell in the sea sand creates high pH levels. Such conditions favour fine fescues more than bents, but even where we want to encourage fescues, we should never lime. Earthworms do not invade, despite the alkalinity, because there is a dearth of humus, which is their food.

It is worth noting that the surface soil above very alkaline subsoils, e.g. chalk downs and limestone heaths, can be quite acid, unless earthworm casting brings up the alkaline base. This is because, with leaching, there is a constant loss of lime. This leaching has led some soil chemists to wrong conclusions, described as the "black-hole theory." They wrongly assumed that without corrective treatment, plant nutrients would be progressively lost, to the point where soils would no longer support vegetation. This is of course nonsense. Levels fall to a point and stabilise. If this were not so, all free draining soils would be sterile. What happens is that the vegetation changes in response to soil fertility levels, and poor soils produce the finest turf. I quote from the late Professor H. W. Woolhouse (1980); "It may seem a trifle odd to suggest that some of the finest scenery in western Europe owes its existence to metal toxicity, but it is a fact that much of our heath and moorland exists on soils where the concentration of free aluminium would be toxic to crop plants. Had these heathlands not been toxic to crop plants they would have been taken over for agriculture long ago."

Liming such acid soils followed by NPK application permits agricultural reclamation for cropping, but the effect is not so much adding calcium as locking up toxic aluminium. This toxicity keeps out more productive agricultural grasses—which are coarser—but permits those aluminium-tolerant species such as bents (*Agrostis*) and heather (*Calluna* spp.) to dominate, thus giving such areas their inimitable character and providing, where relevant, good golfing conditions.

Liming has many other disadvantages in golf greenkeeping, but the prime one is the encouragement of casting earthworms. One has only to look at the old (limed) white lines marking out an old tennis court, and to see the narrow strip of heavily casted and weed-infested lush turf—contrasting with the fine grass of the (acid) court—to realise the harm that can be done on a far wider scale by unwise 'corrective' liming, so happily advised by farmer committee members and, sadly, agriculturally-bred advisers, who should know better. Links turf rarely becomes infested with earthworms, simply because the humus content of the sandy top soil is so low that there is no food for them.

There is an old adage, relating to chemical soil analysis, that is worth repeating—to the effect that the ideal pH is the one you have got—and do not try to alter it. Liming acid turf can induce serious fungal disease. Not just fusarium patch (*Microdochium nivale*) but the far more damaging take-all patch (*Gaeumannomyces graminis*). This destroys the finer leaved grasses, leaving characteristically damaged, spreading, circular areas with the centre colonised by weeds and *Poa annua*. The spread of the disease can be checked by adding phosphates, but this encourages the dominance of *Poa annua*. The answer is not to lime at all. The aims, and therefore the methods, of sound agricultural grassland husbandry and sound greenkeeping are diametrically opposed.

Of course, if you are unwise enough to build pure sand greens without humus to retain moisture and nutrients, then lime has to be given if the hydroponically grown grass is to survive, but again the answer is not to start from there in the first place.

Chapter Six
Top Dressing

This heap of stacked seaweed and sand at St. Andrews is a valuable source of compostable material.

OF ALL THE FIVE basic routine management practices for golf courses, namely aeration; fertiliser treatment; mowing; irrigation and top dressing, it is top dressing which has altered most radically in every aspect since the early 1970s.

Aeration has been increasingly mechanised, but was a recognised and universal practice nearly a century ago, albeit carried out less intensively, as with much less play it was proportionately less needed. Good greenkeepers used fertilisers sparingly, while nitrogen only was the best practice even pre-war; the NPK heresy fostered by agricultural fertiliser manufacturers not having temporarily displaced this tenet of traditional greenkeeping until the 1950s.

Mowing has changed, but only in the sense of being mechanised and carried out more frequently, partly because that same mechanisation made that possible.

Irrigation, too, has been mechanised, but wise men controlling pop-ups still follow the rule of fifty years ago, basically, if in doubt, don't water, and, even then, irrigate sparingly. Pop-ups just make it easier to break the rules.

However, top dressing has changed in almost every possible way. Fifty years ago it was far from being a universal practice. I even had to explain to green committee members—and to some greenkeepers too—that top dressing was not another word for fertiliser treatment. Links courses with free access to sand have always routinely top dressed greens, and the wisest ones mixed the sand with seaweed, composted in heaps, to produce a humus-enriched mix to assist in drought resistance. Conversely, many inland clubs, with no "on course" source of the basic materials, top dressed infrequently or not at all.

In those days, there was no supply of ready-made mixes. You could buy milled peat to mix with sand, but this was not ideal and it was expensive, thus in practice it was limited. If you wanted to top dress, the solution was to build compost heaps with alternate layers, turned every six months by hand, of so-called top soil with any available source of humus (organic matter), which included grass mowings, often full of annual meadow grass seeds. These seeds, of course, successfully survived the low temperatures of such heaps and revelled in the rich mix provided apparently for their special benefit. Some greenkeepers even spread lime on the layers to assist rotting; no wonder *Poa annua* was so common on greens so top dressed. Farmyard manure, coupled with a heavy soil with a high clay and silt content, can never make a suitable top dressing. Sand alone, even in those days, caused root breaks, especially if the practice was spasmodic. Soft greens—thatch was a problem even in those days—were "corrected" by heavy sanding. This reduced drought resistance, so such policies were reversed, and so inevitably courses went back to soft greens and then changed back again to more sand! You can still see this stratification half a century later, with all the evidence needed to pin-point what was the current practice in 1948 or 1965, or at least how many top dressings ago. This dating, on exactly the same lines as with the annular rings of tree trunks, was made possible because top dressing was usually a once a year operation, feasible then because there was so little winter golf on many courses, in those early post-war years.

It was quite a common sight to see golf greens, in late autumn, literally smothered in so-called "compost", which was left on, very nearly unscreened, for a week, before being swept off. With virtually no week-day play on inland courses, few members would be any the wiser. I have actually seen a smothering dressing of (well-rotted admittedly) straight farmyard manure so applied, and left on for many days, until the staff could get round to sweeping off what had not been absorbed. How the green survived the resultant ferocious attacks of fusarium patch disease (*Microdochium nivale*), I do not know. Many did not.

LABORIOUSLY PRODUCED RUBBISH

When one considers all the labour that went into producing this top dressing—for there were few front-end loaders or "buckets" in those days and so everything was turned by hand—it was sad to see the rubbish that so often resulted from all that wasted hard work.

A cylinder (rotary) screener and compost heap. Circa 1930.

There were, of course, some mechanical aids to compost preparation and screening. Rotary, cylindrical mesh screens were, originally, arduously turned by a handle, but were motorised later. In turn, these primitive screens were replaced by shredders and oscillating, horizontal screens. Shredders were capable of a reasonable output, but initially all of them were fed by hand. Later, hoppers fed by front-end loader buckets on tractors reduced the hard labour. Shredders worked on the principle of a fast moving, inclined, continuous belt on which were mounted rows of teeth, operating against spring-loaded bars, through which the material was literally torn apart. Clearly the only efficient way, economically, was in mass production, as with clubs with several courses. In the end, however, shortage of suitable material spelt the death knell of home production.

It is significant that, even in the 1959 edition of R. B. Dawson's *Practical Lawncraft,* top dressing is covered in only seven pages, almost all devoted to making compost heaps, much being made of the value of retaining the fertility of the animal and vegetable wastes. Long before that date, some of us were warning against such materials if we wished to favour fine-leaved grasses and keep out annual meadow grass. A combination of composted farmyard manure and grass cuttings with soils, which it was advised should contain 10–15% of clay, even if left 18 months in the heap is as sure a recipe for annual meadow grass invasion as any I have seen.

Sterilisation was advised, but the sterilisers of those days had such a small output that the idea was impracticable when trying to produce 50 tons or even more a year. One also notes, with some incredulity, advice to apply dung to fairways, even if qualified by not using long or lumpy farmyard manure. And this was in 1959!

One notes with interest R. B. Dawson's stricture against using sphagnum peat, as it caused spongy surfaces. This echoes our concern today on its unsuitability, even if mixed with sand, but more on this subject later.

But all this is in the past, and one cannot sensibly criticise on the basis of 20/20 hindsight. Clearly some courses on light heathland with acres to spare could produce reasonable top dressings from the sandy top spit, after stripping the turf or vegetation, but there was an obvious limit to this practice, which in conjunction with other factors, such as storage and labour costs, led to a complete re-appraisal of the situation.

With the advent of all-year-round golf many things had to change, especially in the top dressing scene. Annual dressings, heavy and smothering, in winter had to go, to be replaced by lighter applications—little and often—when there was growth to absorb them quickly. Screening had to be much finer to make this quick absorption possible, especially if there was to be minimal disruption to play. Dressings had to be sandier—to assist drainage—and had to be uniform, with no extremes of very fine material that would seal surfaces, or coarse particles that would interfere with the mowing machines. Very fine materials may have been less noticeable on greens, but the sealing of surfaces led to poor surface drainage and ponding, which militated against all-season golf. Another problem was the need for speedy application. Players did not take kindly to having to play on the fronts of greens, or on temporaries for a week.

Virtually all today's greenkeepers need no encouragement, or education, to see the many virtues of top dressing (of which more later), and so this trend meant that there was an increased demand. In turn, this led to the development of a quite large specialist industry, supplying ready-to-use top dressings, or at least the ingredients for mixing on the course.

MECHANISATION REPLACES MUSCLE-POWER

Parallel with this came a series of mechanised top-dressing machines, replacing the old way of spreading by shovel (often with remarkable accuracy), brushing or drag matting it in. Some of these were merely pedestrian-led motorised hoppers with an endless belt delivery, but there soon developed a market for self-propelled units, working on the same basis as endless belt and hopper types.

One development was with the hiring of large, motorised top dressers, but this concept suffered from two major disadvantages. First, one was stuck with the material favoured by the operator, and second, one could not choose

This tractor-mounted conveyor belt/shredder at St. Andrews feeds shredded material to a waiting trailer.

optimum weather conditions by delaying the work until surface conditions were more favourable. So the result was often a smeared turf and a muddy mess. It is better to own, rather than hire.

So much for the overall scene, with wide ranging changes in every respect, which have taken place in the last fifty years—a change in materials; methods of spreading; time of application, and a complete swing from one heavy dose in autumn to the little and often principle throughout the growing season. Not only are materials different and improved, but the norm is now to use bought-in ingredients, especially ready-to-use mixes which have been tailor-made to specific situations. No basic course management technique has altered so much. This is partly in response to the availability, or otherwise, of the fundamental ingredients; partly to the influence of vastly increased play all the year round (which was inimical to old techniques); and partly to a better understanding of the functions and benefits that are to be obtained by top dressing.

Spreading top dressing by shovel.

This would seem to be an appropriate moment to discuss the reasons for top dressing turf. It seems necessary to emphasise that not only is this a vitally important aspect of all good greenkeeping and, indeed, for other sports field management, but also that it has a long history. There is nothing new about top dressing. We are talking of a geological process going back to prehistory, many millions of years ago. The sandy links, many on our eastern Scottish seaboard, were created by constant top dressing of the strip between an

Top Dressing

unstable dune structure to seaward and the cultivable farmland inland. In fact at times, once the stability of the dunes has been destroyed, usually as a result of man's senseless activities, the "top dressing" from wind-blown sand can be many feet deep. A classic example is at Culbin Sands, on the eastern shore of the Moray Firth in north-eastern Scotland. Here, fertile farmland, and indeed the big house of a prosperous estate, today lie many feet deep under wind-blown sand, as a result of 100 ft high dunes being blown inland by winter storms. Tales of a sudden and cataclysmic inundation of tidal wave proportions are myths, since even under continuous strong gales, the sand borne by these gales could not exceed 1 in. (25 mm) in depth per day over a distance of one mile. No sudden tidal bore of sand, but enough, over a period, to make cropping impossible, so much so that in 1695 the Culbin Estate went into terminal decline. A prosperous estate in the 17th century, it became a desert 200 years later and is now largely under conifer plantations.

It was the constant top dressing with wind-blown sand which produced the relatively level fine sward on which golf started. The turf came before the game. Grass has obviously got to grow through the smothering sand, and those deep-rooting grasses, better equipped to do this, survive best of all. If the top dressing is very heavy then only those grasses such as marram (*Psamma arenaria*), and sea lyme (*Elymus arenarius*), with a vast network of stabilising underground rhizomes, can survive. It should be noted that if these grasses are not subjected to such an overlay, they do not thrive. Links grasses—bents and fine fescues—survive, and indeed thrive, where smothering is less severe.

The value of top dressing was appreciated by early greenkeepers in "levelling" their greens and producing tolerable putting surfaces. Well over a century ago, the secret of St. Andrews greens was attributed to "mair sand, mair sand."

The only way to level surfaces is, in fact, by such top dressing, but not necessarily with pure sand. One can no more roll out turf level with a roller than flatten out pastry on a cushion with a rolling pin. If the soil is rock hard, the roller has no effect. To be effective, it has to sink slightly into the surface, with the soil pushed in front of it like a shallow ripple. This is fine if the soil itself is uniform but, if a dry place is found, the imperceptible ripple stops and the roller rides over it, to come down on the other side with greater impact. This ridging can occur even on roads—it is called "wash-boarding." If you doubt this ripple effect look at some old cricket wickets. The roller all too often stops and is reversed at the crease and leaves a ridge at each end just behind the wicket.

Levelling is not just a desirable feature to improve playing conditions but is essential to permit close mowing, which, in turn, is vital to the preparation of true surfaces, produced to avoid scalping raised areas or missing low ones.

SOIL CONDITIONERS

There are, however, other useful results from applying bulky low nutrient materials to golf courses—greens and fairways alike. Many of these materials are perhaps best described as soil conditioners and all work effectively if application is preceded by aeration to key the materials into the turf, or to actually introduce it. They produce over many years a better root zone on very sandy or very heavy fairways, than the native soil.

Fewer and fewer golfers tolerate the bleached look of links or heathland courses in drought. The uninitiated even refer to the grass dying. They think that if any grass is other than lush and green it must be dead. They then demand fairway watering, but this costs a small fortune and, in my view, is largely unnecessary and out of character. Sadly however, many of today's new golfers do not understand how to play from tight lies and like to see plenty of grass under the ball, despite such lush courses playing much longer.

The compromise is to top dress heavily, while there is growth to absorb it, after deep aeration with any humus-rich material, such as fen peat, though many other materials, including cocoa waste; sewage sludge; spent mushroom compost; even shoddy (wool waste) have been used. These materials hold moisture and there may also be a mulching effect which keeps the grass roots alive, to regenerate with the first serious rain.

Many have disadvantages; sewage sludge even if dried and digested is offensive, while mushroom compost is often very alkaline from the lime capping of the heaps and encourages worms and weeds.

One undesirable fungal invasion under wet conditions is that of slime moulds looking like a covering of jelly-fish—"squidge" in greenkeeping parlance—which, if pronounced, can render courses or parts of them virtually unplayable. I well remember one moorland course in Scotland, where the greenkeeper, looking rather shattered, apologised for being late for our appointment on the grounds that his tractor and gangs had slid down a sloping fairway into the burn. The secretary commandeered a buggy and raced off to investigate, ending up on top of the tractor! One could hardly keep ones' feet on the slippery turf. Clearly direct control, namely spraying with sulphate of iron, is needed, but this takes time. The short term solution was to dress with coke breeze, when that was available, but now with sintered (crushed) linings of furnaces—glass-like chips—which provide at least traction for feet as well as wheels. In golf we do not have to consider injuries deriving from flying tackles on to sharp materials!

Another material which at times has proved invaluable in firming up

Top Dressing

soft, wet greens is a pumice-like material, baked (calcined) montmorillonite clay, sold under two trade names, introduced in the 1970s. It has near miraculous effects in improving surface drainage on heavy soil greens and in firming soft putting surfaces, but has to be applied when the surface is dry after deep hollow tining, e.g. by Verti-Draining, so that it can be incorporated deep in the soil profile. These products absorb and release moisture and dry up surface root zones. Obviously the deeper they can be "injected" into the soil profile the better they are.

An amusing story involving this material relates to a new course being constructed near a Scottish new town in the early 1970s. This characteristic material was incorporated into the root zone to improve structure. One night, a couple of fly lads stripped a sown green and sold the turf for lawns to new householders in the town. When the police traced them, they still had some of the turf, which was, of course, unique. This clearly disposed of their claim to have bought it. They were duly incarcerated—a first for turf identification by montmorillonite clay.

Top dressing is clearly a very important routine treatment to all turf areas. We are not concerned with other sports, but one cannot conceive any other way of producing the appropriate surface for, say, cricket wickets or tennis courts, although of course the materials used are quite different, if only

The Huxtrux utility vehicle, mounted with HX10 full-width top dresser.

because these are summer sports, so the question of free drainage is less significant. What is even more significant is that in those sports the ball has to bounce, and bounce truly, while bounce is the last thing we want on golf greens (or bowling greens!). Therefore such top dressings are far less sandy and will contain more silt and clay.

Tees and approaches will clearly benefit from top dressing, both to improve levels and the density and resilience of turf, as well as building up better root zones. A stronger root structure, of course, increases resistance to wear.

On fairways we have a different problem, and not merely that of scale. Even in such contrasting situations with soil types of thin sand and heavy clay, the same material can greatly improve soil structure, namely peat or peat-like materials. In these ecologically sensitive times there must be substitutes for sphagnum or sedge peat, but not solely because of finite resources and the effect on the ecology of these extraction areas. Generous applications, to the point of smothering, after deep aeration and working well in by harrowing, brushing or other mechanical means, greatly helps the drought resistance of thin soils. As we have seen, this often makes uneconomical and astronomically expensive fairway irrigation unnecessary. On heavy soils, better turf density results from the improved physical structure of the immediate top soil and associated deeper root development.

So much for "why" and "where," now for "what with." With so many alternatives on offer for those looking for bought-in, ready-mixed, bulk supplies, some guidance on ingredients may be useful. Here, physical soil analyses may help, provided the bulk conforms to the analysis of the sample, which is not always the case.

COMPOSITION OF TOP DRESSINGS

The ideal material should contain less than 5% silt and 3% clay and the total fines content (very fine sand, silt and clay), should not exceed 10% to 12%. Ideally we want a humus content of 3% to 5% by weight, not volume. We need a narrow range of particle size, coarser rather than finer. This is not so difficult to achieve as might be expected.

By far the most important criteria are the shape and size of the particles, especially of the sand component. Clearly we do not want a mix that is too coarse, or the larger particles will damage mowers. Far more significant however, is the other end of the scale. Excessive fines, <0.125 mm in size and even fine sand <0.25 mm, may make materials more easily and quickly absorbed, but they are very harmful to surface drainage. For the sake of just one extra day, when the dressing is still visible though not affecting the trueness of putting surfaces, you may suffer a week longer off the greens in winter because of sealed flooded surfaces.

TOP DRESSING

The ideal mix is to have a high proportion of the particle sizes between 0.25 mm and 0.75 mm, with 80% as the aim. Too coarse is as bad as too fine.

Particle shape is important. Drainage and root development depend on water and roots finding a way between soil particles. Semi-rounded shapes give maximum interstitial spaces, while very angular ones lock together like a macadam road. "Sharp" sand, i.e. sand with very angular shaped particles, is definitely not a good idea. It is as bad one way as very fine sand is another.

A series of typical analyses illustrates the points made above. All are genuine, taken from advisory reports.

DIAGRAM 6-1

Grade	Diam. mm	Sample A %	Sample B %	Sample C %	Sample D %
Stones	> 8	Nil	Nil	Nil	2
Coarse gravel	8–4	Nil	Nil	Trace	1
Fine gravel	4–2	Trace	Trace	Trace	3
Very coarse sand	2–1	6	Trace	1	2
Coarse sand	1–0.5	29	1	1	8
Medium sand	0.5–0.25	55	69	5	11
Fine sand	0.25–0.125	6	27	19	18
Very fine sand	0.125–0.05	Trace ⎫	1 ⎫	12 ⎫	22 ⎫
Silt	0.05–0.002	Trace ⎬ 4	2 ⎬ 3	27 ⎬ 74	20 ⎬ 61
Clay	< 0.002	4 ⎭	Trace ⎭	35 ⎭	19 ⎭
Loss on ignition (humus)		8	2–3	27	1
Calcium carbonate ('lime')		Nil	Nil	Nil	4

Although these results (genuine as they are) go back some years, they are still relevant. Sample A is a standard mix nationally available and test results today are still the same as a decade earlier. The availability of consistent supplies is hugely important. Note especially only 4% fines, 8% humus, while 84% particles are between 0.25 and 1.0 mm.

Sample B was a locally available mix, with lower humus and the particle profile, though still narrow, far too fine. In fact, it was really a dirty sand. There are many materials on the market still with the same pattern.

Sample C was a home-mix—an appalling brew of clay and farmyard manure containing 27% humus and 62% clay and silt. We do not see many of this type today.

Sample D is still available for those foolish enough to buy it—very finely particled and virtually no humus, with 61% of fines. It is absorbed quickly but, just as quickly, seals the surface of golf greens and causes instant ponding after rain.

We have seen, in the chapter on soils, the importance of having a narrow range of particle size, demonstrated by filling separate buckets with ball bearings, golf balls or cricket balls. Surprisingly, to the uninitiated, each bucket will take roughly the same amount of water before it overflows, the water having filled all the air spaces. However, if one mixes the "balls," the amount of water (and thus the air spaces) is drastically reduced, as the small particles infiltrate between the larger ones. Lots of little spaces equal a few large ones, but, for best results, larger particles create a better structure for deep root development, especially as our finer leaved native grasses have, strangely enough, larger diameter roots than that old successful interloper, *Poa annua*. This is why it can invade poorly-structured, fine-particled soils. It bears repeating that these roots do not grow in the soil, they grow in the spaces between the soil particles.

It is important to relate the quality of top dressing to the root zone. With new greens, root zones and top dressing should be the same. If you are unlucky enough to have pure sand greens, use pure sand. Never chop and change. Each change creates a layer and a potential root break. For this reason, sand-only dressings are a mistake if not consistently employed without changes. Pure sand dressings are not ideal in that they reduce drought resistance, but I never advise changing if they have been standard practice for years, as on some links courses.

In passing, this policy of compatibility does not mean that with old, unimproved, heavy soil root zones you use heavy soil top dressing. The aim in such cases is to build up a better root zone as quickly as possible over the inhospitable base.

A consistent policy is the only correct one, which means that supplies must also be of consistent quality and repeatable, with little change in physical analysis.

The make-up of such top dressings is basically sand with a humus-rich additive. The proportion of sand to humus is variable, but should, in my view, not be more sandy than 80:20, or more humus-rich than 70:30. Probably 75:25 by volume is correct. I have no use for 90:10 mixes; they look and act like a dirty sand and the small amount of humus is not only difficult to mix in homogeneously, but can have little or no significant effect on moisture retention or soil structuring.

QUALITY OF SAND

The sand must, of course, be lime free and washed free of clay and silt. Particle size must conform to the guide 75% to 80% in the range of 0.25 to 0.75 mm.

Top Dressing

Drag matting—The SISIS Powadrag.

Particle shape is important—technically semi-rounded. Very angular (sharp) sand locks together, firm enough to take a tractor wheels but not very good for growing grass or draining. There have been some spectacular failures with such angular sands.

The correct sands are not all that difficult to find, but it is not quite as easy to keep on finding them. In other words, good quality can run out, while poorer material from the same source may be delivered and used without being detected.

SOURCES OF HUMUS

The source of humus is more tricky. I have militated for 50 years against using sphagnum peat, not initially, I admit, on ecological grounds but because it is so difficult, even if finely milled, to mix with sand homogeneously. Furthermore, once such a top dressing dries out it is very, very difficult to get it wet again. It tends to separate out and be blown, swept, or mown off top dressed greens, leaving behind just the sand. Ecologically, stripping extensive peat bogs down to the clay base, leaving a desert behind, is quite unacceptable. Nevertheless it passes analysis tests, while those mixes with a more colloidal humus source sometimes do not (nothing wrong with that material, but the laboratory tests cannot cope and produce aberrant figures). The situation is even worse if sphagnum peat is used in a root zone which dries out for any reason. Then even wetting agents are only moderately effective in restoring capillary action.

Sedge peat is not quite so unsatisfactory, performance-wise, but it is just as ecologically unacceptable. There is, however, one source of peat-like material which has been used since the late 1960s, the soil overlying fen peat deposits. These beds derive from alluvial sedimentation over millions of years, on fens which have long ago been drained. Those overlying clay are acid, while other beds over gravel overlying chalk, are alkaline. The use of these materials is ecologically acceptable, because they are being extracted as part of a large wetlands restoration scheme.

There is also growing availability of an ecologically correct source of humus, composted garden organic waste produced by recycling. This must be the way ahead, if only because there is a finite limit on peat and peat-like materials, quite apart from the ecological aspect. Initial problems, such as alkalinity and fertility, are being overcome.

CONCLUSION

Today and in the future, supplying top dressing is, and will continue to be, a big business, one in which more efficient production and delivery have kept costs more or less static. In practice, the only serious limitation on amounts used is cost, even where bulk delivery reduces charges and good storage and handling eliminates wastage. We naturally need such deliveries covered from the weather to facilitate spreading dry material through motorised units (with either moving belt or spinners). Drag mats hitched to the top dressers mean that in a day, two at most, a quite heavy application cannot be seen by even the most critical of golfers. This is subject to dressing being done on a dry turf and when there is growth to absorb it.

Whilst the mower and the aerator are vital machines to help fine turf to stand up to ever increasing and abrasive play, top dressing is still the best way to produce superb putting greens, with true surfaces and resilience, but it is neither cheap nor easy. It is highly labour intensive work, which can be mechanised only to a modest extent. However, the effort is well worth it in terms of resultant benefit.

What one should look for is a material which can be relied upon to be consistent in quality, year after year. It must have minimal clay/silt fraction, but a humus content of between 3% to 5%. There must be a narrow profile of particle size, with 75% at least between 0.25 mm and 1 mm. It must, of course, be finely screened, to eliminate material which could damage mowers or interfere with play. Above all, in my view, the most important factor is the source of humus, though never sphagnum peat, for the reasons stated. Little and often, and as generous in quantity as budgets can afford, well worked in during the growing season, will give better playing conditions all round, be these areas treated greens, approaches (very important), tees or even fairways.

Chapter Seven

AERATION

THE STATEMENT THAT aeration is the most important aspect of management in the treatment, not only of golf courses, but indeed of all sports turf, has always gained support from all but ephemeral, manic minorities. It certainly earns the credence of antiquity, with hand forking of thin, compacted turf being a common practice well over a century ago. There have been one or two maverick opponents but they, like their theories, did not long survive the derision of practical men, despite the initial support given by opponents of any type of aeration, chiefly (guess who?) golfers, who have always blamed an off-day—when their putting left something to be desired—on the poor quality of the greens, or on slit marks deflecting their putts.

So far as one can judge, one opponent of regular mechanical aeration based his objections on the fear that it would destroy soil structure! Others objected that slitting would damage roots. Yet other theories, with an equally short acceptance, included recommending magic mixtures, which it was claimed would do away with the need to aerate turf and so eliminate all disturbance to sacrosanct putting surfaces. Even the most gullible of customers gave that one short shrift.

Today, even if some equally nonsensical theories were to be hyped up by the greenkeeping media, now that we have better education, not just of greenkeepers but, dare one say, club management (though perhaps some golf courses based around hotels may be exceptions), one hopes they would be laughed out of court.

FUNCTIONS OF AERATION

All greenkeeping literature refers to this mechanical, remedial, and routine work as aeration (aerification in America), but, in truth, the literal translation is only one part, not only of the need but of the benefit.

The excellent finish produced with a greens Verti-Drain

The world-famous Verti-Drain, greens model 7316

We are not talking just of getting air into the soil, important for the healthy growth of grass though this is. It bears repetition to remind management that roots do not grow in soil, but in the air spaces between the soil particles. If such spaces become full of water displacing all air, then roots, despite needing water, will stagnate and die.

Before we discuss techniques, it would be constructive to specify just what problem this mechanical treatment of soils is designed to correct.

Certainly it is aimed at improving the air content of soils, while also counteracting stagnation and related toxicity, both by increasing spaces between soil particles and by opening up the structure of compacted soil. It is also an important part of the process of achieving a satisfactory and often predetermined air/water ratio in soils. Thus it forms a vital part in improving drainage and increasing soil porosity, therefore preventing flooding after rain or irrigation. Such flooding is invariably caused by surface sealing, due to the compaction and smearing of surfaces, created not only by traffic but by the use of ultra-fine top dressings. Above all, it plays a key role in controlling and eradicating thatch formation, of which more later.

Conversely, well aerated turf shows more drought resistance. This is partly

AERATION

due to encouraging deeper root growth and partly because what water the turf receives penetrates more deeply, thus less is lost by evaporation, run-off and transpiration.

In curing thatch, aeration on a routine basis is the first step, but with excessive thatch creating soft, waterlogged conditions, it first helps to dry up the surface levels by means of introducing ameliorating materials. Notable among these are calcined montmorillonite clays, granular pumice-like materials which have enormous powers of moisture absorption. They do not break down but absorb and release water. To be really effective, these calcined clays have to be introduced as deeply as possible into the soil, by working the granules down large diameter fork holes, using either hollow tines or Verti-Drains.

Another very important function of aeration relates to the control and prevention of dry patch symptoms, by assisting the penetration of wetting agents.

Routine aeration, before top dressing, keys the applied materials into the surface of the root zone, giving more uniformity and avoiding layering, especially if the top dressing is sometimes, unavoidably, of a different physical character to the root zone over which it is applied.

All these benefits derive from creating a better structured rooting medium, which automatically produces a healthier turf dominated by the desired grasses. Such wanted species, as well as being fine-leaved, are all of them deep-rooting. This is no coincidence, for they occur naturally where drought is commonplace. Only deep-rooting species can survive, and where levels of soil fertility are very low, almost to the point of toxicity, those deeper roots are able to seek deeper seated reserves of food and water. This combination of low soil nutrients and very free drainage means that even though some agriculturally valued coarser grasses are also deep rooted, the low food reserves means that they cannot survive, let alone dominate. Only fescues and bents persist. Species with shallower root systems also succumb, surviving drought conditions only as seed, or through dormant vegetative structures such as bulbils.

Clearly, there are complex reasons why we make holes in every part of a golf course; from greens, tees and fairways to surrounds, approaches and even sometimes the rough. In the rough we need both to encourage desired flora and to reduce surface run-off and flooding of vulnerable parts of the course in play. This will be achieved by increasing permeability.

Early keepers of the green observed that areas of fine turf subjected to traffic—a path or sheep track across links turf, perhaps—changed from the fescues and bents of links turf to annual meadow grass and then to bare ground. By sticking a fork into areas close to such tracks, compared with the

Good root zone physical properties equate with good roots and healthy turf.

Hand-forking. Old-fashioned, perhaps, but eminently worthwhile.

soil under the track itself, the difference in compaction and consolidation was at once evident. From there, it was a short logical step to start forking up the track, when desirable grasses often recolonised without further remedial treatment. It did not stretch logic too far to extend such treatments to the greens themselves and so regular routine forking, showing immediate and obvious benefit, started. No one quite knows when it was, but certainly before the regular use of mowing machines.

Apart from improving drainage, soil structure and deep root development, we have noted the improvement to soil- and therefore turf-health, and especially the related control of thatch. This seems as sensible a point as any to discuss thatch, especially as routine aeration is the best if not the only effective control.

By thatch we mean a surface layer, often very deep, of partly decomposed stagnant vegetation, holding water like a sponge. It is derived from leaves and stems, rather than roots, which will have died long before the thatch became an all too obvious problem. A similar but less serious problem relates to the development of a dry wiry turf, which is differentiated as fibre. In the past there has been much confusion between the two, and one still sees reports and articles from advisers who should know better, referring to "thatch (fibre)" as if the two terms were synonymous. Emphatically they are not, and the distinction is not just academic, since the causes and cures of both are quite different. Fibre is not all that harmful, unless excessive, and indeed we need some fibre to produce the kind of turf best suited to the game of golf.

Clearly thatch formation can be initiated by factors other than bad management, notably over-watering and impeded drainage, particularly where water floods down, without interception, as surface flow from slopes above. Another such factor is the wrong choice of grasses, by using or tolerating grasses which are notorious thatch producers. While annual meadow grass (*Poa annua*) is rarely, if ever, sown, and is generally the result of bad management—especially over-feeding and over-watering—one must condemn, save in special circumstances, the indiscriminate use of *Agrostis palustris* hybrids, so wrongly described as creeping bents (*A. stolonifera*). These are valuable only in certain circumstances, which can be defined in over-simplified terms as on courses where there is no winter, or alternatively

AERATION

where golf cannot be played because of the severity of winter weather. They are not to be recommended, not just because of their long winter dormancy but because they are thatch producers *par excellence*. No amount of surface scarification—of which more later—will ever get rid of thatch, though it may prevent it getting worse. The only effective solution is to identify the cause and correct it.

There was a vogue some years ago for some advisers, who should have known better, to recommend using a turf-cutting machine to remove the surface turf, retain it for reuse, then with another pass of the turf cutter to remove and discard the thatch layer and relay the original turf. Within a year, if the management causing the thatch was not changed, the greens soon reverted to their sickly, soggy, evil-smelling, spongy turf, showing every footprint, and unplayable after the first serious rain each autumn. One of our famous heathland courses was described many years ago as having greens which were soft, soggy and smelling like a sewage farm. This was because the greens were built originally on impermeable clay basins, in the absence of proper irrigation, simply to retain moisture in a dry summer. When pop-ups made over-watering so fatally easy, these dew ponds just filled with water, leaving standing water a foot or so from the surface. The answer was to pierce the clay basin with a soil auger at 1m intervals, keeping the holes open with gravel. The thatch then disappeared, with the resultant improvement brought about by better drainage.

It was very convincing to demonstrate that the discarded thatch, stacked for eventual use in compost heaps, had on exposure to air quickly rotted away to leave a dry friable humus-rich "soil." This convinced even the dubious that air will break down thatch, but to prevent it one must not only aerate regularly, but also correct the causes—primarily over-watering and over-feeding—but also the effects of flooding from surface water running onto greens from slopes above. We have to accept that some golfers liked thatchy greens, which were receptive to their thinned approach shots, but they never played golf under harsh winter conditions, so never saw the flip side of their misguided preferences.

So much for *why* we aerate, but we must now discuss *how*; in other words, all the various methods. Each has its own virtues and each its protagonists. One thing is clear, there is room for all of them. Each has a special function and each has its disadvantages as well as advantages.

If one message prevails, however, it is that shallow aeration is wrong, if it is not augmented by really deep action every so often. Constant aeration at one depth only creates the equivalent of a plough pan. This is caused in farming by smearing and compacting the bottom of the plough furrow, by not altering the depth of ploughing in successive seasons.

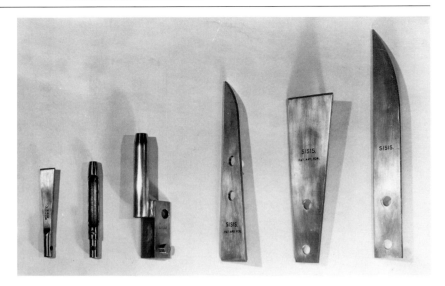

Hollow, chisel and solid tines.

TYPES OF TINES

First we may discuss the types of tines; we can deal with depth and intensity subsequently. There are three basic types used in aeration, namely solid, hollow and slitting or chisel. Each has its merits and its problems.

The oldest method is solid tining, the archetypal garden fork and its sophisticated developments. The advantages are minimal obvious surface disturbance, hence it is often used without depth and is closely spaced, to make many small but inconspicuous holes to aid the penetration of water in summer. For overseeding, it is common practice to use machines with shallow penetrating, but closely spaced, hollow or solid tines.

The problem with solid tines is that, in engineering parlance, they displace the soil laterally and at the base, thus inhibiting the spread of roots outside the aeration hole. We have all seen rats-tails of roots filling aeration holes. What is more rewarding is to see the whole root structure improving, rather than just down the spike hole. The parallel is the effect of planting bulbs or potatoes with a dibber. The plants never do well, because their roots are in such a confined space and cannot spread laterally or deeper because the sides of the hole are so compressed by the dibber. Another problem, more marked with solid tines on heavy soils, is that due to compression of the sides, the clay becomes "waterproofed" and the holes just fill with water.

Where structural strength of the tine is required, as with really deep penetration on heavily packed soils, solid tines are strongest. This especially applies to heavy duty, power-driven tines, as on the Verti-Drain. Even they bend under adverse soil conditions, but hollow tines just snap off.

As long ago as 1910 it was realised that solid tining, as with using a garden fork, exerted undesirable lateral pressure. As a result work began, interrupted by the war, which resulted in a hollow tine-fork being produced in 1919 by Paul's of Paisley. The Paul Fork still to be found in the back of some greenkeeping sheds today.

The main problems with hollow tining are the necessarily greater diameter of hole and the inevitably shallower depth of penetration. This is due to the inherent weakness of the design.

The larger diameter hole, imposed by the need to strengthen the tine, often opens up the way for alien grasses and weeds to invade. How often has one seen a regular domino pattern, coinciding with old hollow tine holes across fine fescue/bent greens, of plants of annual meadow grass (*Poa annua*), each hole colonised by a neat group of invading seedlings. Fifty years ago I was taught by old links greenkeepers that it was not a good idea to hollow tine good fescue greens "as it lets the *Poa* in."

In passing, if you see a pattern of hollow tine holes with the hole becoming progressively more obvious as they open up in the spring, having been nearly closed in over winter, you will be almost certain to find a big fat leatherjacket—the grub of craneflies (*Tipula* spp.),—living happily by day in its secure little bunker, emerging at night to enjoy a feast on the grass round the hole.

The third type of tine became feasible with the mechanisation of the aeration process. This was the slitting tine, developed from the chisel tine. Unlike the others, which were based, even with mechanisation, on near vertical penetration as with a hand fork, this was mounted on a weighted axle, the thin, sharp blades tangentially or radially mounted on the axle, cutting through the turf and root zone, leaving a thin slit on the surface but dividing and cultivating the soil below. From an engineering aspect, this type of tine combines the optimum of sub-soil disturbance, minimum surface effect, and, most important, the least lateral compaction and the greatest stimulation to roots. This side pressure on the soil, caused by lateral displacement around all aeration holes, is in fact less than half that with the much shallower hollow tines. This despite the considerably greater depth of cultivation with slits.

Furthermore, the area of soil face exposed to air is many times greater than with solid or hollow tines, so both aeration—in literal terms—as well as cultivation or soil disturbance of the root zone, is vastly greater, but with less conspicuous surface marks. For routine aeration, slitting is clearly the best choice, but this does not mean that other methods have no useful function and place in this all-important operation.

All aeration, whatever the type, must not, if it is to be tolerated on a regular routine basis, disturb the surface, at least not for any significant period. Pressure by golfers, especially when their cherished putting surfaces

Hand operated Turfman aerator, circa early 1930s. Mr William Hargreaves, founder of SISIS, is at the helm.

are even minimally interfered with, is enormous and vociferous. Many greenkeepers have been assailed by irate golfers, who imagine their putt has been deflected by a transient aeration mark, with the demand "Can't you leave the greens alone for five minutes." To which the correct answer, if not a dignified silence, is "Certainly, Sir, if you stop playing on them."

MECHANISATION SPEEDS UP AERATION

Above all else, even above frequency, the most important factors with aeration are depth and speed of operation. Mechanisation was the solution, but early attempts failed to achieve a significant advance, in that depth of penetration was limited, even if the operation was faster than using muscle-power alone, but it certainly made more frequent aeration feasible.

Early machines developed on two lines but, in both, the tines were mounted on spring-loaded swivel bars, as rigid fixing resulted in the tines tearing up the turf as they came out and, necessarily, leaving long surface slots. This swivel mounting system enabled the tines to be driven in vertically, being withdrawn on the same line, as the spring tension permitted the forward motion of the machine without levering the tine forward.

These earlier machines were hand-pushed. Later, the same machines were adapted to power propulsion by mounting a small engine on their frames. One type, a man-killer and difficult to turn, consisted essentially of a drum which could be filled with water to provide the weight to assist penetration, on which the spring-tensioned swivel bars were mounted. The other, more widely used and developed, consisted of a heavily weighted square box mounted on an axle carrying the swivel bars, which worked by producing a hammer blow effect as the box rolled over as it was pushed forward.

One of the earliest of such hand-pushed aerators was made by Sisis, who started up in 1932, incidentally at the height of one of the worst and longest periods of industrial and economic depression ever experienced in Britain. The first of their hand aerators went to Rye Golf Club in 1934, whose

An Auto Turfman by SISIS.

secretary of the day wrote, with guarded approval, to say that it was an improvement in speed, but at 4 in. maximum depth, it did not compare with a hand fork, and could Sisis produce a machine giving 6 in. (150 mm) deep holes. Needless to say, golfers would not pay, and so developments of deeper-penetrating, powered machines which were both power-operated and propelled, or at least drawn by some kind of tractor unit, had to await the post-war development of golf. Even then, money was very scarce. The comment was made, in those immediate post-war years, that it needed a full green committee meeting to authorise the spending of £5, but one must remember that annual membership subscriptions were often less than that. The agricultural wage, on which greenkeepers' remuneration was almost invariably fixed, was only £3 a week just after the war.

However, early attempts to mechanise did not initially achieve greater depth of penetration, since they consisted merely of mounting a small motor on existing or slightly modified machines in order to assist propulsion only.

To illustrate the delay in marketing such small power propelled units, the first Auto-Turfman from Sisis, virtually only a motorised version of their 1934 hand-pushed machine, was not produced until 1964. This is a sad reflection of the reluctance of golfers, especially those running golf, to fund themselves properly. This applies not only to research and machine development, but to greenkeeper education itself.

Aeration is as necessary on all other areas of a course as it is on the greens, a fact that was accepted more in the mind than on the ground in the early days of the century. It was common practice for fairways to be rolled in order to collect worm casts, tediously scraped off horse-drawn rollers at each pass. This of course flattened and smeared more casts than it collected. This sealing of the surface was criticised, but not acted upon, as there was nothing better than a harrow to deal with the problem on the ground.

In fact it was not until 1935 that horse-drawn aerators were available, though inefficient spiked rollers had been used, with poor penetration and unacceptable damage to the turf. They also clogged up. One is amused to note that "Sisis machines for Horse draft are made in two sizes, for Horse or Pony" (sic). In 1936 the first tractor-drawn units were in use at Hoylake, described by Guy Farrar, their renowned secretary, as "the biggest advance in greenkeeping aids in recent years."

Of course there was much less play in the 1930s, and the need for corrective slitting and spiking was less, though its need was still recognised by some.

Tees, for far too long treated as the poor relations of greens, did not get much special attention until later, though my early reports on advisory visits in the late forties, while concentrating on greens, did even then remind those in charge that the "green" includes tees, approaches and fairways—with the

This SISIS horse-drawn aerator was in regular use throughout the late 1930s.

same compaction problems, albeit spread in many cases over wider areas. In passing, I militated then, as I do now, on fanciful design: bunkers across the entrance to greens, or close packed around them, which concentrates traffic, increasing wear and compaction as well as abrasion. No amount of aeration, however intensive, can maintain good quality turf cover against the effects of such concentrated traffic.

A review of the history of mechanisation shows a programme from sheer brute strength of man-power to hand-pushed green machines and horse-drawn fairway ones, and thence either to putting small engines on such machines or pulling them by tractors. Later more specialised power units were installed to provide propulsion, but not powered penetration. The need to combine speed of operation and depth of penetration was increased by the increase in play, which in turn generated the revenue to make the design and manufacture of machines based on first principles, not adaptations, financially feasible. The old machines simply did not meet this extra demand, but, in fairness, there was never any money from golf or golfers, even well into the 1960s, to pay for special machines. The best that one could hope for was the adaptation of existing hand machines, designed in the 1930s.

An early SISIS tractor-mounted aerator. Scant protection from the elements, above or below.

"Old faithful"—the Autocrat by SISIS.

One problem of towing aerators on greens—with two-wheeled "tractors"—was lack of manoeuvrability, which in many cases resulted in the up-ending of the towed implement.

There was, in parallel with this improvement in the machines, considerable research into the design of tines to minimise the tearing effect, as rigidly mounted tines were withdrawn from the turf. This was initially improved

AERATION

by tangential, as opposed to radial, mounting of fixed tines, mounted on spring-loaded bars to permit forward motion of the machine. In this way the tine remained more or less vertical in the soil, but it was not a satisfactory method.

Long, thin, tapered, high-tensile steel tines, with sharp leading edges, were a step forward, but the real revolution came with the change from just dead weight to power-driven thrust of tines, mounted on arms, driven by a crankshaft. This certainly achieved depth, and could be effective on harder, more compacted soils, because of its positive action, limited only by the strength of tines and the breakage of other parts.

The first machine specifically designed to combine propulsion and thrust was the Autocrat, produced in 1971 by Sisis, mainly for use on greens and tees. This was in response to the urgently expressed demand by, amongst others, me, to produce a machine for under £500 which would give 6 in. penetration and aerate a green in an hour.

THE FINAL BREAKTHROUGH

The final breakthrough came in 1980 in the Netherlands, when the de Ridder brothers produced a machine, the Verti-Drain, which deliberately copied the century old practice of manual raise-forking. This was the best and logical way, because it combines minimum surface opening with maximum sub-surface cultivation, heaving the soil and lifting surfaces *en masse*. Originally developed for football pitches, a few of us saw the potential for golf and were bold enough to put a large tractor on deeply compacted greens. The rest is history, proving that if a machine fulfils a need it will sell all over the world. That need was to combine really significant depth (up to 16 in. or 400 mm), with minimum surface disturbance. In the right hands, and travelling slowly, there need be no disturbance to putting surfaces. Indeed, once properly Verti-Drained greens have been top dressed, even the most critical of golfers would be hard pressed to find fault with surfaces.

Verti-Drains and their equivalent have graduated from being a contractors' machine to being owned by many clubs, who have appreciated the benefits deriving from aerating just when they want it done. This means taking advantage of ideal weather conditions and not just waiting for one's turn in the queue. Fairways, approaches, even paths are now regularly aerated with these machines, as well as greens and tees.

Of course there can be problems, ranging from cowboy operators seeing how quickly they can get the job done, to penetration that is too shallow, causing unacceptable surface disturbances, and too soft greens being deeply rutted. Notwithstanding, this was a marvellous development and the machine, though copied on similar engineering principles, has given its name

The heave and lift tining action of the Verti-Drain.

PRACTICAL GREENKEEPING

Light of tread, nimble and versatile, the compact tractor has become an important member of the greenkeepers' team.

The SISIS HA6 deep spiker was first introduced in the 1960s.

to the generic term for this type of really deep aeration.

For many years, of course, tractors have been taken across golf greens, in circumstances where we needed to achieve depth, often using an old style, heavy duty fairway spiker for the purpose. I well remember one winter advisory visit in the north of Scotland, where the greenkeeper and I were using this method, when he was attacked, almost literally, by an irate lady golfer complaining that, while the head man was using "that dreadful machine" on the greens, she was not even allowed to use her trolley. He had been a regimental sergeant-major of a famous Highland regiment and did not suffer fools gladly. I will always treasure his reply, "Madam, if ye care to hitch this spiker to your trolley, ye can take it anywhere ye like on this course." It was an old Sisis HA6.

MORE PLAY DEMANDS MORE AERATION

Aeration is certainly vitally needed, but equally too often neglected by the fainthearted—club committees and greenkeepers alike—because of complaints by golfers. On advisory visits, a standard enquiry is "how often are you aerating?" The equally standard reply, "as often as possible," is not what was asked and often means virtually no aeration at all. However, be sure one's sins will find one out. I could not even guess how many times I have been assured that "the greens are slit once a week," when I knew full well they were not. Cutting a shallow hole-cut plug and turning it upside

AERATION

The Airdrain deep aerator by SISIS illustrates tangential mounting and long tapered thin tines.

down will show, as soon as the turf is flexed, old slits opening, revealing that it has been done just once, if that. "Once a week! Pull the other one, its got bells on it!" Needless to say, such a conversation is held well out of ear shot of the committee.

Advisory work is, if nothing else, a team effort, and this should never be sacrificed for the short-lived satisfaction of a well-aimed barb, however justified. More often than not, one is dealing with an unsure or demoralised man, rather than an untruthful one, who is trying to find answers that he thinks his critics want to hear. With sound advice, not to mention support, such men can develop into competent greenkeepers. We need to do far more aeration today, simply because there is far more play and especially more winter play. Such play on wetter soils creates far more compaction. Luckily it is an engineering principle that, no matter how heavy a roller is used, it is impossible to compact the soil deeper than, say, 150 mm from the surface. To achieve the desired stability in road building, for example, layers have to be compacted successively. Fortunately this does not often happen in golf, save perhaps in building new courses with massive earth-moving equipment, shifting half the landscape about and creating entirely new contours while destroying both soil structure and drainage in the process. Such compaction cannot be corrected by any normal form of aeration from the surface, especially if the soil has been solidly consolidated to a considerable depth.

There is one method to which I have had recourse on isolated occasions, a relic of my occupation in 1939–45 prior to advising golf clubs, namely blowing things up. The idea is to bore through the compacted layers until more permeable soil is reached, then insert a small charge at the base of the

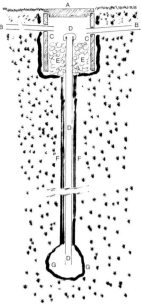

A. LID
B. LAND DRAINS
C. CONCRETE PIPE SECTION
D. LINER
E. STONES IN SUMP
F. BORE HOLE
G. CAMOUFLET

bore to blow a cavity. In earlier days this would have been followed by a much larger charge, the resultant explosion producing a huge crater. The small chamber, called a camouflet, acts as a soak-away. Sometimes the bore was lined and the top surrounded by a large diameter concrete pipe section, into which the liner projected a foot or so.

Drains are run into the stone-filled sump so formed, and the drainage from them overflows down the projecting down-pipe, sensibly protected by a grill, and the whole system creates an effective filter. This provides an outfall in cases where there is a land-locked hollow. Given an outfall, one can drain any land, but water does not flow, though it can be pumped, uphill.

The same principle has been adapted by several variations on the theme, involving injecting compressed gas or air by means of a probe into compacted soils. The probe is driven in by the equivalent of a post-hole "Driv-All".

The main problems are that, if the soil is too compacted to allow sufficiently deep insertion of the probe, then the explosion lifts the turf rather than breaking up the soil below, leaving an impossibly dimpled effect. It is also an extremely slow operation, far too slow for routine work, though it has some promise in special cases of deep seated compaction.

The rapid swing to mini-tractors, fitted with hydraulic lift-bars on which equipment could be directly mounted, led to vastly improved manoeuvrability, as invaluable equally on golf courses as on small farms with small fields.

The comment of Harry Ferguson, who invented and developed this hydraulically lifted toolbar, which made such turning so much easier, is as true as it is timeless. With trailed farm implements, especially ploughs, one needed enormously wide head-rows to turn. In response to fulsome praise as to how much his invention had helped farmers with small fields, he riposted that "there was nothing to it." He was just the first man to realise the difference between a horse and a tractor, namely that "you can't bolt anything to a horse's backside!" Until then, tractors were used as four-wheeled horses.

Today virtually all modern golf course equipment is mounted on self-propelled power units. Pushing something by hand went out of fashion years ago, but pulling equipment is just as inefficient. Not only do we get greater manoeuvrability with direct mounted equipment, including mowers, but in the case of aerating equipment part of the weight of the unit can be transferred directly onto the tines, ensuring maximum penetration. However, as mentioned earlier, the real breakthrough came when Sisis in 1971 designed an aerator with the tines mounted on arms driven into turf positively by a crankshaft, operating connecting rods. It was called the Autocrat. In its day it was just as revolutionary as the larger Verti-Drain, which was introduced

A modern Terralift in action on a putting green.

ten years later and worked on much the same principle. One of the main advantages of the latter was its size and power, giving us for the first time, not only penetration—even into fairly consolidated root zones of well over 12 in. (300 mm)—but a lifting action, which mimicked the legendary old Scottish method of raise-forking, to break up subsoil conditions without disturbing the surface to an unacceptable degree.

To work effectively, and to avoid the age old problem of consolidating and sealing the sides of the hole due to lateral compression, all aeration should be carried out ideally when soil conditions are dry and friable.

One rarely achieves such ideal conditions, but it is counter-productive to

PRACTICAL GREENKEEPING

With this Ryan GA30 one golf course in the south of England cored and dressed 18 greens in a single day.

let play or the golfing calendar dictate timing. Fifty years ago, with no significant winter play, most major aeration was carried out in winter. At least with no play there was no sealing of surfaces or re-compaction of the soil. Today, some still give precedence to the golfing events, delaying deep aeration until early winter with, as a result, much reduced effect. Thinking management, aiming at a compromise between avoiding annoying members and achieving maximum benefit, is increasingly opting for summer programming, not just dismissing golfers' moans in a cavalier fashion, but because on so many courses there is less play, with members on holiday or visiting other courses, in August than in later months. Soils tends to be drier in the summer, and for maximum benefit we need dry soils.

In passing, there is one other type of aeration which is rather less affected by weather conditions, which is based on injecting a fine jet of water under very high pressure into the turf. It certainly leaves no surface signs and so is favoured for opening up the surface in drought to aid the penetration of subsequent irrigation. There are three main problems. It is a desperately slow process, especially if depth is required. It is necessarily shallow, though

AERATION

admittedly it will penetrate deeper if left stationary in one place. The third is that the jets displace the fines in the soil laterally and this might impair permeability on the surface, long term. Linked with this is the fact that the jet will find the line of least resistance down an old closed-in slit, rather than make a new one. Despite these difficulties—and nothing is ever 100% perfect—this machine can be very useful prior to an important summer event, for example to aid penetration when irrigating, because the holes it makes are virtually invisible and do not gape.

Clearly there is a right time and a wrong time to aerate turf, especially greens. If tines will not penetrate because of rock hard conditions, one has two choices. Find a heavier duty machine which can penetrate, or at least aerate deep enough to let water in and to soften the soil in stages to assist subsequent passes, or keep on slitting, however shallow initially. We should never just give up, because we will wait for ever for perfect conditions. Sensible greenkeepers do not slit their greens shortly before captain's day, or, at more exalted levels, just before an Open Championship. However, using common sense and with an eye on the weather, the greens on many of our Open Championship links are aerated as late as a few weeks before the event. With sensible irrigation there is no reason why slits should gape, however severe the drought.

Needless to say, one does not slit when greens are rock hard and dry, but even more important, one should not slit when they are very wet with heavy rain. In the first place, on wet soils the slits close up quickly, while in the

The Hydroject injects water under pressure.

The SISIS Hydromain with deep slitting aerator (guard removed).

second, when greens dry, as in drying them out before a championship, the slits gape. With slitting under relatively dry conditions this does not happen.

As with all operations, but probably in no treatment more than in aeration, the answer lies in doing the work before its need becomes all too glaringly obvious. If you can see immediate improvement from aeration, you most certainly have a major problem.

If greens are aerated regularly and deeply all-year-round, subject only to sensible caveats, then you will not see striking benefits, but if you stop, you will most certainly soon see the deterioration. However, there are occasions when temporary disturbance has to be tolerated by players and management, since neglecting this work, by trying to keep golfers happy in the short term, may well end with disastrous greens and a long period of intensive remedial work.

The more golf courses are used, the greater the need for aeration. Those who yearn for yesterday's conditions should relate that to yesterday's level of play. The only way to emulate that is to pitch subscriptions so high that only the privileged rich could play, and that was never what was intended by those of us favouring the traditionalist view of this Royal and Ancient game, shared from the dawn of history by all, from kings to commoners. In passing, I have often said that I have met more gentlemen in many a Scottish artisan club, than on some of our illustrious and famous courses further south. Such golfers are much less arrogant and demanding, and understand the need for their course to be respected, with time and money allocated to its upkeep.

CONCLUSION

To sum up, aeration in all its aspects and benefits, is more than ever needed with seemingly ever increasing levels of all-year-round play.

There is no one ideal method. Depth is certainly vital, but it must be varied, as in ploughing agricultural land, to avoid creating a compacted layer just below the tines.

Slitting is best for routine work, for it combines maximum air–soil interface and root pruning, together with stimulation and minimum surface disturbance. There is, however, justification for all other types, hollow, solid

Aeration

or even water injection. Hollow tining may prove useful in limited or specific cases, such as introducing soil ameliorants or in over-seeding, or in drought conditions when slits might gape.

If depth is vital, frequency is even more so. I was once accused of advising my clients to use no fertiliser and no water, and to go out and slit the greens every Monday morning. It was not meant as a compliment, but in fact it encouraged the campaign to return to traditional standards. Simply by overstating the principles, it made management at all levels rethink their programmes.

While mowing is the most important operation in the production of good quality playing conditions, with top dressing the best way to produce true putting surfaces and healthy fairways, there is no question that aeration is the most important routine corrective treatment of all types of heavily-used turf, while probably being the most frequently neglected. It does not matter *how* you do it, but how frequently and how deeply it is done really *does* matter. All turf needs aeration, and the more it is the subject of traffic the more it will derive benefit from it. As with all operations, prevention is better than cure, so routine measures are more effective than remedial ones. With this operation the normal rules of greenkeeping apply in reverse: if in doubt, get in there and fork them up.

Chapter Eight

Mowing

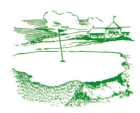

It has been a prerequisite of playing golf ever since it began so many centuries ago, that there must be short, fine-textured turf on which to play. Standards have of course risen dramatically over the centuries, but even a hundred years ago course conditions were fairly primitive, natural if you prefer, and I doubt if today's golfers would be able to cope with them. Yet those champions of yesteryear, using much less developed clubs and balls, managed to produce scores of which many of today's golfers would be proud.

Clearly, in those far off days when golf was confined to a very few links on the eastern seaboard of Scotland, early golfers selected areas of naturally fine-leaved wiry turf, with slow growing grasses and more or less level surfaces. Where better did they find these conditions, which still prevail, than on the natural linksland between mobile dune structures and farmland, with levels produced naturally by wind-blown sand, top-dressing out and making less severe the natural humps and hollows.

Golf, until the advent of some means of mowing the grass, could not be an all-year-round pursuit away from such naturally occurring areas of fine turf on thin sandy soils. This meant that earlier versions from which our game evolved could not be played in summer, when farmed grassland became hay fields or lush pastures and it is impossible to mow fairways with scythes, even if greens could be kept short in that way.

FOUR-LEGGED MOWERS

The earliest mowers, indeed the only ones for centuries, were four-legged; namely grazing animals such as sheep and rabbits. They had, of course, their disadvantages, outweighing their cheap running costs. The localised improved fertility from litter and droppings encouraged more lush, alien grasses to spread and the damage from such scrapes is still a problem.

Mowing

It is a moot point, which came first, sheep or bunkers. Bunkers arose from two main causes. Players taking divots from average drive landing areas started erosion and sheep increased these damaged areas by rubbing away to provide some shelter from wind and weather. Thus these areas came to influence the game, by making it advisable to place shots to avoid such hazards, creating dog-legs instead of dull straight drives.

There were in the later years of the nineteenth century, alternative ways of keeping grass short, chiefly scything. Even in my memory, I can recall greenkeepers mowing tees if not greens by scythe, the only mower being kept strictly for greens use. Others could mow out clover on a green with a really sharp scythe before the days, and even after that, of the introduction of selective weedkillers.

However, the demand for golf increased in the last decades of the nineteenth century, spreading the game to areas initially similar in soil and grass type to links, namely heathland, but even this was not enough to meet

Sheep were grazing golf courses well into the twentieth century, witness this scene in 1914 at Seaford.

Scything the 18th green at St Andrews.

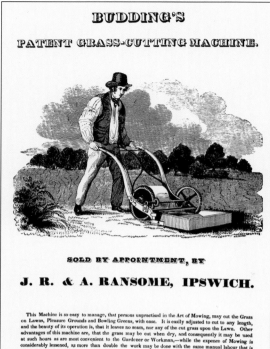

Mr Budding's patent grass-cutting machine.

the demand from unsatisfied golfers around the main cities, whose needs could be met, albeit on very unsuitable heavy soils, only by mechanising the mowing of grass, not just greens but of tees and fairways as well.

MECHANISATION OF MOWING

Around 1830 Edwin Budding, an engineer employed by a woollen weaving firm in Stroud, Gloucestershire, then the centre of a thriving woollen industry, devised a machine with a cutting cylinder with helically arranged blades working against a sharp bottom blade, to shear the nap of woven cloth to produce a smooth surface as with tweeds. Budding developed this concept to mowing grass and its potential was discerned by the pioneer of mowing machine companies, Ransomes of Ipswich, who produced under licence, the first roller-mounted lawn mowers in 1832. By 1858 they had sold 1500 machines, but few, if any, went to golf courses. This machine was fairly primitive, heavy, though with only a 19 in. cutting width. Ransomes then switched to their own design, with an enclosed gear case, which was so successful they sold 1000 in the first season.

Over the years many other firms, up to thirty in all, entered the market, some under licence to Budding and others to their own design, as Budding's patent did not apply to Scotland. Many failed, due to lack of demand or bad

Ransome's motor mower, circa 1911, at St. Andrews. Sharp rotating blades replace grazing sheep.

Ransomes' second motor mower, 1902. A cumbersome beast.

design. In 1869 Follows & Bates introduced the concept of the side-wheel driven machine, cheaper to make and lighter, so increasing the market. Sumner's of Leyland brought a steam-driven machine out in 1893, weighing about 1½ tons, which limited the demand to a few big estates.

Ransomes brought out the first mower powered by internal combustion engine in 1902, mainly for sports grounds. Despite the many makes and undoubted popularity on sports grounds as well as private lawns, mowers were not widely used on golf courses, until the end of the century. They gave a very poor finish.

Fairway mowing was naturally also catered for with a 1914 American patent for gangs of three or five side-wheel driven units to be towed by a vehicle, replacing earlier single unit machines pulled by horse. Many of these original horse-drawn units were fitted with canvas boxes to collect not just the cuttings but flowering heads of weeds to reduce their spread by seed. Nothing changes and we now box off cuttings with modern self-propelled fairway mowers.

In 1926 Ransomes developed the first mains electricity mower, later replaced in popularity by the battery powered models.

The first rotary mowers with power-driven, horizontally spinning blades came in 1934, capable of dealing with longer grass than any cylinder cutter, however large the diameter of their cutting cylinders. The hover mower, the Flymo, was first introduced in 1964.

With all this plethora of types and constant improvements it is really quite surprising how slowly they were adopted in golf. The first specialist greens mower, the Certes, was not produced by Ransomes until 1924, really

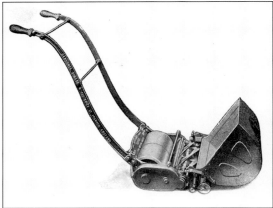

Ransomes' Certes mower—an all-time classic.

The Ransomes' Auto-Certes—natural progression.

a surprisingly late date, indicative perhaps, as much of the poverty of golf clubs as their lack of concern about a superb finish. It was manufactured for 30 years.

It is not always appreciated that the first motorised mower of a quality to produce really good putting surfaces was not marketed until 1950. This was the Auto Certes, again by Ransomes, still going strong nearly half a century on. There were a number of similar quality machines, nearly all now out of production except Lloyds Paladin—a name to conjure with!

Prior to that, greens were mown by hand-pushed machines, not of course every day as is the current norm. Sometimes the greenkeeper would get some help from a youngster pulling the machine with a rope as he pushed it, but the effort to mow 18 greens in a day was daunting, and remember that, post-war, most courses were maintained by a staff of two, three at most, and often by a man on his own. This was one reason why old greenkeepers did not use much (if any) fertiliser; the resultant growth was a rod for their own backs. Skilled men realised that it was easier, on them and their grass, if they mowed frequently, as often as six times a week, even with hand-pushed machines. Not only was this kinder to the greens, but it also avoided the problem of coping with too much grass in a period of flush growth.

Clearly, as the influence of a really good multi-bladed cylinder mower used at frequent intervals became more fully appreciated, especially as golfers played more golf over more months, the need for speeding up the job became paramount, if only to keep out of the way of the golfers. This need to speed up the process stimulated demand for mechanisation. The waste of time in the old days, as greenkeepers stopped mowing to let play through, was unbelievable.

This need was understood even before the war and in 1937 Ransomes produced the Overgreen to meet it. This was essentially a long handled, pedestrian-operated, two-wheeled tug, pulling three Certes mowers. It was extremely difficult to manoeuvre and the units could not be raised for turning off the green, so much so that there was no question of mowing in alternative stripes. One half of a green was mown one way and the other

Ransomes' 'Overgreen' 1937.

half the other. This left characteristically light and dark halves and, would you believe it, golfers complained about the two halves putting differently. It is all in the eye and demonstrations by myself and others to show that a properly hit putt would find the hole failed to convince some of them.

This machine, unhandy though it was, did release scarce labour. Introduced pre-war it survived until 1963, though many were still being used long after that date.

The biggest change came with the importation of triplex mowers from America in 1969–70. I well remember at a somewhat later date, an over-enthusiastic salesman trying to sell one such machine to Shaig Logan, the redoubtable head greenkeeper of The Honourable Company of Edinburgh Golfers' course at Muirfield, claiming that with his machine, all the greens could be cut inside $2^1/_2$ hours. "Very interesting, I'm sure, but at the moment, it takes me an hour" was the reply. Six men with six Auto Certes cutting three greens each, were all back in the sheds inside the hour!

KEEPING AHEAD OF PLAY

These machines did permit not only more frequent mowing, but enabled mowing to keep ahead of the players. Many still think they do not do quite as good a job as hand mowers, if only because with the latter the greenkeeper could ease the machine over weak areas. It does make mowing on a daily basis feasible, even if, for special events, hand mowing puts that final finish on the end product. Triplex mowers also have another advantage, now at last shared by some hand mowers, in that they can be fitted with interchangeable reels mowing vertically not horizontally i.e. verticutting and grooming, of which more later.

Triple gang circa 1923. Slow work for man and beast.

The mowing of fairways developed on parallel lines. The old horse-drawn single unit fairway mowers introduced first in 1914 from the United States, with the horses wearing large leather "boots", slowly gave place after the First World War to tractor-drawn trailed gang mowers, with a range varying from three to nine units. These were fairly difficult to manoeuvre and this stimulated engineers to design the first power-take-off driven trailed gangs in 1964 which were more compact, and then, later, units direct mounted on, and under, tractors which were hydraulically driven. The first was Ransomes Hydraulic 5 (or 3) in 1967, which showed vastly improved performance and manoeuvrability over trailed gangs. The next stage was the development of self-propelled, specialist, permanently mounted, multi-unit mowers on their own compact power units, sometimes fitted with boxes for collection of cuttings. For special presentation, fairways are sometimes mown with conventional greens type triplex mowers, to give a striped effect.

There were of course many firms and many different types of mowers supplying this growing market, but it is not the function of this book to itemise a catalogue of all grass mowing machinery. Quite apart from lack of space (and interest), it is significant that mechanisation of mowing came late to golf. There were of course many motor mowers in use on sports fields and domestic lawns long before they were used on golf greens. Partly this must have been due to the innate conservatism of early greenkeepers, strong in the arm though not invariably thick in the head. Many, as I can confirm from first hand experience, feared the compacting effect of heavier powered machines, and the risk of vibratory consolidation resulting from the motor. Others felt their hand-pushed machines did a better job, and often they were right. Some hold the same opinion still and hand mowing is the hall mark of superbly presented greens.

Mounted hydraulic five-gangs combine high output with efficiency on large areas of grass. The Ransomes' Hydraulic 5/7 pictured here was first introduced in 1967.

As a result, although many firms and many different mowers were actively supplying the domestic and sports ground market even from the mid 1800s and especially in the years after 1945, many were unsuitable for golf course work. It would be invidious to single out any of these once famous household names, especially now the domestic market has switched to rotary and hover mowers, but Lloyds of Letchworth deserve commendation in their range of green to fairway mowers, long recognised as being at the top of the range.

Of course when triplex mowers took over there were the usual fears about compaction with a heavier machine, although strictly the weight comparison should have been between one triplex and its mounted operator, and three greenkeepers on foot with three hand motor mowers, covering the same width of cut.

Pleasing to the eye—criss-cross striped mowing patterns at Chateau des Vigiers, France.

PRACTICAL GREENKEEPING

Lloyds Paladin—favoured by those who appreciate the finish achieved by walk-behind mowing.

Triplex mowers made it possible to mow turf in a vertical as opposed to horizontal plane, by means of spirally-mounted, multi-bladed "teeth" or serrated blades on high revving axles mounted between the front roller and the normal cutting cylinder. This could cope with routine scarification with much less disturbance, even less evident with the introduction of much finer bladed grooming reels designed for routine use as opposed to corrective scarification.

SCARIFICATION, OR VERTICAL MOWING

Scarification is obviously a form of mowing. It was much advocated in the 1960s and 70s to remove dead growth as part of an anti-thatch programme, the thatch being caused by bad greenkeeping. It did not in itself, of course, cure the cause, so the thatch returned. Severe treatment, especially when growth was slack, left quite deep slits and opened up the turf. If one scarified when there was little or no growth it was an open invitation for our old enemy, annual meadow grass, to invade. Attempts to savagely scarify out prolifically seeding annual meadow grass were almost always a failure, because the shed seed (in early days there was no attempt to box off the rubbish) simply secured a foothold in the opened up turf.

The motto is never scarify when there is no growth or when *Poa* is seeding. The verticut reels are less severe and so can be used more frequently and what is more, most of the clippings and seed can be collected in the box.

Grooming is even less severe and indeed is primarily aimed at mowing

Below: *The SISIS Hydraulic Veemo fairway scarifier.*

Below right: *The Auto-Rotorake Mk 4 scarifier by SISIS, who invented the process.*

Mowing

straggling, surface stems and encouraging a more upright growth habit. It can be carried out as a routine, even thrice a week if the need is there, but, as in so many greenkeeping operations, if there is no need, do not do it.

The advent of verticut reels in the first place and then of grooming reels, which can be used with greater frequency and discrimination has meant the end of putting surfaces marred by the straggling surface stems of creeping bent (*Agrostis stolonifera*) and to a large extent, of Yorkshire fog (*Holcus lanatus*), whose soft broad prostate leaves are more penalised by vertical mowing than finer leaved species. In the old days we used to slash the pale, disfiguring patches with a sharp knife, though in truth they did not affect putting, only appearance. Then gadgets with a dozen spaced razor blades mounted on a forked handle speeded up the operation, but there was always some residual scarring. Grooming reels solved the problem.

It has long been one of the basic truisms of greenkeeping that the most important machine on the golf course is the mower and the better the greens mower the better the green. Few would disagree. However, mowing is an operation qualified by many criteria, not least height and frequency of cut, collection or otherwise of clippings and altering the direction of cut, amongst others.

At Augusta, a platoon of greenkeepers cut fairways with triplex mowers, travelling in echelon. The speed and discipline of these experts has been likened to that of the Red Arrows display team.

119

PRACTICAL GREENKEEPING

A lightweight fairway mower. Jacobsen model LF 3810.

"THE QUICK AND THE DEAD"

On greens, increasing the speed of putting surface has been the target for some years. It was not always so, but golfers and greenkeepers recognised that firm, fine-textured natural links and heathland greens were naturally faster than soft *Poa annua* ones. The pursuit of speed began in earnest, I suppose, in the 1970s. All manner of, frequently disastrous, methods were adopted, chiefly of course shaving greens, which speeded them up temporarily, but soon killed the finer grasses which gave naturally faster surfaces, but eventually even *Poa annua* will not survive the stress. Hence the description of such shaved greens as the quick and the dead.

Mowing at a height of 3 mm for any length of time, measured in days rather than weeks, creates excessive stress and kills all grasses, which simply have not enough leaf surface left to provide the food to keep the plants alive.

Various other methods were employed to speed up greens, including verticutting, heavy sand top dressing, brushing, reduced irrigation and rolling.

Tests at Pennsylvania State University were both surprising and revealing, but they did confirm that the age-old greenkeeping method of speeding up greens by running a hand mower with the blades set up and a sand bag in the box was still the most effective. Rolling with specially designed motorised rollers may have some undesirable side effects but it works. The harm done

Mowing

by compaction must of course be counteracted by deep aeration, but the harm so done to the turf is minimal compared with that caused by shaving. Verticutting on a weekly basis and grooming two or three times a week helped significantly but the effect soon wore off once the treatment ceased.

Shaving greens speeded them up by lowering the blades to $^3/_{16}$ in. (5 mm) from $^1/_4$ in. (6 mm), but lowering the blades even lower, gave no really significant worthwhile increase in speed, while regular cutting at $^1/_8$ in. (3 mm) was lethal after a few days.

Brushing has no effect. Heavy sanding, either little and often, or heavily four to five times a year showed no effect. Surprisingly, watering studies carried out in a period of drought contradicted the usual belief that dry surfaces are faster. There is little difference.

The answer to producing fast greens is to produce the right grasses, but this is easier said than done. *Poa annua*, however intensively managed, will always be slower and more accident-prone than fine fescues, which, in turn, are faster than bent (*Agrostis*). There are well authenticated cases of fine fescue greens cut at even 7 mm being significantly faster than *Poa annua* greens cut at 3 mm.

The answer to speeding up greens is therefore linked to sound, long term, greenkeeping, to achieve the best balance of fine-leaved grasses, coupled with short term remedies such as grooming and especially rolling. Harmful side effects must be counteracted by aeration against compaction. Never shave greens to speed them up even in an emergency. This results in some spectacular disasters, all too often "as seen on TV."

A word of warning on an invention that has often turned out to be a rod for greenkeepers' own backs, namely the Stimpmeter. This is essentially an inclined chute down which a golf ball is released at a set angle. Distance run is measured in two directions and averaged. If this machine were used solely to measure the speed of one green against another, well and good. All too often greenkeepers are instructed to produce greens with a specified Stimpmeter reading—and that way lies disaster and disappointment. My advice to greenkeepers

Motorised rolling of greens. Used sparingly, a motorised "turf iron" can increase green speeds without stressing the mown sward.

The groomer attachment with grooved rollers. Used intelligently, this is a positive boon. Brushes and mini-spikers can also be incorporated.

The Ransomes' lightweight T-Plex 185D.

is to hide your Stimpmeter and certainly never let your chairman of green have his own!

The same basic rules on mowing apply to every part of the course, save that frequency is clearly greater on greens and tees. Daily mowing is less severe on grass than mowing it spasmodically. Less weight of mowings are removed by frequent (even daily) mowing at a modest height and the worst damage is done by shaving at infrequent intervals.

Today, few would argue in favour of letting the cuttings fly, but it is not so long ago that half the domestic lawns in Britain became soggy, thatched, spongy areas of turf as a direct result of the introduction and use of the hover (rotary) mower. This created a deposit of a fine mulch of decomposing tissue, which was a breeding ground for fungal disease, encouraged worms, weeds and annual meadow grass and produced turf so soft that it foot marked. Why, then, if we religiously collect cuttings on greens, and tees, do we let them fly on fairways. The answer in the past was there was no machinery equipped to do the work. There now is, and unquestionably the best way to improve turf density and texture is to mow it regularly, collecting the cuttings. This is highly effective in improving approaches so that they are in effect fore-greens, identical to putting surfaces save only in their raised height of cut, regularly mown with boxes and top dressed and irrigated when the necessity presents itself.

The same argument applies to tees and to surrounds, both of which deserve to be treated on the same lines, if not so intensively as the greens themselves, save only in not being mown so tight. Any converse argument that collecting cuttings exhausts soils of nutrients, should be countered by observing that virtually every course in Britain is over-supplied in such nutrients, especially measured against the very low demands of fine turf, and in fact by such exhaustion we are encouraging the finer grasses.

To sum up, mowing and the quality of the mower is still the most important single factor in producing really good playing surfaces. Frequency not severity of cut is the prime factor in such mowing. Never, never shave for any reason, certainly not to increase the speed of the putting surface. Collecting cuttings from all parts of the course in play, if feasible or possible, improves turf quality and reduces weed and worm invasion. Mowing in a vertical as well as a horizontal plane helps to eliminate undesirable grasses and habits of growth, as does changing the direction of cut. As for the vogue of leaving stripes on fairways for the benefit of TV cameras, if it pleases some there is no harm in it, but it does not impress traditionalists, and golf surely of all sports, is the one most based on tradition. Finally, whatever economies have to be made, never apply such restraints over mowers—buy the best. It will save money in the end and produce better turf, as well as better appearance and better playing conditions.

Ransomes' Fairway 250 is a dedicated lightweight fairway mower combining low ground pressure with a 2.5 m (98 in.) cutting width.

Chapter Nine
IRRIGATION

IRRIGATION! WHAT AN emotive word in golf greenkeeping. It immediately conjures up battles between the traditionalists and the "feed and water" brigade. It is often wrongly assumed that over-watering was an unwanted import from America, but this is far from true. If any one body can be blamed, and the blame goes back a long way, it must be laid firmly on the shoulders of the professional golfers—whose aim has always been to take the element of chance out of their game—and their income. Yet chance, or luck, is surely part of the fascination of golf. Many of us treasure the remarks of Bernard Darwin, who dismissed the moans of his opponent, who had suffered a rub of the green—that it was "not fair"—with the all-encompassing remark "my dear fellow, golf is not supposed to be fair."

There have been as many, and as fervent, supporters of the need to control both water and fertilisers in the United States as here. In any discussion, reference to the late and inimitable Al Radko, past national director of the USGA Green Section, is inevitable. Two of his many sayings, all of which will be remembered with affection and support, were, "Green is not great," and "Over-watering is the cardinal sin of greenkeeping." Yet still some golfers equate green with quality and some greenkeepers chase colour to please their members.

We play golf on fine turf, not on colour. It is less damaging to dye grass green than to feed and water it to make it match the false standards expected by too many golfers. "Nice and green" is a contradiction in terms. You cannot have it both ways. The problem of over-watering, which is inextricably linked with over-feeding, is that first it changes the grass species to *Poa annua* (annual meadow grass), with all its inherent problems, and then it produces soft, spongy, target greens, which is very much what traditional golf is NOT about!

Irrigation

The change started in earnest in the late 1940s, encouraged by the crusade of Bobby Locke, the Open Champion on four occasions. Oh, what responsibilities lie on the shoulders of champions, and not all of them use their influence for the good of golf as opposed to the good of themselves. Locke had seen American courses watered, and watered heavily, merely to keep the grass alive in arid climates. He was no greenkeeper and completely failed to understand the effects of heavy watering in a cool, temperate and often wet environment. All he wanted was to aim at the hole, not just the green—target golf, played in the air—rather than the pitch and run-up game, which is the mark of traditional golf.

It would not be so bad if those who water and feed (the one following the other as night follows day), merely wanted to alter the way the game of golf is played, but none of them understood the effect on the grass type or the turf itself. All too soon, good, firm, fast, fine-textured *Agrostis* (bent) greens became soft, soggy, thatchy, bogs of annual meadow grass.

However, we progress too fast. If over-watering really is such a sin, why did it not rear its ugly head before? The answer is two-fold. First, the relatively late emergence of the influence of American golf on the British scene, and especially of their professionals, together with the much greater post-war contact between the professionals on both sides of the Atlantic, who were spending their spare time telling us how to look after golf courses to suit

"If it's brown it must be dead," is the eternal cry of the pessimist. This picture, taken at Hillside during drought conditions, disproves the myth, for the course quickly reverted to a fine and natural grass cover, none the worse for its browning, following steady rainfall.

their game. Second, there had to be some way to make serious over-watering feasible. This was made possible by automatic night-time watering. In other words, over-watering was made all too easy by the advent of pop-up watering, not wrong in itself, but so prone to abuse simply because all the greenkeeper had to do was to turn dials and press switches. Up until then, there was a built-in restraint on excessive irrigation, simply because of the man-power involved in night watering, or the interference to play by the use of hoses and sprinklers in daytime.

It is worth going back to the early days of greenkeeping, when there was no irrigation. A few enterprising greenkeepers might have filled tanks from the nearest stream or burn and emptied them on to the worst affected greens, but in most cases, even in my memory, the greens became pale khaki in colour, mowing ceased, and play continued on faster but still true putting surfaces. There is an old Scottish greenkeeping adage that "a good drought gets rid of a deal of rubbish." One has, however, to consider that there was far less play, even in summer, and far more tolerance by golfers of the effects of weather on courses. Certainly, while native bent/fescue turf will quickly green over again with a few days of rain, annual meadow grass turf, especially if damaged by heavy play in drought condition, is slower to recover and may be left very scarred.

DEW PONDING

New courses, constructed on drought-susceptible heathland and links land at the turn of the century—built without piped water supplies, of course—aimed to give some drought resistance by constructing the greens on saucers of impervious clay or sometimes puddled chalk, which were about two feet below the surface. This is often referred to as dew ponding. This certainly retained summer colour, but it did little for winter drainage. This did not matter so much when there was little winter golf, but later, when all-year-round good playing conditions became important, the system failed utterly, especially in the early 1970s after automatic watering had been installed and grossly abused. I well remember cutting holes in soggy *Poa* greens, which had been built at the start of the century on such dew ponds of clay, looking down at standing water reflecting back at me less than a foot from the surface. The stench of rotting thatch was discernible a long way from the hole. There is one true story of a greenkeeper who had been hollow tining by hand on such a green being overcome by methane gas, and laid out unconscious on the green.

The first answer was, of course, to pierce at 1 m spacing the clay or chalk basins, through to the underlying native sand, keeping the 3 in. auger holes open with pea gravel, and then increasing aeration and reducing watering.

IRRIGATION

The start of watering putting greens is credited to Scotland in the 1880s. There are records of digging wells or impounding streams. For example, a well was reputedly dug at St. Andrews expressly for this purpose in 1894.

It is surprising, nevertheless, how few even of our links courses had piped water to greens before the last war. Certainly in the early 1930s the over-enthusiastic implementation on links of the acid theory, designed more for those courses on heavy clays, burnt up the moisture-retaining humus and a series of hot dry summers literally killed greens, which had too much vulnerable annual meadow grass anyway.

Instead of increasing aeration and humus-rich top dressings, and cutting back on the fertiliser, too many lost their heads and faith in what was a sound general principle. They just went straight back to heavy NPK feeding, along with over-watering with their new piped systems.

Piped water supplies became more common in the post-war years, but even so, some new courses being built in the late 1940s relied on primitive watering systems. In one new Scottish links course, we merely dug sleeper-lined wells into the sand, down to below the ground water level, and used old war-time auxiliary fire pumps to flood the greens once or twice a week. That course today, 50 years old, now has pop-ups, but we still had very good fescue greens with nothing save primitive irrigation at the start.

The idea of watering greens by hose and sprinkler was clearly uneconomic and inconvenient. It was also disliked by golfers, who were prone to pull the sprinkler off the green, or, worse still, onto a part that had already been watered and forget to replace it. Leaving sprinklers on all night to cut out interference with play was no answer, and even 50 years ago I was preaching against this silly practice.

AUTOMATION OF IRRIGATION

This is where automatic pop-up watering came into its own, stimulated by a couple of dry summers in the 1960s. By that time most clubs of any standing had installed piped water to greenside hydrant boxes and some made the mistake of trying to run pop-ups on the existing system. This was particularly relevant where the pipe lines had been fairly newly installed with say $1^1/_2$ in. non-rigid, heavy duty polyethylene. This is notorious for friction losses, so that even greatly increased pressures got very little more water down the pipe, even if it did swell a bit. By the laws of physics, increasing flow increased friction losses, thus reducing delivery. For example, with a 2 in. pipe and a flow of 50 gallons per minute (gpm), a loss of 50 ft head per 1000 ft of run is created. Increasing flow to 100 gpm increases the loss to 180 ft head per 1000 ft of run, while increasing the pipe to 3 in. diam. at 100 gpm involves only 30 ft loss per 1000 ft.

PRACTICAL GREENKEEPING

The parkland course at Château des Vigiers, with automatic irrigation pop-ups at full-throttle.

Pop-ups were first introduced into five English courses in 1964. They had, of course, been widely used in the United States long before that, partly because golf clubs always had more money over there and partly because of the far greater need for irrigation. This applied not just in the arid Southern states, but because America enjoys a more predictable, continental weather pattern with hot, dry summers and cold winters. In addition, American golf had long succumbed to the feed and water school of greenkeeping and to target golf.

The first pop-ups were by Buckner, installed in 1912 at Pebble Beach in Monterey, California. Other systems followed. The term pop-up was first used, in 1916, to describe a retractable head which lifted out of the ground by the pressure of its own water supply when operated by various types of valves or switches.

Later agricultural/horticultural impulse heads were enclosed in "pots" sunk into the edges of greens. They worked well but were much larger. The choice, then as now, was between two principles, an internal gear-driven, turbine-powered head, or the simpler impulse or impact method of slowly rotating the head by the jet impinging intermittently on a spoon, which knocked the head round slightly at each impact.

The first English installations were with very small turbine heads, quite

IRRIGATION

inadequate to cover large greens and originally designed for gardens. These were soon superseded by larger gear-driven heads, with improved impulse heads coming in fast over the next few years. Their popularity was linked with the fact that they were much easier to adjust in arc of spray.

As with so many new toys, pop-ups were soon abused. There was, and is, nothing wrong with automatic irrigation, only with the operators who, through ignorance or incorrect motivation, clocked on the system for far too long, applying the equivalent of a month's rain overnight. Furthermore, irrigation layout design and engineering was often in the hands of totally inexperienced and unqualified "engineers," resulting in poor coverage, and worse still, gross local over-watering contrasting with missed areas. Many is the time I have stood in the middle of a green, asked the greenkeeper to turn on the pop-ups and got just the odd drop on my shoes. The biggest cause was the obduracy of those advocating three heads per green and insisting that this triangulation gave the best cover, and of course a cheaper price! It may well have done, if it had been part of a wall-to-wall triangular layout, but positioning two heads close together and facing each other at the front of the green, with the third some 25–30 yards away at the rear, resulted in a very uneven cover. This system killed itself, but it did emphasise the need for head to head cover. In other words, the throw from the pop-up on one side of a green must reach almost, if not quite, to the other side, to achieve uniform cover. This applies in both theory and practice.

One problem with so many imported, American-designed, pop-ups was that they were engineered to cope with far higher irrigation levels than were either necessary or desirable here. Consequently it became very difficult to cut them back to apply the very small volumes of water demanded by austere traditional greenkeeping. When clocked back to these low levels, some large gear-driven heads did not even complete one full (sometimes not even a 180°) rotation. All this is now history, but these teething problems gave pop-up irrigation a very bad reputation in the 1970s.

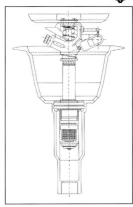

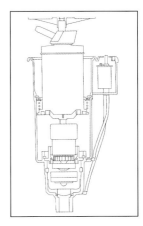

Sectional drawings of modern sprinkler assemblies. (Drawing A—The GR3 sprinkler by Watermation. Drawing B—The GD 186 VE sprinkler by Watermation.)

I speak feelingly from experience, almost from the start, certainly from 1967 onwards. Trying to prevent the proud owners of new systems not to abuse them, and not to risk losing their excellent fine-textured greens, as good in winter as in summer, just for the sake of making them "nice and green" was bad enough. It was much worse coping with members who demanded that, as they had paid for the system, it must be used according to their misguided idea, and especially so that they could pitch and stop on greens in summer droughts. There is no golfing law which says that one should always be able to stay on any green irrespective of the line of approach or the weather.

I well remember one club, where despite the head man protesting that he had set the timers to apply only six minutes a night, over-watering on a gross scale was clearly being carried out. The installer confirmed that the control system was functioning properly. An overnight watch caught the culprit, a low handicap player who had been nipping in at night, resetting the timers and then coming back before dawn to re-set them. His excuse was that he could not maintain his handicap on such under-watered, hard greens. The club solved his problem. He was banned from every course in the county and lost his handicap as well as his hobby. Would that we had the same firm leadership in clubs today. This particular club was run by an amiable dictator, who maintained that as long as "his" course was in good order, that was the way things would remain.

Perhaps one should deal briefly with pop-up system design in broad terms. Clearly any system should be able to apply the required low level of irrigation accurately and uniformly in response to the planned programme. Note the word uniformly. Even the most complex computerised system, with control panels looking like the pilot's view of Concorde, cannot do better than apply water uniformly. Yet contoured greens do not require uniformity. High places

Hand-held hose watering of dry raised areas to top up minimal pop-up irrigation is absolutely vital.

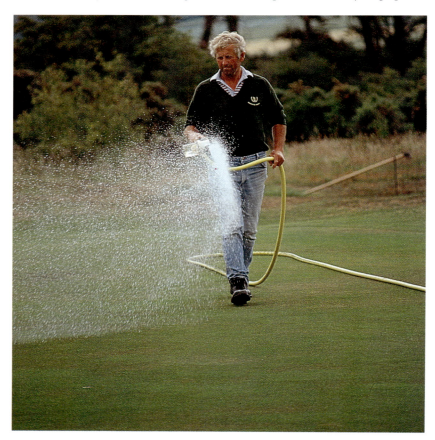

need more and low ones less, and this can be achieved only by topping up watering of high or dry places with a hand-held hose, with penetration aided by aeration and the use of wetting agents. Merely stepping up watering only gets the wet places wetter, while the dry ones stay dry.

We also need easy adjustability of arc of spray to cater for surrounds being watered periodically, but not permanently, as in most cases they are less well drained than greens.

STANDARD SPECIFICATIONS ESSENTIAL

Before installing a new system it is sensible to get competitive quotations, based on a standard specification. It is commercial nonsense to merely ask a number of irrigation companies to price their own ideas. In that way lies disaster, because the risk is that a rubbish specification will be inefficient though cheap; badly designed even more than badly installed; and will never give satisfactory performance. In many well authenticated cases the entire cost has had to be written off, with a fresh start unavoidable.

This is not the place to detail every aspect of a good contract specification, nor to stipulate precise methods to be employed, for such specimen specifications are available. It is, however, sensible to emphasise the most important points, bearing in mind that outside factors such as limited water supplies, big changes in elevation on the course, or the impossibility of upgrading single to three phase electricity supply, may have repercussions on the whole design.

It goes without saying that the installer must be qualified and responsible. Too many cowboys, whose main qualification might be described as limited to gluing pipes and wiring up 3-pin plugs, left a trail of expensive disaster in the first few years. Ask for a list of clients and go to see them, to learn of problems. Check not only on installation but on back-up servicing facilities and performance.

We are more concerned with performance specifications, the most important being that the system shall be capable of delivering 30 mm precipitation per week to greens, 25 mm per week to tees, 20 mm to approaches and the same for fairways. This does not mean that this is a standard delivery, only a potential maximum. It also must be confirmed that these delivery rates are inside eight hours, though there are still very bad systems recently installed which take up to 18 hours to complete the irrigation cycle.

Pipework must be related to demand, but anything less than a 3 in. main throughout the course needs a lot of explanation, and leaves no scope for expansion of the system. Mainline PVC pipes must, in my view, be joined by a combination of rubber ring seal and solvent adhesive. This method enables mechanically sealed pipes to be mole ploughed. Solvent welded-only pipes are not recommended for mainline pipe sizes greater than $1^1/_2$ in., as experience shows that stress-related joint failure tends to occur in a relatively short time (ten years). If installation is carried out in winter weather conditions, solvent welded joints can easily be substandard, resulting in small, almost undetectable, leaks.

In recent years there have been a switch from PVC to medium density polyethylene for convenience and cost. Note that this must not be either high or low density polyethylene, both of which have major disadvantages. MDPE is supplied in coils up to 90 mm diameter (equivalent to 3 in. PVC) and above that in 6 m lengths up to 160 mm diameter.

Pipes must be deep, a minimum 600 mm cover to avoid damage from the surface. Trenching is therefore essential, save on very light soils.

If drainage is being installed, as on new courses, whichever goes in first has to be deepest, usually the drainage, at 1 m depth, otherwise one damages the other.

Control cables should be laid with the main pipe runs. Commonly, most systems today work on a two-wire system, with encoders and decoders.

Sprinkler heads should provide cover on a head-to-head basis and be spaced in accordance with the manufacturer's specifications to achieve this. If spacing is further apart, then either the centres of greens get over-watered or, in extreme cases, the centre is missed.

Most would advise that all the heads on one green can be operated simultaneously, though they need not necessarily always have to do so. This enables dressings to be watered in by hand-operation, which facility should be incorporated in the greenside hydrant box. Such boxes should also contain snap-on hose-connection points for localised hand hose watering of those areas that are somehow missed.

It is absolutely essential that the arc of spray can be adjusted easily and quickly, to cover surrounds periodically but not permanently. Old-type turbine heads were either fixed-arc (half or full circle only), or adjustable only with difficulty. Newer gear-driven heads can now be altered very quickly and effortlessly, while impulse-driven heads have always been relatively simple to adjust.

I have no patience with heads that take ten minutes to alter. Because this has to be done with the heads operating, one needs a wet-suit as well. Consequently, only the most dedicated of greenkeepers will keep altering arcs to cope with changes of wind, or the need to cover surrounds, unless this is quickly and easily achieved. As one head man explained to me, he had to play his pop-ups just like a piano.

Another so-called improvement arose just to reduce costs, namely

IRRIGATION

watering greens in a zoned system, with only one head operating at a time in each zone. Of course, to operate and supply all the heads on one green simultaneously you need larger diameter pipework, which raises costs. In all too many clubs, discussion on which competitive tender is accepted rests with worthy committee men, whose expertise rarely lies in irrigation, so the cheapest bid is nearly always accepted. Subsequent problems are rued by all, not least the greenkeeper. If all heads on a green operate at the same time, this makes it easier to start watering at night before the last players come in. Nothing is more disconcerting than one head coming up without warning on the 18th green just before dusk, with the last four ball putting out!

Tees are best covered with a staggered double row each side, rather than a single row of larger heads down the centre.

Approaches are generally best covered by a pair of green-type heads on each side, though sometimes bunkering and contours make central siting with a fairway type head unavoidable.

CHASING COLOUR

Fairways again are best covered with a double row, as a single row spaced out to the maximum to cheapen costs can produce a very unsatisfactory series of non-overlapping circular irrigated turf, with dry segments between. With fairway watering, we are talking not of irrigation on a regular basis,

Greenside mole ploughing of horse-shoe pipe work for pop-ups.

133

thereby changing heathland and links into meadows, but of insurance against drought. Many good greenkeepers use their fairway systems very sparingly, applying perhaps no more than 10 mm per week. We must always remember that we aim to no more than top up deficiencies or short-fall in the average rainfall for the month. This is rarely more than 100 mm per month, with a short-fall of perhaps 50 mm at most. Never chase colour with water—use the water merely to stop the grass actually dying.

There must be better education of members and especially the new entrant golfer, whose enthusiasm is exceeded only by his ignorance, and whose battle cry is "we paid for it as members and so as members we must determine its use." It has to be a very strong-minded greenkeeper who can stop that ploy. This is where perhaps a good agronomist could independently lay down the rules.

Much nonsense is talked about water quality. The only real quality that is needed is that the water should be wet. Clearly one must consider toxicity, even salinity, but even where bore holes are drilled close to the sea, the risk of other than minimal pollution by tidal water, even when bores are excessively lowered by over-extraction, is minimal. I have never found serious levels of salinity, especially bearing in mind that most links are exposed to salt-laden spray and rain, and links grasses are indeed adapted to a quite high level of salinity. Flooding by inundation from the sea is of course another matter, but the most serious problem is not so much salt as the flooding. It is often forgotten that underneath even the driest links turf one frequently finds a raised water table of excellent potable water. This was the case at St.

Booth Concrete's underground reservoir at Halliloo Golf Course, Surrey. Now covered, this ambitious project is completely invisible.

IRRIGATION

Andrews, where drainage of wet, low-lying fairways produced some million gallons a day of clean water, which normally just dispersed seawards, but was then collected and diverted to their reservoir, and, in effect, circulated back via the fairway system.

Before any decision or debate is started on the extent of irrigation, it is vital to make sure there is enough water to supply ambitious schemes. The sources of water are varied, ranging from water impounded during the winter, to reservoirs and bore holes. Impounding of an actual water course is not allowed, especially in summer and especially where users, including anglers, down-stream might be adversely affected. Generally speaking, you could bore as many holes as you liked, but you needed permission to extract and often this was difficult or denied. Today, in many cases, you need permission to drill.

A word to the wise is necessary in relation to constructing reservoirs. It should be noted by all proposing to install fairway irrigation facilities, that you need huge reservoirs. Looking to the future, with global warming threatened, even if we take this with a pinch of salt—as it is not so long ago that we were equally threatened by a new ice age—it is sensible to make provision for all contingencies. The average 18-hole course with complete greens and fairway watering may need, in a long drought, say five million gallons of water, but with contingencies to consider, it is sensible to provide even more volume. Each million gallons occupies 4545 m^3, so a 10 million

Once a major source of irrigation for The Belfry, this lake at the 18th has been replaced by an 11 million gallon purpose-built reservoir.

Lakes doubling as a source of irrigation can sometimes suffer a lowering of the water line, especially during drought conditions, leaving unsightly banks.

gallon reservoir, with a depth of say 4 m, would occupy an area of at least the size of one and a half football pitches, probably more. Such large reservoirs take some hiding. It is not a good idea to get them to double as water features, if only because at the end of a dry summer they have all the charm of an African watering hole at the end of a long drought. One also has to find a home for up to 50,000 m^3 of excavated subsoil—and when you need a dump, there is never one to be found.

You may argue that by deeper excavation you need less surface space, and thus less surface evaporation. However, here are two cautionary examples, involving excessively deep excavation. In one case, because the spoil was being used to create features on a very flat site, excavation proceeded with abandon despite my expressed concern. Eventually and inevitably they hit water, a real gusher of an underground stream. Apart from problems in trying to get machines out of what looked like a deep open-cast mine, all regarded this as a bonus. They were most surprised when the reservoir obstinately refused to fill to less than half its capacity, leaving unsightly exposed slopes. What these enthusiasts failed to realise was that, when the head of water exerted downward pressure equal to that of the gusher, the resulting equilibrium meant that no more could enter from below. Trying to top up from other sources increased the head pressure, and so the water merely reversed back into the underground stream. This defeated the experts, despite its simple logic. The cure was costly and included massive pumping, capping the stream, filling in half the depth of excavation with clay and then refilling. The water feature now keeps its constant desired level.

In another case a very deep excavation in chalk was lined with butyl rubber, and then filled. Crevices, indeed veritable crevasses, opened in the deep, previously undisturbed, chalk. With 20 m head of water no normal butyl liner could hold, the problem was not just losing the water but wondering where it went—and the effects on say house foundations might show a long way from source.

Having constructed your reservoir you now have to fill it. The concept, so dear to American architects used to dealing with rock hard surfaces and flash floods, of diverting surface drainage into sealed storage lakes by contouring, backed by what is, in effect, a sewer down the centre of fairways, is very ineffective with the soft wet surfaces with which we must cope. Winter playing conditions with contour drained fairways can be very poor, and indeed field drainage has had to be installed to back up this type of drainage.

The choice lies between filling reservoirs in winter from mains supplies;

IRRIGATION

pumping into lagoons; impounding winter flow on streams; or from bore holes. The latter solution has its own problems and you need prior permission to extract. Before drilling you need a survey indicating likely delivery at stated depth. I remember one case where my geological knowledge told me that if there was water it was probably 350 ft down. The amateurs involved were sure they would find water at 180 ft. When they finally gave up, they were pumping a few gallons of fluid looking like Guinness. Geological surveys are never wasted, even if you sign a contract specifying "no water, no charge." Not all of us are dowsers (fortunately, I have that gift), but we can all read geological maps and use common sense, such as not drilling for water where one knows there is 400 ft of permeable subsoil under the rig and no impermeable bed below to trap water.

An exposed bore hole.

Having provided the water, we must decide to which parts of the course to apply it, and at what level. Clearly greens are essential, but we should also be able to water surrounds periodically but not permanently and that means quick, easy and effective adjustment to the arc of spray.

We need independently controlled approach watering, so that we can produce veritable foregreens by mowing (collecting the cuttings is very important), aeration and top dressing, with limited irrigation. The last things we want are lush, soft approaches where balls are slowed down even if they do not plug. A ball, pitching just short of the over-watered approach, could bounce on hard fairways over the green, whereas one landing a yard or so further could stop stone dead.

This huge machine is mole ploughing and feeding waterproofed electrical wiring from a spool directly into the mole channel, for a new irrigation system.

137

Design and head siting must be based on each site, but personally I favoured paired heads each side, echoing the green pattern and obviating that annoying bulls-eye around the larger head of a fairway type pop-up dead centre on the approach-line.

Tees clearly need water, even if one uses it sparingly and perhaps only to facilitate repair work, such as over-seeding, in summer. With many tees not being built on drained bases, for example on stone carpets, the need is for restraint if we are to produce tees you could putt on.

FAIRWAY IRRIGATION

Fairways are now increasingly being given irrigation cover, for various reasons, none favouring tradition. Many of today's golfers think that if grass isn't green it is dead. Others also want more grass under the ball, as their lack of skill militates against taking a ball cleanly off a tight lie. If they cannot do this, then clearly they cannot apply back-spin, so at once they demand that the greens are watered more heavily to make them more holding. Too many of this kind of player are fair-weather golfers, so the resultant poor winter conditions are no concern of theirs.

Many lovely heathland courses, whose committees I used to advise, now have lush fairways and play much longer. This may not be seen as such a disadvantage with modern clubs and balls, but such over-watered courses play like 7,000 yarders and are tiring to the majority.

Ardent defenders of the traditional game are no match for the mass of new golfers, to whom the old standards and the traditional summer appearance mean nothing. Televised tournaments have much to answer for, encouraging demands for Augusta-like perfection and wall-to-wall green grass. It does not matter to them what that grass is (almost certainly annual meadow grass) and equally certainly, if it did, they might well prefer lush, leafy lies, so that they could take a big divot without hurting their wrists. The skills of imparting backspin from a tight lie are lost on them.

In my view, and it is I know old-fashioned and out of fashion, fairway watering is justified only for televised courses and major events—attributed to demands for visual niceties—or possibly on very free-draining links and heathland courses. It removes yet another element of luck, which is what the game is all about. However, I am all too well aware that I am in a tiny minority. Most golfers today refer to nice and green conditions. This in my book is the worst insult to pay any greenkeeper who is aiming at all-year-round perfection. Of course, even if you do have fairway watering you do not have to use it. You can reserve it solely as an insurance, to be used against the combination of the effects of drought and ever more intensive play. But how many greenkeepers, unless supported by their club management, can brave

IRRIGATION

Installing fairway pop-ups. The early stages.

the complaints of members that their money paid for the system and they reserve the right to say when it should be used.

The first wall-to-wall full course irrigation in the United States was not installed until the early 1950s. Fairway watering, even for championships on UK links, was rare before the advent of pop-up irrigation, simply because of practical limitations. The use of quick-coupling valves on old oil pipelines, laid on the surface in the rough, gave fairway watering facilities in the United States in the 1920s, but it was very labour intensive, in moving sprinklers and in interference to both play and mowing.

Travelling sprinklers work tolerably well on level terrain, the best types being the self-winding hose type, compared with those winching themselves back on a wire cable onto a drum. The problem is that the long rotating arms make the machine unstable and, if they tip up, they do not automatically cut out, but can leave a huge crater on sandy fairways, where the jets wash out turf and soil all night long. It requires at least three of the large winding-drum type and six of the winch type, as well as the commitment of one man, to apply the barest amount of irrigation effectively to an 18-hole golf course.

The design of fairway watering must avoid the worst problem of contrasting wet areas around heads with dry spaces between. This is best avoided by correct pattern and spacing, but especially in staggered double row layout, with efficient head-to-head cover.

This brings us conveniently to when, and how much. In my book, April is still a winter month and the start of irrigation should be delayed until May. One hears, even on our old traditional links, of committees over-riding experienced course managers and starting watering in mid April, only to be astonished at seeing icicles on fairway pop-ups and frozen standing water. It takes weeks to restore good growing conditions after such a set back. Equally important is the end date. It is vital to go into winter with dry greens. No one can forecast the weather with total accuracy. If one continues irrigation into September, and the autumn turns out to be exceptionally wet after a short dry start, where does that leave us? With sodden greens, which even with intensive aeration leaves no chance of drying them out: the end result is disease; thinning of turf density; soft, soggy, greens; poor winter wear; and very slow recovery next spring. Is it really worth the gamble? My rule over many years is stop at the end of August, whatever the weather. If September does turn out dry all month, no real harm is done except to those whose putting skills depend on total uniformity of surfaces and colour.

In between early May and late August we have to consider irrigation levels carefully. In an ideal world, irrigation should simply top-up rainfall deficiencies. Here again we find a repeat of the chemical soil analysis situation. Below what level do we assume we need to report a deficiency, whether of a manurial element or water?

In many cases, over-enthusiastic topping up results in the equivalent of monsoon conditions with waterlogged turf and soft greens. It is not easy to theorise, there are imponderables such as losses by evaporation, and poor penetration due to inadequate aeration (accepting that excessive aeration may cause problems on putting surfaces in drought). For my part, I have never regarded greenkeeping as an exact science, lending itself to computerised controls.

The third rule of good irrigation practice after "start late" and "finish early" is "if in doubt, don't water." Little and often is the best answer. Better a light shower every night than a thunderstorm once a week. As a very rough yardstick, in the early, less computerised, days I advised no more than 250–300 galls per 500 sq. yard green—or about six minutes. Circumstances alter cases, but while exposed windswept greens may need more because of losses, they should not get significantly more.

There was a silly vogue a few years ago, to water greens heavily once a week and let them dry out before re-watering. Quite apart from being wrong horticulturally speaking, the practical difficulties were insuperable. To counter the criticism—that there were simply not enough hours in the night to achieve this—it was proposed that six greens were watered one night, another six two nights later and so forth. How does one play a course with six greens literally waterlogged bogs, six drying out and six rock hard? More to the point, how do you get those dried out greens wet again, even with intensive slitting and wetting agents?

The function of water on golf courses, it must be repeated, is merely to keep the grass alive, not green, or even growing, and certainly never to make surfaces more receptive and holding.

If it is to do good to the right grasses it must go deep, so aeration and irrigation go hand in hand. The aim must be never to lose the capillary connection in the root zone between surface and deep root depth, but to avoid flooding the pore spaces between particles, which for healthy growth should be slightly more air- than water-filled.

CONCLUSION

To sum up, water on a golf course should be used as a servant, never allowed to become the master. We play golf on grass not colour. The chase after the great god green has ruined many of our traditional courses, but thankfully nature is very forgiving and recovery from all but the most irreversible mistreatments is often gratifyingly rapid. Remember the old adages. Cold wet greens start growth later than cold dry ones, when growth eventually starts. Water sparingly, little and often. Start later (early May at soonest), and finish by the end of August, whatever the autumn forecasts say.

Vary levels of irrigation according to need, not just on a day by day setting of the timers, but by adjusting arcs of spray and giving some greens more and others less, according to perceived need.

If you have wall-to-wall irrigation use it sparingly and never, never overwater approaches (which is why they should always be quite independently controlled in relation to the greens), as this ruins the run-up game.

Furthermore, remember strict irrigation control is a key to controlling *Poa annua* invasion or in reducing it, with a return to the bent/fescue turf so characteristic of all our best courses.

Finally, remember that even under ideal working conditions, the best pop-up system can cover turf uniformly, but only uniformly, and most contoured golf greens do not want uniform coverage, but some method whereby low places get less and dry places more. It is pointless merely increasing duration times and volumes, because the dry place stays dry and the wet areas get waterlogged. The answer, at any rate so far, is to top up the dry areas by hand-held hose, with penetration where necessary aided by slitting and the use of wetting agents.

Above all, someone has to control golf club members, who, because they feel they have paid for the irrigation, they and they alone should decide how it is to be used. I always treasure the irascible comment of one of my favourite golf club secretaries— long retired—who expostulated on a similar situation: "Members? We take no notice of them. They should consider themselves very lucky indeed to play on our magnificent courses."

Chapter Ten
Turf Grasses

THE STUDY OF those grasses which form fine turf is the basis of all good greenkeeping. While other sports also are played on turf, in no other sport than golf has the quality of that turf such a profound influence on the game, nor indeed on the way it is played. Not only does the golfer want uniform, fine, firm, fast putting surfaces, but he wants to play to full greens all year round, from well-drained, wiry, fine-textured fairways, subject only to the effect of very severe winter weather. These qualities are determined more by the grasses than even by their correct management.

It is therefore surprising to find how relatively few of those concerned with either management or advice really know their grasses. It is perhaps more excusable for agriculturists, horticulturists, or even botanists, however eminent, not to recognise grasses in mown swards, but they should refrain from venturing their opinions on management if they make fundamental errors in identification. Less pardonable are those advisers who wrongly identify dominant grass species in a mixed sward, because this can lead to inappropriate diagnoses and thus wrong management. The number of times I have been assured that the dominant grass on a green was bent (*Agrostis*) when it was an almost pure stand of *Poa annua* are countless. The usual defence is that "it must be *Agrostis* because we spend so much on over-seeding every year with creeping bent." Conversely, when advisers can report that greens they have just examined "are some of the best annual meadow grass greens seen for years," when in fact they were 50% or even more *Agrostis tenuis*, this is inexcusable.

Hopefully, training in the correct identification of grasses in mown turf may rectify some of the errors. Part of the problem derives from the sad fact that far too much education is based on identification of grasses in the flowering head stage and one does not get many flowering heads on golf

Turf Grasses

greens, save those of *Poa annua*. Thrusting a bouquet of flowering stems of grasses under the noses of students is clearly misdirected and a waste of time. The problems of identification are more apparent than real. As with any parallel education—such as bird-watching—the beginner is both appalled and confused by the apparent size of the task. Only when he is over the first stage, with extra confidence and, above all, a competent mentor, does he realise that the problem is not so complex and that he is dealing 99% of the time with very few species.

Pure bentgrass

Confusion arises, also, because there seem to be not only so many grasses, but also sedges and rushes. In fact, some of these grass-like plants are found in fine turf, e.g. field woodrush (*Luzula campestris*), which is a sedge, and toad rush (*Juncus bufonis*), which is found in wet conditions. Sedges have triangular section stems, while rushes have cylindrical solid or pith-filled stems. In both, the leaf sheaths form a continuous cylindrical sheath around the stem, whereas in grasses the leaf sheaths overlap.

Grasses belong to the order *Graminae*, as also do cereals. There are no less than 106 species of grasses which can be found in northern Europe. Of these the majority have been found—not all on one course, naturally—on our golf courses, many admittedly in the rough.

The task of their identification, even in the flowering head stage, is daunting. Naturally there is a limited period when identification on this basis is possible, though in mown turf the problem has to be narrowed down.

It is not within the scope or space of this chapter to try to produce a botanical key to the identification of all temperate European grasses. Nor can we hope to cover, not only the main species found in mown turf, but the strains of those species, let alone the varieties. Evaluation of these would take more than a chapter on its own.

FRIENDS AND FOES

What needs stressing from the start is that, while there are many interesting rarities to be found on golf courses, only a tiny handful of grasses are on the one hand desirable or, conversely, harmful nuisances.

It follows that if anyone can accurately identify half a dozen in each category, they are automatically experts. Furthermore, you do not need to be a botanist talking knowledgeably about ligules and auricles in order to identify grasses in mown turf. If you do make mistakes, virtually no one

Red fescue with bent

knows enough to take you to task, though I have to admit at times I have been rightly corrected by the occasional skilled course manager, when I made too hasty an off-the-cuff identification.

An interest in grass identification was programmed into me at a very early age by my professor at university before the war, who made it clear to me that if I was going to be any use as a farmer (yes, I came from farming stock), I was going to have to be able to identify a handful of useful grasses—ryegrass, cocksfoot, timothy, meadow fescue and a similar number of weed grasses, meadow grasses (*Poa* spp.), bents, fine fescues and dogstail. After the war, during which for six years farming was not uppermost in my mind, I was forced to opt for the golfing as opposed to the farming scene. I had to reverse everything I had been taught—the goodies became the baddies and vice versa.

In half a century of "grass watching" I have noted no fewer than 65 different grasses on golf courses, with some 25 others in rough areas and woodland nearby. You have to be grass-mad to be that keen, but for normal, sane mortals all one really needs is confidence to pick out a very few, and to know which are desirable, and which are weeds.

Before dividing up the commonest grasses into friends and foes, let alone providing a guide to identification, a few tips may not come amiss. Grass identification is rather like bird-watching, with enthusiastic beginners always believing they have spotted some extreme rarity. Later, instead of poring over guide books and pretty pictures, they learn to recognise the "jizz of the thing," as they say in Ireland. Even before getting down to eye-level with a magnifying glass, take in the general look and colour of the turf, especially where it has not been masked by being painted green by fertilisers. Learn to differentiate in a mixed turf between the blue- or grey-green of *Agrostis* and the yellow-toned green of *Poa annua*, especially marked when the grasses are growing in zones rather than uniformly mixed.

Then look at texture. Is the turf dense and compact, or open and rather coarse? Start with pure stands. These are rarely found on greens, but look at surrounds, often so much better than greens, grass-wise, because not only do they not get so much abuse from feed and water but they get less traffic. Many is the time I have promised clients that our aim is to get the greens as good as the surrounds, since the latter are dominated by the desired grasses. Few will ever mistake the wonderfully fine texture of pure fescue of links and downland turf for anything else, once they've had it shown to them, or they have enjoyed discovered it for themselves.

The presence of diseases can sometimes help. While fusarium patch will attack bents (*Agrostis*) as well as *Poa annua*, the latter is most susceptible. Fescues are virtually never attacked. On the other hand, red-thread, always still called Corticium, attacks only the finer fescues and bents and never *Poa annua*. Take-all patch goes for *Agrostis*—not fescues or *Poa annua*—while Anthracnose attacks only *Poa annua*. It is all confirmation that your initial diagnosis is correct.

Having got the long-view sorted, switch to close range. Never mind auricles, extensions of the leaf clasping the stem (see illustration), or ligules, extensions of the leaf sheath arising where the leaf subtends from the stem.

Pull an individual plant out by the roots and look first at the colour of the base of the stem, where the roots start. You may have to pull the leaf sheath back to expose the basal stem. Not every plant will show the characteristic colour of the species, but enough will be revealed for you to find them. Is it maroon red, yellow, with mauve stripes, plain green or very pale and light in colour?

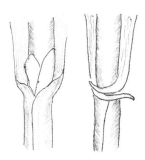

Left: *"Ligule" (extension of leaf sheath).*
Right: *Auricle (clasped round stem).*

Then look at the stems themselves; are they rounded or flattened? If the latter, are they just folded or severely flattened?

Finally, look at the leaves. Is the ribbing obvious? Is there a double mid-rib (two parallel lines) which shows quite clearly, especially under a lens? Or is the ribbing close and parallel, or merely a central rib? (See illustrations.) Are the leaves parallel or tapering? Above all, are the undersides dull or shiny—a really glossy green. Then, and only then, can we pick up the different grasses by checking on their characteristics in the list below.

First, however, we must limit our choice by selecting only a few grasses in the good and bad groups. Frankly, any others will be so rare, or of such minor importance, that their presence will be of academic interest only.

PRACTICAL GREENKEEPING

Top: *Transverse section of leaf of fine fescue. Closed up, as in drought conditions. Note needle shape.*
Centre: *Similar fine fescue leaf. Opened up, as in wet weather.*
Bottom: *Transverse section of bent* (Agrostis) *leaf. Note uniform, fairly shallow ribbing.*

Desirable species making the best turf
- Bents (*Agrostis*)
- Fine fescues (*Festuca rubra*)

Undesirable species forming poorer turf
- Meadow grasses (*Poa* spp., especially *Poa annua*)
- Perennial ryegrass (*Lolium perenne*)
- Timothy (*Phleum pratense*)

Weeds, or positively harmful species
- Yorkshire fog (*Holcus lanatus*)
- Crested dogstail (*Cynosurus cristatus*)
- Early hair grass (*Aira praecox*)
- Cocksfoot (*Dactylis glomerata*)

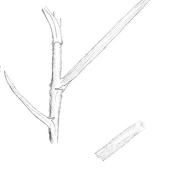

Top: *Stem of perennial ryegrass* (Lolium perenne). *Very shiny dark green backs to leaves.*
Centre: *Shredded ends of ryegrass leaf defying all but the sharpest of mower blades.*
Bottom: *Transverse section of ryegrass leaf. Note fibrous structure.*

Top: *Transverse section of Yorkshire Fog* (Holcus Lanatus) *leaf. Note hairs and absence of strengthening fibres.*

Bottom: *Plant of Yorkshire Fog. Note prostrate habit of growth and hairy leaves.*

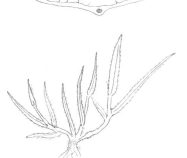

Top: *Transverse section of annual meadow grass (Poa annua) leaf. Note marked double line of motor cells.*
Centre: *Plant of Poa annua. Note short, stubby leaves.*
Bottom left: *Flattened tip of Poa annua showing split end.*
Bottom right: *Boat-shaped tip of Poa, characteristic of entire genus.*

146

Turf Grasses

There are, of course, very many more grasses to be found on golf courses and some may be locally very common, though restricted, such as *Molinia coerulea*—flying bent in semi-rough on low moorland courses; *Nardus stricta*—mat grass on hill pastures and sandy heaths, and *Bromus* spp.—bromes on thin soils, *Agropyron*—couch grasses, *Anthoxanthum odoratum*—sweet vernal grass (with its sweet-scented but unpalatable hay), and many more. Two rarities can be found on some links, such as *Sesleria* and *Koeleria*; which can be useful in confusing theoretical experts when in the field! On sea marshes, normally dominated by fine fescues, in wet slacks one often finds *Pucinellia maritima,* adapted to such wet conditions where fescues cannot survive. This is of interest primarily because it quickly dies if taken away from its maritime environment and subjected to close mowing. It was a frequent cause of bowling greens, laid with poorer sea marsh turf, failing within a year of the turf being laid down. All these may safely be ignored by all save the most obsessed enthusiast.

We will not at this stage start talking about the break-down of species in such huge genera as *Agrostis, Festuca* and *Poa,* because in identification we are not concerned with such divisions: more of them later. Now for identification features.

Tip shooting on Agrostis

Agrostis (bent)
Uncoloured basal stems, round section; many obvious, very close, parallel leaf ribs (no central rib) and dull blue-green colour. May go purple in cold weather.

Festuca (fine fescues)
Uncoloured base and round stems, needle-shaped leaves, which will open up in wet weather but close up in dry; characteristic, light khaki-coloured leaves, forming close knit wiry turf.

Poa spp. (Meadow grasses)
Pale coloured base, folded stems, parallel-sided, rather short leaves with characteristic boat shaped tip (illustrated), with pronounced double mid-rib. If the leaves are flattened the tips split (see illustration). Forms open turf and often looks yellow-green and less than healthy under adverse conditions.

Lolium perenne (perennial ryegrass)
Bright maroon coloured base to stem, a feature shared only with *L. italicum*

(an annual), and *Festuca pratensis* (meadow fescue), which is a larger-than-life relative of the fine fescues. You will find neither on a golf course. Stems semi-folded to oval, rather than flattened. Leaves slightly keeled below, with distinct ribs above and very shiny glossy dark green under-sides of leaves. Forms a less than compact turf, rather coarse in texture. One tip on identification is that because the leaves are so fibrous they tend to strip or shred between cutting cylinder and bottom blade, giving a characteristic browned ragged end in mown turf.

Phleum pratense (**Timothy**)
Found in wetter fairways, but also on sandy links. The leaf base is bulbous (very characteristic) and the stems very rounded. The leaves come off at right angles ("T", for Timothy). This is distinctive and only otherwise found in crested dogstail. It does not blend well with other grasses in turf. Its colour is a characteristic grey-green.

Holcus lanatus (**Yorkshire fog**)
Very obvious parallel mauve stripes on pale basal leaf sheaths. Round stems with very hairy leaves and sheaths (which characteristic helps control, as herbicides adhere more to these leaves and run off smooth ones, so the Yorkshire fog gets a double dose). Very prostrate habit and very pale in colour, especially after frost, showing as disfiguring patches, but not, in fact, affecting putting.

Cynosurus cristatus (**Crested dogstail**)
Used to be included in mixtures for tees and fairways, but the wiry stems are so difficult to cut that the mown turf was left with a mass of unsightly stripped stems (whinnel straws). Base of stem bright deep yellow or yellow-brown, very obvious. The leaves also come off at absolute right angles and are fibrous, so they 'strip', as with ryegrass. Stems are very slightly flattened. Leaves are keeled and very dark shiny green on the lower side, ribbed above, short and tapering.

Aira praecox

Aira praecox (**Early hair grass**)
This is included because it is both a nuisance and easily confused with fine fescues to the unwary eye. This is a very short-lived grass, surviving summer droughts as seed. It flowers early, around May, seeds and dies in early summer. Leaves are needle-like, but the plants are tufted, not creeping. The problems with

identification start once the dormant shed seed germinates *en masse* in autumn, when it can be mistaken for seedling fescues. The dead plants with dry tufts of seed heads survive into the autumn and give the game away. Nothing else is like it, so if you see masses of seeding heads in May on fairways, though never greens, it is not *Poa annua*, nor is the mass of new seedlings in autumn fine fescue.

Dactylis glomerata (**Cocksfoot**)

This is included only because it is sometimes mis-identified as Yorkshire fog, because of its very pale colour. Leaf bases are very pale but very, very flattened and prominently keeled, hairless and vigorous. Leaves are very folded and keeled, broad, tapering, long and hairless. It is never found on greens—mainly fairways and semi-rough. Like Yorkshire fog, its broad leaves do not appreciate vertical mowing or scarification.

If you get to know this relatively limited number, you will know far more than most, and can ignore other grasses as being of no economic importance. However, failure to identify half of them is a severe slur on the technical ability of any greenkeeper. After all, these are the bricks with which he must build his course and wrongly identifying dormant grasses can lead to wrong measures being adopted or, worse still, to a false sense of security. I do not know which is worse, the man who swears he has good bent greens when they are pure *Poa annua* and will not be persuaded otherwise, or the chap with good bent or fescue greens which are a bit off colour so he thinks he should tart them up with a bit of fertiliser.

Good putters will be the first to tell you if you have good bent greens or slow, stubby *Poa annua* ones, though none will be able to identify the species. The trick is to keep one jump ahead of all the members, producing good conditions which they will appreciate even without knowing precisely why and explaining when it is necessary to impose on their tolerance, so that the best grasses can be encouraged.

Hopefully, with perseverance and enthusiasm, the budding botanists will be able to identify, within reason, the above nine grasses in mown turf, and may even be encouraged to start linking flowering heads in the rough with vegetative identification features. The most enthusiastic may then consider themselves experts and, while it is true that an expert has been described as someone who knows marginally more than those around him, it is worth considering that there are nearly a hundred more grasses. If that were not daunting enough, most of the genera described earlier have many species. *Agrostis* has no fewer than six turf species and many strains or cultivars, while the three main species (out of six found in turf) share no fewer than

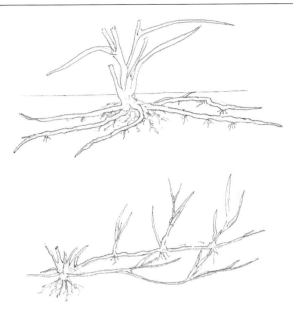

Top: *Rhizomes (underground stems) of couch grass* (Agropyron repens).
Bottom: *Stolons (surface running stems) of creeping bent* (Agrostis stolonifera).

77 cultivars between them. Perennial ryegrass cultivars have 122 strains and rising. These are just the cultivars being trialled.

But does it really matter, unless botany is one's hobby? The most important thing is to be able to identify the handful above with accuracy and confidence, because assessment of change in dominant species is the first warning, or encouragement, of the results of his management policies that the greenkeeper will receive.

SPECIES AND VARIETIES

Agrostis species (bent grasses)

There are a number of grasses within this genus, which in fact is arguably the commonest grass, because it is dominant on so much of our unspoilt natural grassland, whether used for golf or not.

A. tenuis. The archetypal browntop, the desired companion of fine fescues as the ideal partnership for all parts of golf courses, greens, tees and fairways alike. In selecting which one of some ten cultivars to use, the main criterion is to rate them against the desired performance for each specific use. Ratings are on turf density, fineness of leaf, shortness of growth, freedom from red thread disease, and summer and winter greenness.

A. castellana. A more vigorous, somewhat coarser-leaved, old strain (Highland), still the best for tees or indeed in my opinion, for over-seeding in remedial work on greens, as its extra vigour is a plus.

A. stolonifera. Our native creeping bent, with characteristic and annoying creeping surface stems (stolons) which can be kept in order by regular verticutting etc. If it is, then it makes good putting surfaces.

A. canina. Velvet bent, sometimes found in wet or over-irrigated turf, a desperate thatch former and very susceptible to disease. Once it was touted as a lawn grass established by stolons, but in practice it was much better appreciated by sparrows making nests. Very fine leaves and deep green colour, which distinguishes it from fescues.

A. palustris x. The practice of referring to Penncross and allied strains as creeping bent (an American distinction between it and colonial bent) is bad enough, but to re-christen this hybrid as *A. stolonifera* is appalling. It bears no botanical similarity. A fine-leaved grass, tolerant of warmer climes, it was bred to provide better greens than strains of Bermuda grass which used to be the choice for such hot climate courses. It is aggressive and spreading. It needs constant verticutting or grooming. It plucks up badly with spikes. It suffers from disease, both fusarium and especially take-all patch. It produces soft spongy turf due to its thatch-forming habit. All this is bad enough, but in European temperate conditions, as opposed to hot Mediterranean ones, its habit of dormancy in winter makes it quite unsuitable for winter golf in the former zone.

Never once have these strains out-performed European brown top bents in trials. Penncross and allied strains show spectacular early establishment, but rapidly deteriorate. Partly this is because those who specified its use in the past also seem to have gone for sand-only greens. This, coupled with the combination of heavy (hydroponic) feeding and watering with a grass with a severe winter dormancy problem, inevitably means *Poa annua* dominance, sooner rather than later.

To sum up, Penncross is fine where there is no winter—or where the winters are so severe that there is no winter golf.

One would care less if we had not seen all this before. After all, Penncross was bred in 1955, and even one of the most recent introductions—Cobra—in 1987. Its introduction and predictable failure in colder northern European conditions, save under very intense skilled management and minimal play, was partly due to the inexperience of American designers, copying what they knew worked in the United States, with a somewhat under-researched launch by a seed firm who possibly may not have known of its faults, or chose to ignore them. After all, they could always blame the subsequent deterioration on bad greenkeeping rather than bad grass.

There are other species of *Agrostis* —the larger ones found in the rough

Practical Greenkeeping

Above: *Slender creeping red fescue (Barcrown)*

Above right: *Slender creeping red fescue (Barcrown) close-up*

and some small localised ones in turf—which are rare. They can be ignored in greenkeeping, if not in botany.

Festuca species (fine fescues)

Here again there are five species found in turf, which are, with the exception of the *F. rubra* group, of academic interest. There are also much larger broad-leaved fescues, typified by *F. pratensis* (meadow fescue) with very broad long flat leaves and red bases to the stems. The largest grows to 150 cm in height. One case history illustrates how careful one has to be in advising seeds mixtures. This was for a practice ground and I stipulated no ryegrass, but a bent/fescue mix. The club sowed earlier than I expected, and, when next I saw it, the field was like a silage crop. The seedsman has supplied bent and meadow fescue. We talk glibly of bent-fescue, and I was once taken aback when asked in all seriousness, whether straight, not bent, fescues could be used—and he did not mean pure fescue mixes!

F. ovina. Sheeps fescue is common enough, but useless to us as it has a whorled, tufted habit of growth—not creeping— and so never forms a knit turf, resulting in very unsatisfactory pitted lies. One curiosity is *F. vivipara*, which does not produce seed but tiny plantlets, which drop off and colonise under suitable conditions.

F. rubra. This is the main species. It is reputed to be difficult to manage and perhaps it is, in that one cannot make a mistake or it goes! The commonest mistake is to mow it too closely. This is quite unnecessary, as these fine fescues produce superlative, fast putting surfaces even when mown at 7 mm, let alone 5 mm. Using complete fertilisers or over-watering will rapidly kill them.

There are three main groups:
- chewings (*F. rubra*, ssp. *commutata*)
- slender creeping red (*F. rubra*, ssp. *litoralis*)
- strong creeping red (*F. rubra*, ssp. *rubra*)

This last will not withstand close mowing, so is restricted to fairways, tees etc. It is sensible to use at least one strain from each of the first two groups for greens, in order to spread the risk of disease. Remember that the variety at the top of the cultivar list will be the most expensive and in the shortest supply, so ask yourselves whether you really need all those characteristics, such as greenness, for run of the mill use. My personal advice is to use the best strains only for greens, with cheaper, but still good ones, for the whole of the rest of the course, and to use basically the same mix for everything—greens, tees and fairways alike.

Poa species (meadow grasses)

Here again there are a number of varieties, from our old enemy *Poa annua* (itself very variable in its growth habits), to perennial species covering a wide range.

P. pratensis. Smooth-stalked meadow grass (the Kentucky blue grass of legendary fame). Not a lot of use as it cannot survive closer mowing than 50 mm, but it used to be valued for its rhizomatous underground root habit, to knit together loose soils. It was in my view over-rated and short-lived.

Poa annua– *bent mixture*

Perennial ryegrass

P. trivialis. Rough stalked meadow grass, a fluffy, surface-growing stoloniferous grass, of no use whatsoever to golf.

P. nemoralis. Wood meadow grass, often included in so-called shade mixtures, but goodness knows why, as it will never survive either wear or mowing.

P. bulbosa. Bulbous meadow grass, found on thin open sandy links etc. Its interest, academic only, is that it survives drought in the form of little bulbils, swollen bases of stems. When the main plant dies, rather like *Aira praecox* survives as seed and *Festuca vivipara* survives as plantlets produced instead of seed, it survives as bulbs.

P. annua. Annual meadow grass is the target for a battle that we never quite win, to keep it out of bent-fescue turf. It, too, can be variable, from very coarse, prolifically seeding, almost ephemeral plants through to very prostrate fine-leaved almost biennial forms sometimes called *P. angustifolia* or *P. reptans*. There is insufficient evidence to justify differentiating these forms as separate subspecies, because a change of management can sometimes produce a change of characteristics.

Lolium species (perennial ryegrass)

By my book this has no place on any golf course. If our aim is fine bent-fescue turf, even for fairways, why start with a football pitch plant which never forms a really close knit turf, aggressively smothers finer grasses, takes a lot of mowing (and with very sharp bladed machines) and never blends with other turf grasses. All too often, one ends up with a patchy mix of *Poa annua* and ryegrass, unattractive, unsuitable and poor wearing.

Even so-called dwarf varieties are not all that dwarf. Ryegrass does not wear better than, say, bents and fescues, but it may, because it is so aggressive, survive poor quality management longer.

There may well be conflicting views, but I deplore the attitude that says there is a case for ryegrass on municipal tracks. Presumably their golfers know no better and should not be offered quality conditions. In my not inconsiderable experience and trials over many years, I have concluded there is no proven case even for dwarf ryegrasses, even for paths or tees.

Turf Grasses

Other grasses

As for the rest of the weed grasses, Yorkshire fog can be controlled by vigorous mechanical treatment—slashing etc.—on its soft prostrate leaves or by spraying with herbicides, which adhere to its hairy leaves more, while running off smooth and upright ones.

Timothy is sometimes found on golf courses but is of botanical interest only. There are dwarf cultivated forms but they have no economic use. Cocksfoot is so obvious and unsightly that it deserves a mention, but again this can be controlled mechanically.

Early hair grass is certainly a serious problem locally on drought susceptible fairways, and once established it spreads, because it fills the gaps in autumn that would normally recover naturally (without that intense competition) with bents and fescues. Too many look at the mass of fine-leaved seedlings and think, "Oh good, we have fescue," only to find next May that everything has died on them.

Yorkshire fog

Thus grasses are not all that daunting in identification or control. There are really so few that have significance in greenkeeping that anyone who can accurately identify bents, fine fescues and annual meadow grass, and assess the relative proportions in turf, has a head start over many so-called experts.

Cocksfoot

Do not be afraid to challenge anyone who makes a dubious identification. Insist that they demonstrate the botanical characteristics on which they have based their mis-diagnosis. This is often a very effective way of gaining an initiative, or demolishing charlatans. This technique was used by Tom Simpson, the famous architect of the inter-war years, who used to turn up at a client's course in a Rolls Royce, establishing at once that he was no cheap fly-by-night. His point was that he controlled from the start, while the Rolls won him the first few holes outright.

The best way to check the credentials of any adviser is to ask him to identify grass from small plantlets taken from mown turf. If he does not know them, it is a safe bet he might not know much about other facets of greenkeeping.

Ryegrass - Yorkshire fog - Crested dogstail

RUSHES AND SEDGES

Only one in each of these genera is of direct interest to greenkeepers.

Toadrush (*Juncus bufonis*)

Symptomatic of wet conditions and often associated with over-watering, it shows as individual tufted plants with solid round leaves and is often found with seed heads in early spring. It can ruin putting surfaces, but it can be sprayed out with approved selective herbicides. The main line of attack must be to reduce waterlogging by aeration and by cutting back on irrigation.

Field woodrush (*Luzula campestris*)

Actually a sedge, not a rush. It is not of great significance as it is not found on greens. In slightly longer turf its very early seeding and brown hairy tufted leaves make it all too obvious, but it does not interfere with golf. It can be sprayed out if its presence is resented, but most tolerate it or ignore it.

WEEDS

With progressive bans on the use of specialist herbicides, logically leading eventually to a total cessation of their use, we may have to revert to cultural, rather than herbicidal, methods. Selective weedkillers, developed during the war as a weapon and turned into plough-shares of inestimable value, revolutionised weed control.

I well remember, on one long six-week tour of Irish courses for the G.U.I. just after the end of the war, going to course after course which were almost unplayable because of starweed (*Plantago coronopus*) and daisies *(Bellis perennis)*. I had organised that supplies of the then only available herbicide would be provided. Initial disbelief—that this miracle powder would clear greens—gave way to delight. Because of the lack of public transport I relied on each club to get me to the next, so I was often going back over my tracks. One small nine hole course, seen some weeks after my visit, had the members ecstatic about the improvement—"shure, it would be a lasting disgrace to the club to let the boy'o away sober." They tried, but did not succeed. But that is, or was, one of the joys of advisory work—every so often one can work miracles.

Prior to selective herbicides, which today are household products, we had to rely on scorching broad-leaved rosette weeds with sulphates of ammonia and iron applied on damp surfaces and relying on hot sun to do the work, or to keep soils acid to discourage clover. Close scything was carried out, against clover and yarrow, the nearest today being grooming and verticutting.

Hand weeding was commonly practised on links courses against starweed. One well remembers the line of kneeling women on Lothian links, recruited from potato pickers, definitely not relishing polite enquiries from young advisers as to the state of their knees or backs.

There really is no point in itemising all the weeds found in turf. A weed is a successful plant out of place, and that covers a lot of plants.

Suffice to say, until growth-regulating herbicides are permanently banned by narrow minded bodies and ignorant authorities, on pretexts varying from being kind to weeds to contamination risks on water supplies, there is really still one specific effective weedkiller for every weed, though some are more difficult to kill than others.

Weeds have to invade through scars in dense knit turf, which is why there is an age-old resistance to hollow-tining fescue turf on links unless other methods fail. If this is done in spring, when the *Poa* is seeding, every fork hole will soon be sporting a plant or so of invading *Poa annua*, in a classic domino pattern.

Growth herbicides quite naturally need growth to work, yet can be easily washed off by rain before they can become effective. Timing is therefore important—actively growing conditions and 48 hours dry weather are ideal but not always achievable.

Worm casts provide excellent conditions for weed seeds to germinate, so we must control earthworms. Collecting cuttings to hopefully reduce the dispersion of weed seeds is something which goes back to the start of the century with canvas boxes on horse-drawn gang-mowers. It certainly is very important in improving turf density and quality—as in mowing approaches—and collection also stops the cuttings acting as worm-food.

With a possible ban on herbicides, it may have to be our first line of defence in future.

Controlled irrigation is another factor. Over-watering helps weeds and weed grasses to thrive, while "a good drought gets rid of a deal of rubbish."

All these management patterns may have to be used against weed invasion if selective herbicides are progressively banned. Though this is unlikely it is possible, despite the enormous lobby of intensive arable farming, which would be impossible if weeds could flourish and dominate as they used to seventy years ago. One is reminded of the cartoon depicting two lady hikers, complimenting an irate looking farmer on the fact that he had the prettiest fields for miles around!

One hardly ever sees a starweed, even on links greens these days, and one hopes that we will never again have to putt over surfaces which were literally pock-marked by the rosettes of this seaside plantain, touching each other and smothering the weak grass between the weeds. We do tend to take weed-free turf for granted, and overlook the enormous debt we owe to the chemists who developed growth-regulating herbicides.

Chapter Eleven
.....
TURF GRASS DISEASES AND THE GOLF COURSE

For as long as there have been plants, there have also been diseases. The science of plant pathology—the study of plants and their diseases—has been continuous for over 300 years in the UK, yet began comparatively recently for grasses maintained as turf on golf courses. Around 80 years ago, Fusarium patch disease was described as the most damaging and disfiguring disease of fine turf in the UK. Despite decades of research and practical experience this is still true today. What does this teach us of the abilities of disease to survive, particularly as greenkeepers charged with their prevention and control? The lesson to be learnt is that, despite all the advances in plant breeding, cultural means and chemicals, diseases are still able to cause a significant detraction from the high quality standards we are trying to achieve. In effect, unless some new revolutionary treatment is on the horizon, about which the author has no knowledge, diseases are here to stay and we must think in terms of *managing* them effectively rather than imposing unrealistic targets of complete eradication or control.

Think also of the standards we are trying to maintain on the course. A farmer with 1% disease infestation in his crop would generally not consider this significant, as there would be little effect on yield. On a golf green, 1% surface area affected by fusarium patch translates into several thousand scars, a situation that is quite intolerable. Thus, greenkeepers are unique with respect to diseases on the course as their standards are probably the highest of any situation.

Having begun by painting the negative picture, let us now turn to how UK greenkeepers fare in comparison with their foreign counterparts.

World-wide there are over 60 grass species recorded as being maintained as turf, with approximately 150 disease problems to consider. In the UK there are principally only three turf grasses—bents, fescues and the ubiquitous annual meadow grass. Furthermore, as we have a fairly consistent cool temperate climate (the significance of which will be explained later), across the UK, the potential for disease attack is further limited. This chapter contains information on only five major diseases and their related problems—fusarium patch, anthracnose, take-all, thatch fungi and dry patch. While at times these may cause serious damage, do not get the importance of disease, relative to other greenkeeping matters, out of context.

Disease is often portrayed in isolation from other problems the greenkeeper may have in attempting to produce the highest possible quality playing surface. In fact, every greenkeeping operation, be it mechanical treatment, fertiliser application, or seeding, to name but three examples, has a direct bearing on the nature and severity of turf grass diseases. Disease should be considered together with the other major factors in producing a quality turf grass surface for golf.

DISEASE DIAGNOSIS AND IDENTIFICATION

In common with the medical world, the importance of making a correct diagnosis at the beginning is paramount, as all further decisions and treatments will depend upon this. A mistake in identifying a disease could lead to inappropriate treatment, which may even exacerbate the problem and make it worse than it was at the beginning. During the dry summer of 1995, this mistake was made—and the consequences were clear for all to see. Furthermore, as corrective treatment is most successful if made early, when the first symptoms appear, correct identification is clearly important. Each section appearing below and covering the individual turf grass diseases gives detailed information on the key features of each disease from which it may be identified. If in any doubt, expert advice should be sought. This is readily available from qualified plant pathologists based at the following institutes:

Institute	*Location*
ADAS	Laboratory in Leeds, service nationwide
Scottish Agricultural Colleges	Ayr, Edinburgh, Aberdeen
Service Chemicals	East Midlands and northern England
PSD Agronomy	Lancashire, service nationwide
Institute Grassland & Environmental Research	Aberystwyth, Wales

Integrated disease management

Integrated disease management (IDM) is defined as the complementary use of cultural, biological and chemical methods to maintain disease at an acceptable level. This essentially means doing everything possible to prevent diseases from occurring and, when they do, in keeping them at a very low level by using all the tools at our disposal. This can include cultural methods such as modifying the irrigation or fertiliser programme, biological methods such as choosing cultivars resistant to disease, and also the careful and judicious use of chemicals. IDM is a recurring theme throughout this chapter and specific disease prevention methods are given for each disease below.

The disease triangle

Virtually every text book on plant pathology contains the diagram shown. It illustrates very concisely how the environment, the host (i.e. the turf grass), and the pathogen (the fungi that cause the disease) are all inter-related.

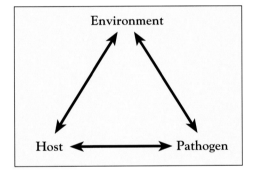

The turf is there all the time and is not like, say, a crop of wheat in a farmer's field that is harvested and a new crop planted. Not as obvious is the fact that pathogens are also present all the time in the turf and soil as well. Why then do we not get all diseases all of the time? The answer is that the environment plays a major part in determining when disease strikes and *how* it spreads. For example, fusarium patch thrives on wet, cool, high nutrient conditions, whereas red thread likes a warmer, low nutrient regime. This is important, for we know from research and experience the principal environmental conditions that favour each disease. Armed with this information we can manipulate the environment— for example by promoting a drier turf surface throughout the winter—to the detriment of disease development.

Fusarium patch disease (*Microdochium nivale*)

In Europe, fusarium patch disease is by far the most common disease that can cause significant damage on a golf course. Whilst other diseases mentioned herein may cause severe problems in certain situations, none are as widespread and prevalent as fusarium patch. Virtually every golf course has an outbreak of this disease sometime during the year and it is fair to say that fusarium patch is the number one disease problem faced by the greenkeeper. For this reason alone, fusarium patch is covered in detail.

As with all diseases, it is essential to recognise fusarium patch from the visual symptoms of the disease. Furthermore, it is vital to be able to recognise

Characteristic symptoms of fusarium patch disease.

the disease in its *early* stages of development. The reason for this is that the chances of a curative treatment being effective are much greater if remedies are applied at an early stage. The first step in recognition is to identify the grass species affected. Fusarium patch disease is primarily a disease of annual meadow grass, with fescues and perennial ryegrass generally more resistant to attack, although bents may also suffer severe damage. Be it annual meadow grass or bent grass, the early symptoms are similar in that the disease usually first appears as orange, water-soaked spots, typically 2–3 cm in diameter. These spots may coalesce to form larger affected patches. Under cool, humid conditions, spots may increase in diameter to form scars up to 10 cm wide. In all cases one will find the characteristic orange to straw-coloured patches, which appear water-soaked and slimy to the touch. Under very high humidity, a wispy white or pink mycelium around the edge of the scar may also be seen, which indicates very active disease. In time the centre of the patch may turn straw or bleached in colour, which indicates less active disease.

Reiterating, environmental conditions play a major role in determine the nature and severity of turf grass diseases. Fusarium patch is no exception and the principal environmental factors, along with what may be done from the cultural control point of view, are given here:

Fusarium patch is favoured by a cool temperate climate. It is in fact highly suited to our cold winters, with temperatures above freezing and up to around 10° to 15°C being the optimum for disease development. Fusarium patch may also occur in warmer weather in the spring and autumn. Sub-zero temperatures will check the disease, with the frosty conditions of winter effectively halting disease development. Of course, temperatures are outside our control, but these points serve to explain the point: that turf grass on UK golf courses is being maintained in semi-ideal conditions for the development of fusarium patch. The disease may also spread under snow cover, in which case it is often referred to as pink snow mould.

The next environmental factor favouring this disease is water. Fusarium patch is favoured by moisture in the turf surface, e.g. due to poor surface drainage or water-retaining thatch. This is one reason why mechanical aeration (described in chapter seven) is so important. Promoting a dry turf surface, especially in the winter months, is the principal cultural method for the prevention of the disease. Fusarium patch is also favoured by dew on the surface, which should be dispersed by manual switching or a mechanical method or by an application of wetting agent. Again, this is a simple, effective method of disease prevention.

Surface alkalinity also has an effect on fusarium patch disease. Alkaline materials may find their way onto the turf surface in many ways, for example by sand splash from bunkers, by hand-hosed irrigation water or deliberate (ill-advised) applications. Thus, for disease prevention, choice of a lime-free topdressing is important, while irrigation water may be acidified prior to application. The whole principle of maintaining turf under acidic conditions is described elsewhere in this text. Let me emphasise how important this is with respect to fusarium patch disease. Acidifying fertilisers and the use of iron sulphate or the new "liquid iron" materials can greatly assist in this process. During the winter months leaf surface acidification, with hardening treatments such as iron sulphate, may have a major preventative effect on fusarium patch.

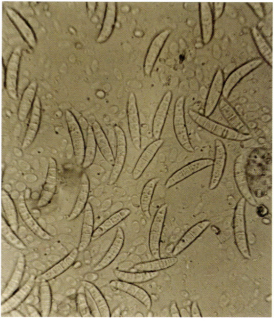

Fusarium spores. Magnification X 900.

"Smothering" the turf, with heavy top dressings as well as a snow cover, will also induce attacks of the disease—which often starts where putting surfaces are locally smothered by sand blasted out from greenside bunkers.

The nutrient status of the turf also has a major effect on fusarium patch. High nitrogen conditions, particularly those devised from organic materials, favour the disease. Soft, lush growth produced by excessive nitrogen is a major factor in predisposing turf to attack. The judicious use of nitrogen is emphasised, while avoiding any application after August at the latest.

Biological factors also have a major impact on fusarium patch. Anything that helps to reduce the annual meadow grass content of the sward will effectively remove the host for the disease. Thus the favouring of bents and fescues, to the elimination of annual meadow grass, is the way to have the most impact on the disease in the long run. For other diseases there are cultivars which show a certain degree of resistance to attack, but this is not practicable for fusarium patch.

Thus it can be seen that several cultural methods exist for the prevention of fusarium patch disease. However, even if all the aforementioned methods are implemented, the fact remains that fusarium patch is still a significant problem on many UK golf courses. The reason is simple—our conducive climate and the prevalence of the susceptible bents and annual meadow grass, aided by over-feeding.

As part of an integrated disease management programme, pesticides are often necessary. I advocate the careful and judicious use of chemicals as part of a IDM programme, for it is complementary to preventative, cultural and biological methods. There now exists a fairly wide range of chemicals from which to choose and the following points will show how to get the best from them.

First, treat the turf at the first signs of the disease. All chemicals are much more effective applied at this time rather than curatively. No amount of chemical is going to bring dead grass back to life! Second, do not over rely on chemicals. Typically, a UK golf course will make between two and four spray applications per year. Any more than this may mean that cultural methods are being neglected. Third, use systemic fungicides during periods of active plant growth (spring to autumn), and curatives during the winter months. Certain new materials being marketed have two active ingredients, one protective and one curative in the same product. Fourth, apply the chemical exactly according to the manufacturers' recommendations. Most complaints concerning chemicals are usually due to the material being applied too late, i.e. when the disease has already caused its damage, or mis-application, e.g. poor sprayer calibration. Finally, "ring the changes." Do not apply one product repeatedly but rotate them to ensure different chemistry is being applied. Consideration must also be given to the use of biological control sprays. These are not fungicides, but they promote natural resistance and inhibit the activity of the fungus causing the attack.

Anthracnose (*Colletotrichum graminicola*)

Anthracnose is a relatively new disease. It is only over the last 10–15 years that it has been recorded on golf courses, principally causing damage to golf greens. It has risen in both evidence and severity to become now a significant problem on turf grass during the winter months. In certain circumstances it may require control.

From the practical viewpoint anthracnose is confined to annual meadow grass. Indeed its attacks are so selective it can often be viewed as having a beneficial effect; in that it will selectively remove annual meadow grass from the finer grasses. However, in situations where the surface of the golf green is largely made up of annual meadow grass, it may be disfiguring and cause substantial loss of cover.

Anthracnose may be recognised in that it affects annual meadow grass only. While it is very rarely recorded on the leaves, it is usually the stem base of the plant that is destroyed. From the surface, affected plants may appear sickly yellow in colour with the youngest leaf being affected. If affected plants are held between forefinger and thumb and rubbed, they are readily detached

Yellowing of individual annual meadow grass plants affected by anthracnose.

from the surface of the green and the black rotted base may be seen. No other disease produces these symptoms.

Mirroring fusarium patch, anthracnose is favoured by a wet turf surface and again mechanical aeration and surface drainage are important. The principal factors favouring disease are cultural conditions that produce a stressed annual meadow grass plant. Since the overall aim of good greenkeeping practice is to produce conditions that favour bents and fescues, while discouraging annual meadow grass, it is not surprising that the disease has developed in recent years. Low fertility situations are often those where anthracnose develops, thus a sensible balanced approach to the fertiliser programme is necessary. Anthracnose is also especially prevalent in compacted areas and slitting/aeration treatments are known to be detrimental to the disease in this situation. Thus, to prevent anthracnose, the key cultural means are to maintain adequate fertility and good surface drainage and to reduce compaction wherever this is possible. From the biological viewpoint, reducing the annual meadow grass content of the sward is the only practical method. There is thus a conflict between austere management—aimed at starving out the annual meadow grass—and maintaining a soil nutrient level which is sufficiently high to avoid overstressing the meadow grass, and a positive decision needs to be made as to which is more important. If you opt for killing the meadow grass then members should be warned accordingly.

Despite there being a wide range of chemicals available for fusarium patch only one is labelled for anthracnose. However, for this chemical (see Table 1) it is known to be considerably more effective when applied as as preventative rather than curative treatment. It is fair to say that once anthracnose has developed, many of the affected plants are already dead, thus chemicals will have little effect except to prevent further spread.

PRACTICAL GREENKEEPING

TABLE 1—*Major Fungicides and their Uses*

Systemic Fungicides	Fusarium Patch	Anthracnose	Red Thread	Fairy Rings	Seedling Diseases
MBC Group Carbendazim Thiophanate-Methyl Thiabendazole	✔ ✔ ✔		✔ ✔ ✔		
SBI Group Fenarimol	✔		✔		
Contact Fungicides Iprodione Vinclozolin Chlorothalonil	✔ ✔ ✔	 ✔	✔ ✔ ✔		
Seed Treatments Systemic/contact combinations	✔	✔	✔		✔
Other Fungicides Benodanil Oxycarboxin Triforine				✔ ✔ ✔	

MAJOR FUNGICIDES AND THEIR USES

Take-all patch disease (*Gaeumannomyces graminis*)

Take-all patch disease, measured against other disease problems on golf courses, is comparatively rare but increasing. However, it makes up for this by being extremely damaging and disfiguring. This is particularly significant in two ways. It is a disease of bentgrass, the principal turfgrass species of good golf courses, and when it occurs there is no readily available and effective control method available.

Take-all patch disease is a disease of bents in the turf grass situation, with fescues and annual meadow grass not being affected. The disease may be first noticed in late spring and throughout the summer, while being particularly prevalent in the autumn. Affected bentgrass appears bleached in colour during the spring and summer, in turn appearing as a very characteristic bronze colour during the autumn. Affected patches are usually around 30 cm in diameter with an irregular ring of dying bentgrasses at the edge of each patch. The centre of each patch is usually colonised by grasses and other plant species resistant to the disease—fescues, annual meadow grass and broad leaf weeds.

Take-all may be further recognised by looking closely at affected plant

Turf Grass Diseases and the Golf Course

material. Roots and stolons of affected bents may have dark brown threads (termed runner hyphae) across their surface and in some cases black pinhead-sized dots may also be seen. These are fungal structures highly characteristic of take-all. They can just be seen with the naked eye, but are best viewed with a hand lens.

Much has been written about the factors that favour take-all patch, particularly in agricultural situations and this information is often applied to turf grass. The following are the main cultural factors that favour the disease.

Characteristic symptoms of take-all patch disease.

It is widely stated that take-all patch is favoured by alkaline conditions, yet one wonders why the disease does not become endemic under naturally alkaline conditions, e.g. courses based on sand dunes? It is more accurate to say that take-all is favoured by a sudden increase in soil pH, for example when lime is applied to acidic soils low in phosphates or by topdressing with sand containing lime. This is often the major reason why the disease occurs. Obviously it is important therefore to consider the implication of using alkaline materials, be they sand, water or fertiliser. This is especially true where new constructions are being made using alkaline root zone constituents.

As with other diseases, surface wetness is also important with respect to take-all. The fungus that causes take-all produces its spores in the autumn and they may be spread rapidly by surface water. Promoting a dry turf surface through good aeration and thatch control will again help discourage the disease. From the nutritional point of view there is some information to suggest potassium and trace elements such as manganese have beneficial effects, in that they may help the turf fight off take-all patch. While this is far from being proven for the turf grass situation, it is sensible for other reasons as well as disease prevention, to ensure an adequate supply of these elements. Adding phosphates or ensuring a higher phosphate level will avoid the disease, but encourage annual meadow grass. The obvious solution is to acidify the soil. Take-all commonly attacks new greens built on sand root zones, primarily because the leaching of nutrients from such over-drained "soils" results in very low phosphate levels. One recorded case was of 1 p.p.m., despite such greens receiving 150 kg/ha in the growing season alone.

Take-all patch is named after take-all disease of wheat and other cereals, which was a serious problem with continuous cereal cropping 70 years ago. Even then, farmers were advised not to lime on any account and to keep phosphate levels high. The three main epidemics of take-all, previously called

PRACTICAL GREENKEEPING

Take-all patch disease at an advanced level.

ophiobolus, can all be blamed on man-made causes. Two, before and after the war years, were certainly due to unwise liming based on soil analyses, when misguided advice recommended "corrective" liming of any soil showing the slightest acidity. The third and most recent epidemic has been triggered off by the combination of using alkaline (sandy) root zones and very low phospate levels in subsequent nutrition, with the laudable aim of discouraging *Poa annua* invasion of pure bent seedings. The answer is to select acidic root zone constituents, rather than applying phosphatic fertilisers, otherwise the stark choice is between serious take-all patch attacks (to the extent of a total kill of bent), or for the bent to be replaced by *Poa annua*.

From the biological viewpoint take-all is very aggressive against all species of bent, which appear to have little natural resistance to the disease. Cultivar trials in several countries have found some differences in resistance to attack by take-all, although it suffices to say that these currently offer little practical benefit. When cultivars vary between very susceptible and extremely susceptible to take-all, there really is no practical choice at all. The important point is that bents are very susceptible to take-all, which may cause rapid and severe damage. Everything must be done from the cultural point of view to prevent the disease occurring. Once take-all occurs, severe damage almost certainly follows.

If take-all does occur then the only real hope lies in a phenomenon called take-all decline, which is a process in which the disease naturally declines in severity over a period of time. The major reason identified for this phenomenon is due to a build up of antagonistic fungi and bacteria in the root zone, which are able to out-compete the disease and offer the plant some protection from attack. Typically, in turf grass this process takes two or three years from the disease first being recorded on site. Once an attack has taken place and the decline process has been completed, further attacks are rare. Therefore, promoting the decline process by using those cultural methods listed is advised. Some agronomists advise using as little fungicide as possible, for fear of affecting the beneficial microbes responsible for antagonising the take-all. While this appears logical and sensible, there is no hard evidence to support this statement. I would say give priority over fungicide treatment of fusarium patch, rather than concerning yourself over affecting the take-all decline process. In any event there are currently no approved pesticides for control of take-all patch, though some applied at high rates can check it at an early stage. This must be qualified by the risk of scorch and inhibiting beneficial micro-organisms.

FAIRY RINGS, THATCH FUNGI AND DRY PATCH
Fairy rings (various *Basidiomycetes*)

Fairy rings are an extremely common sight on golf courses and have been the subject of much study, both academically and from the control point of view. It is important to state at the outset that, to date, there are around 65 fungal species recorded forming fairy rings. Fairy rings have not been shown to cause direct pathogenic damage to turf grasses, i.e. they are not diseases in the strictest sense. However, they may be disfiguring in that their green rings are unsightly or may cause indirect effects, for example by killing turf through producing a very hard dry soil. For this reason control is often recommended. In my opinion, whether this is worthwhile or not, depends largely on the site of the fairy ring. They can, in most circumstances be tolerated on fairways and other areas, but if they appear on putting surfaces

Type 1 fairy rings.

Type 1 fairy rings.

and possibly on tees, then it may be necessary to limit their spread.

The classification of fairy rings, their biology and life cycle, while extremely interesting, are beyond the scope of this brief chapter and readers are referred to the further reading section. However, one fairy ring, that caused by the fungus *Marasmius oreades*, deserves special mention in that it is the principal one capable of causing damage to the turf grass. These fairy rings are easily identified in that they are large, growing quickly like a ripple, and have typically a dead ring, either side of which appear stimulated zones of lush grass growth. In the dead zone, copious fungal mycelium may be found which is very dry and has a very characteristic "dry rot" smell, not unlike mushrooms. It is believed the turf grass dies due to drought stress, as this area is extremely water repellent.

Prevention of fairy rings is generally not possible, as their occurrence is often erratic and fits no general pattern. Some authorities say thatch control is beneficial as it removes the food supply for the fairy ring. From the control point of view, the greenkeeper has essentially three choices. The first is to dig out the fairy ring and after fumigation to replace the soil and turf with fresh material, although this is hardly practicable for golf greens. The second choice is to use nitrogen fertiliser or iron based treatments to darken the turf surface as a whole, thus making the fairy ring less noticeable. This is easily achieved using the "liquid iron" type products available commercially and offers a simple and fairly effective temporary solution. Finally, one may apply fungicides to kill active fairy ring mycelium in the soil. There are currently several materials available for this purpose. Whichever material is chosen it is essential to first drench the fairy ring with a wetting agent, in order to break the hydrophobic materials in the soil and to allow penetration of the fungicide into the mycelium. Many commercially available fairy ring killers include wetting agents, but success hinges on getting the fungicide into intimate contact with the fungus by intensive aeration first.

Thatch fungi

Thatch fungi, or superficial fairy rings as they are sometimes known, are in many ways similar to the fairy rings already described. This is because they are caused by the same group of fungi, the *Basidiomycetes*. Thatch fungi deserves special mention in this chapter as they may cause severe damage to

Turf Grass Diseases and the Golf Course

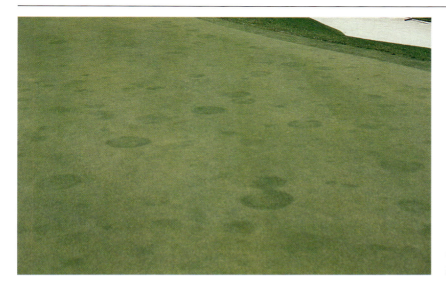

Thatch fungi on a bentgrass green.

golf greens. The fact that yellowing of the sward and sometimes plant death may be seen would suggest these fungi are pathogens, i.e. true diseases, although this has not been proven conclusively.

The name thatch fungi is in fact a misnomer in that the fungi are not confined to the thatch, but are generally to be found in the surface layers. It is thought that many species of fungi are responsible for this problem, although as few produce toadstools they have not been identified. Thatch fungi may be identified in that they form either rings or patches, usually circular, up to 30 cm in diameter.

Occasionally during the winter, the edge of each patch is bleached in colour, where a dense web of mycelium may be found. More often between spring and summer the edge of the patch is sickly yellow in colour, which is especially prevalent in an annual meadow grass sward. These types of thatch fungi simply cause a mild disfigurement of the surface and are best treated cosmetically, as described previously for fairy rings.

In some cases thatch fungi may also cause physical damage to the turf surface, in that the surface fibre or thatch may be reduced to form depressions in the surface. This has a marked effect on the playing qualities of the surface and can be a serious concern. It is believed the thatch fungi do this by utilising the thatch as a food source, thus breaking it down and causing a subsequent collapse of the surface.

Little is known about the cultural and biological factors that favour thatch fungi. It is possible that a surface thatch layer predisposes the turf to attack, thus good thatch control practices are important. In some cases aeration operations have been felt to increase thatch fungi, although the benefits of aeration probably outweigh this point. All turf grass species in fine turf appear to be equally susceptible to attack by thatch fungi. As with fairy rings, the greenkeeper has three choices for control. The first is to do everything to keep the thatch layer at the lowest possible level. The second is use of cosmetic treatments to hide the symptoms of thatch fungi. The third is chemicals, which again must be preceded by a wetting agent to increase the chances of penetration by the fungicide.

Surface depressions left by thatch fungi may be levelled by selective applications of top dressing.

Dry patch

Again, dry patch is not strictly a disease in that there is no known pathogenic organism responsible for its occurrence. However, it has been widely reported that fairy ring fungi are at least in part responsible for its occurrence. As a major problem faced by the greenkeeper, it is included in this chapter.

For many years the term dry patch has been used to describe any area of turf that dries out and is for whatever reason difficult to re-wet. Recent thinking has tended to confine the term dry patch (called localised dry spot in the United States), to where there is a definite water repellent soil and the occurrence of this is a legacy from fungal activity. Other factors that lead to a dry turf profile— compaction, thatch, inadequate irrigation, root breaks and the like—may be simply referred to as drought stress. Initially, dry patch

Dry patch.

Dry patch.

is easy to recognise as the symptoms of grass wilting due to lack of available water are readily obvious and do not warrant description here. The root-zone below dry areas may be snuff dry. Attempts to re-wet affected areas usually fail in that water is often reluctant to penetrate into affected areas. These areas may have seen extensive fairy ring activity in the past. Another key symptom of dry patch is that dew will not settle on affected areas.

The rooting in dry patch areas is often also poor. Dry patch can often be caused by type one fairy rings. *Marasmius oreades* produces a waxy mycelium, which is water repellent. This creates localised drought, which will account partly for death of grass. Water-repellent conditions, due to fungal deposits on soil particles, may also cause dry patch. Due to intense fungal activity in the thatch and root-zone, waxy materials may be deposited on sand or soil particles immediately below the thatch layer. The condition is worse in coarser sands and often sand particles may be bound together in a completely impermeable layer.

Physical causes of dry patch may be alleviated by additional aeration on the areas worst affected. Commercial wetting agents specifically designed for use on turf are now available and are used widely for the alleviation of dry patch. Wetting agent applications should begin at the start of the growing season.

Slime mould and algal slime

These are caused by a number of primitive organisms (*Nostoc* spp. and others). Known to greenkeepers as "squidge," these are not strictly diseases as they do not attack grass, but their jelly-like growths of dense slime create problems for golfers and machines alike by being so slippery, as well as unsightly, and by smothering. Invasion is linked to wet weather in autumn. The cure lies in a combination of aeration; top dressing with gritty material (sharp ash, sintered furnace linings etc.); spraying with high rates of sulphate of iron; and squeegeeing off the material and physically carting it away.

OTHER DISEASE PROBLEMS

One area which raises the most questions from greenkeepers is the number of potential disease problems that may occur. Textbooks on turf grass disease, written by American authors and in wide circulation here, list as many as 150 different diseases. This may be applicable to the American continent, where there are many more species of grasses maintained as turf, i.e. more hosts and also great variation in climatic conditions. In northern temperate Europe the range of diseases is restricted, due to the narrow range of both turf grasses and climate. This essentially reduces the number of practical disease problems to twelve, the main five of which are described in this chapter.

The other seven diseases are listed below though they have little significant effect on greenkeeping—in fact they create few problems on fine turf.

Corticium on fescue.

Corticium, or red thread disease (*Laetisaria fuciformis*)
This attacks primarily fine fescues and bents in mid season and autumn and is often an indication that greenkeeping techniques are on the right lines. Fungicidal treatment is never necessary, as a light nitrogenous feed will soon control it.

Dollar spot (*Sclerotinia homeocarpa*)
This is in effect confined to slender creeping red fescue and is so rare that it can be ignored as being of academic interest only.

Leaf spot diseases (*Drechslera siccans* and others)
Even if they occur they are never of serious importance.

Pink snow mould (*Microdochium nivale*)
This is really an advanced stage of fusarium patch, developing under prolonged snow cover. We do not get enough snow generally for it to be widely found in Britain.

Grey snow mould *(Typhula incarnate)*
Another disease linked with prolonged snow and very rare.

Seedling turf diseases
These are uncommon, occurring as a result of a combination of poor management and high humidity. Prevention is always better than cure. Avoid high humidity and keep seedling grass topped but not shaved. Watch for it especially where growth stimulating covers are used on new seedings.

Corticium on fescue (close-up).

BIOLOGICAL CONTROL OF TURF GRASS DISEASES

In the mid 1990s, biological control products were introduced and early results in the inhibition of turf grass disease, especially fusarium patch, are promising.

Some of these products contain, or actively encourage micro-organisms whose activities compete with or inhibit the fungi causing turf disease, in some cases by antibiotic action. Others are directly parasitic on the disease-producing fungi, while some compete for available space and nutrients and inhibit the fungi in that way.

To get the best results, their use must be related to other management, for example by care in the use of other fungicides which might adversely affect these biological products. They also need to be applied in the growing season and, obviously, sufficiently ahead of a potential attack of disease for them to inhibit the harmful fungi. Certainly, encouraging results warrant both further investigation and continued use.

CONCLUSION

Clearly with so few diseases warranting remedial action it is folly to look for unheard-of diseases recorded only in the United States and rarely, if ever, found in Europe. The cause of problems almost always turn out to be due to errors of management, especially over-watering in drought and excessive fertiliser treatment, especially in autumn.

With austere greenkeeping regimes, fungicides are rarely needed, whereas with artificial levels of management in artificial environments—sand-only greens—and with disease susceptible grasses, even fortnightly intervals may not be sufficient to give control. The answer is that prevention by sound management is always better than cures with fungicides. Turf grasses which are not over-stressed will stay healthy and disease-free, whatever the weather.

Chapter Twelve

CONTROL OF PESTS

WHAT IS A PEST? The most simple definition is that it is any animal or insect that interferes with the running by the human animal of the environment which that human wants to manage to *his* satisfaction. Fortunately in golf course management in this country we have few serious pests compared with, say, some areas of America, and fewer still which are difficult to control. In fact, most damage linked to insect pests is caused by other pests digging up hallowed turf in search of insects.

Rabbits
If we start at the top end—relating to size rather than pecking order—the main animal pest on golf courses must be the rabbit. The damage they do can be very severe, primarily, of course, burrowing and scraping, thus undermining tees, destroying bunker faces and creating holes in playing surfaces. They also cause annoyance in two other ways: by urine "scalding," and by nibbling, especially irrigated putting surfaces, below the height of cut. Scalding is not just the unsightly effect of scorched turf with a stimulated green rim, but its effect on the grass species. Looking at a typical rabbits' lavatory, one notes that when the turf recovers, the grass type has changed to one dominated by annual meadow grass (*Poa annua*), which has displaced the fine-leaved grasses. Coarser-bladed grasses, almost untraceable in the original turf, have also been stimulated by the increased fertility. This is because rabbit urine and droppings are high in phosphates, connected with the fact that these pests have the anti-social habit of recycling their own droppings. It is the high phosphate levels, rather than nitrogen, which encourage phosphate-demanding grasses, especially annual meadow grass, (*Poa annua*), to displace those fine-leaved species which thrive best on the poorer soils and form the desirable, fine, wiry turf on which the game of

Rabbit scraping on edge of bunker. Note shallow face and effect of run off water on too shallow a bunker.

golf is so dependent. The only justification, in my opinion, for the existence of rabbits is to provide a graphic example of the results of NPK fertiliser application to fine turf in the education of young greenkeepers (and green committees!). Such patches of alien grasses can be seen on links fairways long after the rabbit which caused the scald initially had died.

A determined hungry rabbit will take a lot of stopping. The best method I know is a lead pill propelled by gunpowder. The great advantage of shooting, especially at night, is that the bag is predominantly does, which gets to the root of the problem. This is primarily because does sit tighter, while the scary bucks scamper away more quickly. Trapping and ferreting, even gassing, all have their place, but cannot do more than nibble at the problem. I wonder how many of my readers have been long-netting with poachers, as I have. A long net about a yard tall is very quietly run out at the foot of a grassy slope so as not to disturb the rabbits. It is supported on small forked sticks with a slack fold at the base. A lurcher is then sent round the hill—the rabbits bolt and get entangled in the mesh. The skill is to administer the *coup de grâce* swiftly, before the net gives way under the sheer mass of entangled bodies. It works well on some golf fairways, but the problem is that few are wide enough to be able to string out the net without disturbing the pests. Frankly, night shooting with powerful lights is a lot more efficient, but noisier!

Rabbits can sometimes be deterred by running a soft rope soaked in animal oil (with a repellent smell), or with foxy-smelling compounds around an affected area. Operators are socially unacceptable for days, if they are careless in handling this evil oily liquid.

Rabbit fencing.

Few can afford to erect proper rabbit-proof fencing, buried at least a foot in the soil, with the lower end turned outwards. However, this is not always necessary, neither is the netting-off completely of vulnerable greens. On one such links course, we were very successful in erecting low fences of close mesh netting with the foot turned outwards, flush with the turf, but not buried, half way round the back of greens and set well back from the putting surfaces. This did not inconvenience the members, while the rabbits put two and two together and nipped round the front. The secret was to startle them by an unexpected foray, whereupon they dashed for safety to the rear only to find their line of escape blocked. Those we did not shoot or club must have been sufficiently scared to try somewhere else. Anyway, it worked and cost very little.

In mentioning rabbit-proof fencing, I do remember vividly one links course in Ireland which was polluted with rabbits of all colours and sizes. They dug burrows, even on the edges of greens, and a careless putt could disappear for ever. No amount of discouragement worked, because of constant invasion from surrounding dunes.

On one of my visits I was astonished to discover the problem had been solved by the erection of a tall link fence on concrete posts, cut deep into the ground, lower edge turned outwards—a classic and astronomically expensive construction. When I enquired if they had won the Irish sweep, they admitted it was done on an E.C. grant. To my incredulous enquiry as to how they got the grant, they said that "to tell the truth it had been entered in the club records as a road!"

There was, however, an unexpected twist to this story, which proves that one man's meat is another man's poison, or more specifically one man's pest is another man's pet. When I advised that we must now exterminate the colonies inside the fence, they protested that we could not do that to the poor little bunnies because the ladies would not like it. What they proposed was to build ramps up inside the five foot high "wall" so that the rabbits could jump over but not get back! The bunny huggers of the world cause so many imbalances—by their misplaced and anthropomorphic sentimentality—that they are really one of the worst pests of true conservation.

Man—the worst pest

In considering pests, pride of place must unquestionably go to that subspecies *Homo subsapiens viridis*. Every golf club I know has them in profusion. They are instant experts in everything from architecture to agronomy, characterised by their really daunting, as well as vaunting, ambition to serve on the green committee. This they regard as the easiest route to their hearts' desire, captaincy of the club. Their claim to fame is the captain's bunker, which is promptly filled in by their successor after their year of office is over. Surely the secret of being a good and respected captain is to avoid, so far as humanly possible, making any decisions; to resist trying to leave a memorial, and to enjoy ones term of office socially. It is however a wise man, and not his subspecies, which follows those age-old and proven rules.

Evidence of the harm this particular subspecies can cause is clear to see after hoar frost has thawed.

Classic proof of the thoughtlessness of that worst pest—the golfer—and the damage caused by crossing a green covered in hoar frost.

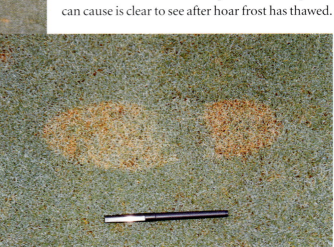

CONTROL OF PESTS

Selfish individuals who ignore COURSE CLOSED notices leave their footprints in crushed frozen grass, which turn brown when the frost thaws. Equally, it is nonsense for any greenkeeper to tear round his course when it is covered in rime, leaving the wheel marks of his utility vehicle and his footprints to the flag, as he moves it to a temporary green. Far better to close the course and ensure that it is kept closed until the hoar frost disappears. In passing, the man to make a closure decision *must* be the head greenkeeper, as he is the first of management on the scene.

We digress. In order of size we should have started with sheep (and, less commonly, grazing cattle and horses), but luckily, few courses are now shared by golfers and livestock. Those that do, suffer electric fenced greens, damaged bunkers and litter. Only those whose ball finishes in a cow-pat, or who have to thread their way past sheep droppings, are perhaps appreciative of the removal of four-legged lawn mowers which were so common in earlier times.

I well remember a links course which was partly tenanted and partly owned. The tenanted half was grazed with sheep. The landlord delivered every year several tons of granular fertiliser "to help the grazing." The greenkeeper and I, equally assiduously, used to go out at night at low tide, and tip it into the sea. However, while this reduced the damage to the links turf, while making the contrast with the ungrazed half less dramatic, we still had serious problems, chiefly scalding on greens and destruction of bunker faces. A policy of revetting faces—building turf "walls"—made it more difficult for the sheep to get in under them for shelter. The former problem was resolved by noting flock behaviour. In severe weather the sheep would find a lee under a stone wall, but normally they followed a primeval instinct to move to the higher ground at night, thus severely damaging a few of the top greens, with their unwelcome attention coming at crack of dawn. We resolved this by mowing out a "sheep green"—well away from the firing line—and herding the sheep off the true greens for a few nights. They quickly got the message, which rarely had to be repeated.

Badgers and foxes

Badgers and foxes can sometimes be a nuisance in scratching out turf, which they do in the hope of turning up grubs. Indeed it is not the damage done by grubs eating roots which is serious, but the "ploughing out" of entire fairways by rooks and crows (even starlings) and of course badgers, whose insatiable craving for chafer grubs can cause total chaos.

Even when the grubs have been killed, the predators keep on working in hope. The answer is to apply approved insecticides well before signs of the pest are all too obvious. Bleached areas of turf are usually the first signs, but earlier warning of leatherjacket attack can be detected by noting abnormal

Badgers, amiable creatures but no respecter of sacrosanct turf in their search for grubs.

cranefly activity and egg-laying the previous late summer. In chronically affected areas, egg counts can be made.

Moles

Moles are extremely successful pests. Every man's hand has been against them for centuries; farmers, gardeners and latterly managers of sports turf, yet the mole thrives and more than maintains its population levels.

The life history of the mole is worthy of detailed study, especially if you are trying to catch them. On golf courses, their activity in pushing up mole-hills is normally confined to the rough or rarely on fairways, virtually never on greens. This is simply because they are no fonder of working for nothing than the next creature and will not waste time burrowing into land where the earthworms which are their major food source have been controlled.

In the old days one often saw mole-hills right up to the edge of a dewormed green, but never on the putting surface. They can, however, cause trouble in creating very shallow surface runs, often just in the surface thatch, when extending territories or searching for mates. The problem is so slight that it can be ignored, as repair work is simple.

Moles can be controlled by authorised trappers placing strychnine baited worms in runs—not a job for amateurs. They can be trapped along runs to water which are used every four hours or those between mole-hills, never in

CONTROL OF PESTS

Moles can be a problem.

the hill itself. Shooting at a "moving" mole hill with a 12-bore at close range is very effective. The best way is avoidance—get rid of their food, namely earthworms, and they will soon depart.

Incidentally, trapping is made difficult because moles are very sensitive to disturbance in their runs. They can detect the smallest foreign bodies or crumbs of soil or any change in their tunnel roofs. This is achieved by very sensitive hairs on their snouts and tails. Travelling up tunnels, their tails are held erect and even when travelling as they do at up to 4 km/hr they will stop instantly. They do not have particularly good hearing though they can detect high frequency sounds. Likewise they have a poor sense of smell and are proverbially almost blind, but they have become highly adapted to life in a dark tunnel, a solitary existence for most of the time, except during mating, and apart from that they will fight to the death any other mole they meet.

Insect pests

There are only three significant insect pests which can cause problems worthy of treatment, leatherjackets (the grubs of craneflies, *Tipula* spp.), chafers (three kinds), and fever fly grub (*Bibio* spp. and *Dilophus* spp.).

Leatherjackets are the commonest, but not an insoluble problem if early signs, such as bleaching of turf, trigger off timely action. The list of permitted insecticides gets less every year as persistent insecticides are banned, yet

Leatherjackets.

persistence is what we need. However, there are still some left which receive grudging acceptance—Dursban is one—but the answer is to seek professional advice and apply what is permitted as early as possible. There are old dodges to check on grub populations, such as leaving a soaked piece of carpet, in lieu of the old heavy hessian sack of yore, on wet grass. The grubs will come up to the surface overnight and estimates of numbers can be made.

We may yet have to resort to the old method which was displaced by the use of DDT (now banned of course), namely a solution of orthodichlorobenzene and Jeyes fluid. This is an expellent and useful for testing, but one needs to sweep up swiftly or the grubs pop back in again!

A forest of pupal cases sticking up out of the turf and a host of egg-laying craneflies in August is warning enough to lay in stocks. Female craneflies go for short, green, watered turf so they aim at the greens for egg-laying. One solution is to pray for a very windy August, when the craneflies get swept downwind in their thousands against fences or in bunkers, and cannot lay their eggs where they would prefer.

Chafers.

Chafers are much more difficult to control because of the long life cycle (as against a yearly one for other grubs), of some species—up to four or five years for cockchafers (*Melolontha melolontha*)—with the ever-growing grubs descending deep into the soil over winter.

CONTROL OF PESTS

Control has therefore to be in the summer, and in severe attacks there is little warning, until that given by birds and badgers. An old trick which still works is to roll affected turf heavily. Some grubs are squashed. Others find it more difficult to move around and the root-damaged turf is pressed more closely with the soil and is less likely to suffer from drought.

Fever fly grubs (*Bibio* and *Dilophus* spp.) can often be very numerous. They occur in small nests of small white grubs with brown heads. Sheer numbers make up for small size, but the damage is generally localised, though still worth treating with a permitted insecticide. The adults are like very small house flies with larger wings to body size ratio. They emerge in May, earlier than craneflies, and nest clusters can sometimes contain hundreds of grubs. The problem is disturbance to surface levels rather than root damage.

With all insect pests a balanced view on their extermination is needed. Can one ignore small numbers, or are they a sign of worse to come? Wholesale application of insecticides is not the answer in every case. As with fungicides, one kills indiscriminately and may upset the balance of soil health. Only experience can give the right answer. Whereas prevention is always better than cure, with insect pests there is little scope for preventative measures.

The answer is to act quickly, if you act at all, and remember that the more

Birds in search of grubs can tear a precious green to shreds in a single frenzied feeding.

Damage caused by badgers ripping up turf in search of chafer grubs.

185

serious damage to grass is generally from predators tearing up turf in search of food, so discourage them by bird scarers or night-time forays for birds and badgers respectively.

Earthworms
We come now to the last and worst of the pests, the casting earthworm. There are still some "rabid envirogreens" who deplore their eradication, yet earthworms are the worst problem on fine turf, more especially the casting ones. The damage is manifold, with smearing and flattened casts creating muddy uneven surfaces, weeds invading the open tilth left by worm casts (which also often contain dormant seeds brought up from below the surface), subsidence, impeded surface drainage and even in extreme cases the turf being killed.

The problem with casts is that they contain mucus, so they dry rock hard. If wet, they are sticky and smear. Not all earthworms cast, but the point is academic because, so far, we have no selective worm-killer. Indeed we have hardly a worm-killer left.

I have always questioned the logic of banning persistent worm-killers. Operator risk is a factor of toxicity combined with operator exposure. I was brought up on the use of lead arsenate, admittedly toxic if ingested in quantity. In all the thirty odd years I used it, I never had the slightest problem. One took sensible precautions over disposal of empty drums, but in all those years of operating (without protective masks, of course,) I "never lost a greenkeeper" or had any problems with livestock. The material was heavy—in fact it could be applied only by a conveyor belt type spreader—and did not blow in the wind. It lay where it fell and did not leach, wash to the drains or pollute waterways. It gave protection for up to seven years.

In my view, the risk factor was much less than using a fairly volatile spray twice and more times a year with an insecticide which is, wrongly I think, suspected of undesirable health risks. Bring back lead arsenate—it was in fact never prohibited, it just became too expensive and unavailable—all is forgiven.

However, this is academic. We have to use what is permitted and available. Chlordane has gone, with absolutely no scientific evidence to justify its prohibition. Carbaryl must soon join the prohibited list. We are then left with no choice save to use massive doses of a permitted fungicide—Carbendazim—which has worm-killing side effects. The prospect for greenkeepers is not appealing.

More promising is to avoid the problem of not encouraging earthworms in the first place. The first action must be use acidic-reacting materials and never alkaline ones. Lime in any form is anathema, worms love it. Lime can come in many disguises, for example as shell in sea sand. Such alkaline sand on links causes no problems because the other necessary ingredient is lacking, namely, food in the form of humus. On inland conditions, however, lime has destroyed more fine turf by encouraging casting worms over the years than almost any other cause, yet farmers on golf courses still advise it. "The land is too sour," they claim. Well, they would, wouldn't they! Earthworms may be the farmer's friend, but they are the greenkeepers' enemy and we are still suffering from the philosophies on the benefits of casting earthworms on farmland, first propounded by Charles Darwin in 1881.

This leads us to the most promising line of attack, acidification of the soil. Sulphur and sulphur-based products oxidise in moist soil to sulphuric acid and the drop in pH has several effects. The acidity discourages earthworms, which depart for less irritating soil conditions. It also flocculates the tiny soil particles of fine clays into larger ones, creating more air spaces, a better soil structure and better drainage. Admittedly lime will also have the same effect, but its use encourages casting worms. Thirdly, sulphur creates a soil which discourages annual meadow grass, while locking up phosphates and favouring bents (*Agrostis* spp.) which compete better in lower fertility soil conditions, which are not appreciated by other fertility-demanding species. Sulphur thus turns a muddy morass into fine, wiry, worm-and-weed free, better draining turf.

We may see developments of specific worm-killers in future years, but the total market for worm-killers is so small and specialised that it will not encourage or justify costly research. The best chance is from the department of serendipity—the sheer accident noted and observed by a seeing eye—which is how most of the world's greatest discoveries arose.

In contrast to fungal diseases—most of which arise because soil balances and natural equilibrium's have been disturbed by misguided watering and feeding—pests are a natural phenomenon, not a just retribution for bad greenkeeping. With the exception of casting earthworms, they just happen. The trick is to act quickly. To do this you need to look for the first signs— bleaching of turf locally when there is no drought, holes in the turf which should not be there, bird damage, even such minor points as hollow tine

Worm casts, the greenkeepers' nightmare.

fork holes staying open in spring, because a fat leather jacket is using them as a haven from which to emerge at night to graze on the grass around.

A knowledge of life cycles is helpful to observe egg-laying adults or to detect the early signs of over-wintering grubs coming up from below. As with all greenkeeping, the benefits deriving from correct observation are incalculable. The secret is to spot at once the first signs of something that is slightly out of normal for the season or the circumstance. Never wait until the symptoms would be evident to a blind man. All in all, we can live with a few parasites on our hallowed turf; it is when numbers explode that our problems begin.

Chapter Thirteen
. . . . .
DRAINAGE

ALMOST AS SOON AS our early ancestors abandoned their way of life as hunter-gatherers and became tillers of the soil, the draining capacity of the land they cultivated so primitively became of prime importance. Not every community would necessarily be blessed with light, well-drained, fertile soil.

Early farmers learned to improve soils by intercepting or cutting off the downward movement of water, either surface flow on fairly impermeable soils, or subsurface seepage water. Ditching around their primitive fields helped the soil to dry out earlier in the year, so vitally important in encouraging better crop yields, while making earlier sowing possible.

Centuries later, when heavy soils had to be cultivated to provide food in times when there were serious shortages, this was made possible by so ploughing the land—splitting furrows—as to leave steep-backed ridges. In practice, such rig and furrow land was croppable only on the raised areas. On especially heavy land, this was accentuated by leaving a wide open furrow for drainage between the cultivated strips. This rig and furrow land is still evident on very heavy soils, but much has gone with the creation of prairies to aid cereal farming—the eradication of hedges and the deep effective drainage of the land. Not so long ago I surveyed some land, optimistically ear-marked for a golf course, where the old rough grassland was in just such a formation, and promptly rejected it. Drainage had defeated generations of farmers and would have defeated us. Without an outfall the only option is pumping.

Open ditches provided the outfall from the furrows and some would say that an open ditch is still the best drain, though fearfully expensive to maintain. Very often, these ditches followed a contour line along a change of soil type. Early farmers appreciated that some lighter soils warmed up more quickly and, rather than have half fields of different soils, they enclosed

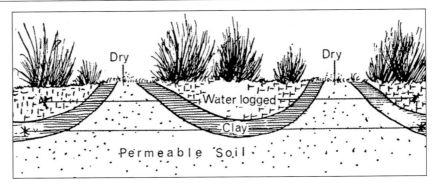

Characteristic strata of a patchy field

such different land, separating it from more productive, lighter soil, fields. This is not just of academic importance, for when such farmland is proposed as the location for a golf course, an old field survey may well indicate, by the long since grubbed out hedges, where the main ditches and drains were sited and often where soils are of quite different character, although separated only by an old hedge line.

The early history of drains and drainage is largely of academic interest in golf course work. It is sufficient to note that early drains were often merely deep slits, dug as narrowly as possible by hand, with stones, brushwood, heather or even stones at the bottom before the soil was backfilled. Later, more sophisticated versions were laid, with two upright stone slabs topped by a third, mostly confined to main conductor drains. Some are still functional despite being well over 200 years old.

Another form was to cut a very narrow slit at the base of the drain to leave a ledge on which fibrous turves were laid. Although the turf has long since rotted, one can sometimes still see the drain line, with the original narrow slit showing as a thin black line in the clay, but still carrying some water. Many of these primitive drains date back to the mid-seventeenth century.

A turf drain

A major fillip to land drainage occurred at the turn of the nineteenth century, at the time of the Napoleonic wars, when there was a desperate shortage of food and the need to grow wheat especially was acute. In those days, farmers could still show a profit in growing $3^1/_2$–5 cwt per acre of wheat, and heavy land suits wheat. Consequently much clay land, barely suitable for cereal production, was ploughed in steep rig and furrow, with field drainage augmenting the furrows.

The secret of good land drainage is to go deep—

DRAINAGE

Construction of a plug drain

certainly three feet. This is primarily because, at that depth, soil movement is minimal, whereas shallow drains soon silt up as a result of disturbance by cultivation or weather. How those old drainers, working entirely by hand in very poor conditions, produced such long-lasting results I do not know.

I have seen many cases of very small diameter drains at that depth still functioning perfectly, often 150 years after they were laid, simply because the surrounding clay had never moved since the drains were laid.

Tile drains came later—first, thin, foot square slabs of clay laid over pole formers and fired to form an inverted 'U'—sometimes laid on a flat tile and later with elaborate flanges on the low (open side) to stop tiles sinking into soft subsoils. These were the horse-shoe tiles of the early 1800s. In a few cases these modified horse-shoe tiles were laid, the upper reversed over the lower, to form a channel. This, though expensive, had many advantages in their elliptical channel shape.

A double horseshoe drain

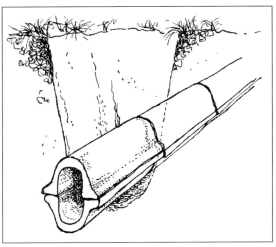

THE ADVENT OF TILE DRAINS

The first cylindrical, fired, tile drain was made by John Reade in 1843. Two years later, the invention of a tile-making machine by Thomas Scragg, revolutionised both costs and efficiency. It is worthy of mention, however, that as early as 1787,

An early drain constructed with slabs prior to the introduction of tile drains.

a certain Stephen Switzer was recommending using pipes made of potters' clay, fabricated by pipe-making machines. How long it takes for good ideas to become common practice! One is reminded of Budding's mower, invented in 1832, which did not become widely used until fifty years later.

Larger diameter tile drains were favoured, since small diameter ones tended to block if they were not accurately aligned. The old familiar red tile drain dominated land drainage for over a century, but is now virtually extinct.

This was because the sheer weight of larger diameter tiles needed for, say, a fairly intensive system, encouraged drainers first and then manufacturers to look for alternatives. Light, flexible, perforated, plastic tubing was introduced in the 1950s and, while slow to take-off initially, it now totally dominates the field drainage world.

There were early attempts with rigid PVC with slits, but the advantages of flexibility and ease of handling of coils of flexible piping were clearly apparent, especially to those who had to manhandle them.

Earlier generations of field drainers were extremely knowledgeable. I nearly said surprisingly, but they knew their craft and knew their soils. They drained deep and they drained well and some of their work is still effective a century later.

BASIC RULES

There are a few basic rules, as true today as long ago. Perhaps the first and most serious is to find an outfall! It was Archimedes who claimed that if he were given a fulcrum and a big enough lever he could move the world. Many a drainer has proved that given an outfall and a fall he could drain anything. Today even the existence of a fall is not so vital with zero-drainage, in which the water in a virtually level drain moves laterally under the influence of the head of water in the drain—in other words the incoming water pushes the static water out of the end of the pipe.

I remember one project for a golf course built in the early 1970s, where various so-called experts proposed impracticable methods of draining some virtually flat, cleared, woodland with deep, water filled, craters where oak stumps had been blown out, looking for all the world like a First World War battlefield. One bright spark proposed to take the water up-hill. Accurate levels showed we had only six inches of fall on a 500 yard run, thus demanding extremely accurate levels, with laying and supervision by a genius of a drainer. It worked, and still continues to work 25 years later. The drainer, who had to be instructed in laser beam levelling, was most efficient and will long be remembered for his appreciative remark, "It has been a great privilege working for you, I've never had to work with a feeler gauge before."

As I have said before, the next most important rule is to go deep. The deeper you go the less chance there is of soil movement and so minimal risk of silting up. This silting is much reduced, of course, with flexible perforated plastic.

Another is to lay the pipes or tiles straight onto the subsoil itself, which has, of course, to be accurately graded. Laying pipes on gravel merely

The laying of perforated flexible plastic piping in a narrow slit drain. The pipe is fed directly onto the base of the slit from a coiled roll.

encourages the water to flow under the pipe, not in it, and this can cause problems. By all means cover the drains with stone etc., to ensure better collection, while sometimes it even pays to bring the stone right to the surface, leaving a narrow open slit with turf cantilevered over the wider drain. This will act as a cut-off drain to catch surface flow.

Another rule is to run drains across slopes, never at right angles to the contours. Another memory—again recalling my old, long-deceased, drainage wizard—was in connection with the drainage of a new course in the south. This was laid out on lower levels of London clay with Bagshot sand overlying the upper slopes. Another bright young man installed a system, luckily at first (and last!) on only one fairway, with close spaced (2 m), shallow drains at right angles to the contours. This produced several undesirable results.

First there was no interception, so only the land a foot to each side of the drain was dry, with the strips in-between bogs. Second, it cut the irrigation pipe up into neat 2 m lengths. Third, it cost a fortune, and as I pointed out, it would have been cheaper to buy some extra land!

What we did was based on prevention rather than cure. It is always cheaper to stop water getting to vulnerable areas than to try to drain it away after it has done the damage. A deep open ditch was excavated on a contour line just above where the clay emerged on the slope, a cut-off ditch set a foot deep into the clay under the sand. The ditch, with a slight fall, intercepted all the subsurface flow, and any surface flow for that matter. With intensive aeration and only minimal back-up drainage, for example in low places on the fairways and to collect tee and green drainage, the fairway dried up. The cost of the effective scheme for the whole of the valley was less than 8% of an ineffective, badly conceived disaster. A good axiom I have always followed is that if one does not know, one should ask a man who does. While much drainage is logical and self-evident, every so often one comes across a situation where the lifetime experience and skill of a born and bred drainer finds a not always obvious solution, which both works and is cheap.

There are some other basics, such as not running subsidiaries into main drains at right angles, and protecting outfalls into open ditches, not just against vermin, but against collapse of the bank and frost damage. My personal preference is to avoid many outfalls into ditches by running the subsidiaries into a main parallel to the ditch, which involves only one substantial outfall at the end of the run.

Finally, never fall into the trap of trying to judge falls by eye. You do not need to go to the chore of taking levels by theodolite or dumpy level. Our rude forefathers used simple devices. Two glass tubes connected by a rubber pipe filled with water will give you a very accurate level sight line, and a man standing at the other end of the line can act as a good measuring staff. I

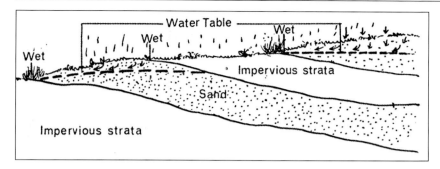

Strata and water table

often used my soil auger, held between finger and thumb with the boring tool acting as a pendulum and the handle giving a reasonable horizontal sight. With this aid, one could often dispute successfully with DIY experts about the true fall—so many times have these bright characters planned systems depending on water being able to flow up hill!

One of the worst cases I suffered was when a motorway engineer, who was also a club member, took over the job of draining a golf course on heavy land. His main drain, laid to extravagant motorway standards, started too deep and came out of the ground after a few hundred yards and would have accepted the flow from several hundred acres with a three foot concrete pipe. On the same course, close shallow mains were planned, with close spaced subsidiaries. Our plan involved really deep mains, 15 m apart, laid with a trencher drainer and the narrow slits shingled to near the surface. Mole ploughs were pulled diagonally across the entire slope through the shingle, and the system, costing a quarter of the original proposal, still works well today. In any eventuality, re-moling across the slit drains will keep it effective for many more years.

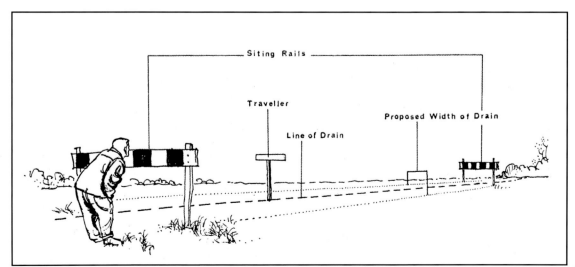

Method of using boning rods

Of course, as with all drainage, systems are more efficient if soils are deeply aerated to assist absorption. Surface sealing by traffic and unrelieved by deep slitting may cause problems with excessive run-off.

CONTOUR DRAINAGE CONDEMNED

This is a convenient place to condemn contour drainage—an irrelevant importation from America—designed to cope with the rock-hard impervious soils and those rare but very heavy down-pours of the southern arid states of the USA. Anyone who has suffered from the total snarl up of traffic on a freeway, in California for instance, which automatically follows a torrential if short storm, will know what I am talking about. There are no roadside drainage gullies, everything depends on run-off. Flooding, albeit temporarily, is the rule. Meanwhile, everything stops.

On golf courses, the theory is that really heavy rainfall cannot be absorbed, so it must run over the surface. Courses are designed with massive earth moving operations, destroying any natural drainage in the process, to shed water to the centre line of fairways, down which is run what is literally a sewer, with gratings at intervals to deal with the flow. The water is collected in storage lakes, doubling as the water features which seem such

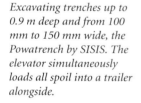

Excavating trenches up to 0.9 m deep and from 100 mm to 150 mm wide, the Powatrench by SISIS. The elevator simultaneously loads all spoil into a trailer alongside.

Drainage

an intrinsic aspect of American design. Golf is not a water sport; water features are not easy to manage and the concept is, to the eye of traditionalists, most unnatural.

However, the system works tolerably well under those arid conditions, but it does not work well here. Primarily this is because of our climate rather than our soils. We have more winter than summer months and a more even spread of rainfall over the year. Wet fairways absorb more water than bone dry ones. Run-off becomes minimal and, in any case, the centre lines of fairways taking the water become bogs at the end of the winter, demanding subsidiary drainage to produce dry surfaces all-year-round. There is one form of contour drainage which is acceptable, namely the formation of shallow valleys or swales behind greens or tees cut out of slopes, but to work efficiently even these should have a stone-filled drain run to an outfall or existing drain, in the bottom of the swale.

We have dealt mainly with field drainage, namely with tiles or plastic pipes. On heavy soils this can be supplemented by moling—pulling a bullet, mounted on a vertical blade—as deep as is possible with a powerful tractor, or even a winch. This works best, in fact it works only, where the soil is a uniform clay and obviously is not feasible on stony or sandy soils. One tip, impressed on me in my agricultural university days pre-war, was that you must always pull the mole uphill, as any small "disturbances" are pushed back by the downhill flow. That stated, many people opt for the easier way of pulling the moles downhill, so that the flow displaces and gets behind any "flakes" peeled back by the bullet, even if an expander is fitted behind it. Moles have, of course, to be pulled through stone-filled slits above main drains. It is unsatisfactory to pull them from the ground at the end of a run.

One specialist form of drainage, which I have often used with great effect in very wet or poorly drained sloping sites, is a cross between a slit drain and an open ditch. Even the thickness of a turf can prevent surface flow from reaching the stone-filled slit drain. I therefore would bring the stone right to the surface, cutting the slit as narrowly as possible. Even this degree of narrowness is not acceptable where such intercept drains are close to putting surfaces. The effective answer was to

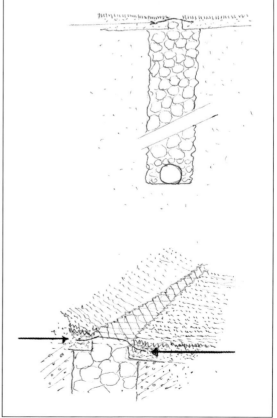

Top: *Section of intercept drain. Note narrow slit, with turf cantilevered out over drain. The slit is protected by strip of wire netting.*

Bottom: *More detail of intercept drain. Note that the stones cannot be dislodged, neither is putting affected, due to the small gauge wire netting—See arrows.*

cantilever turf out from the soil each side, leaving only a 2 or 3 in. (50–75 mm) gap, stone it to the top, and insert a narrow strip of wire netting cut into and flush with the turf but covering the stone. This deals with every drop of surface flow, but one can putt over the slit with confidence, and the stones cannot be dislodged.

RUNNING SAND

A treatise on golf course drainage would be incomplete unless we mention that dreaded problem, running sand. I have seen conventional narrow slits, cut deep into such areas with a trencher, become crevasses, with collapsing walls a metre and more wide, in a matter of hours. The solution is, of course, to go deeper than the water source. This is sometimes easier said than done. Coir-wrapped, flexible piping will take water without silting up, while on occasions one may have to use rigid piping to conduct water over unstable land.

Running sand has always been a problem for drainers, but with modern techniques the problems caused by it can be overcome. I refer to the practice of de-watering.

This operation is carried out by sinking well points into the ground, down to a depth approximately 1 m deeper than you want to lay the drain. These well points consist of perforated tubes inserted into the area requiring to be de-watered, at usually 3 m deep and 1–2 m apart, with each well point surrounded by very fine grit to filter the sand. They are usually driven into the ground by water pressure, but can also be inserted into the ground with a suitably sized excavator. Each of the well points is then connected to a pipeline, which in turn is connected to a pump. The pump is started and water is sucked from the sand in the area requiring draining and carried, usually by flexible pipe, to the nearest suitable outfall. It can take anything up to ten days, with the pump running day and night, to remove sufficient water for the sand to become stable enough to work in. It is not a cheap operation and should be used as a last resort.

Other problems with drains involve tree roots, with poplars and willows the prime culprits. On occasion I have had to take conductor drains in seamless pipes through badly conceived plantations of such trees, as blockage by tree roots left the land above and below the woods totally waterlogged. In other cases, rows of Lombardy poplars, planted each side of a wet clay fairway, had to be pulled out by a big crawler. In every case massive roots, encased in shattered tiles, came up with the stumps, while every tile drain had become solidly blocked by first minor and then main roots.

Draining peaty land has its own difficulties. To avoid insoluble subsidence problems in building greens, it is necessary to excavate the peat to a firm base, usually a wet clay, and then build up a solid base with imported fill. Using geotextile membranes will not stabilise soft bases, and the sheets get displaced during construction, leaving ruts and hollows.

CONCLUSION

All in all, since golf is played on many other sites than the ideal light sandy soils of heath or links land, drainage is still a far more important factor, in relation to all-year-round play, than almost any other consideration.

The rules are simple, perhaps the most important one being to drain deep and back up the main system with subsidiaries, mole ploughing, or deep aeration. Uniformity of falls is vital. Falls can be minimal if not imitating a roller coaster drive. Remember, a good system can last for more than a century—and some have lasted even longer—so it pays to take sound advice and go to someone who has done it all before. There is nothing like learning from other people's expensively acquired experience. Modern machinery greatly simplifies and speeds up installation, but there is no substitute for a sound plan supervised by an experienced drainer.

There are all sorts of tricks of the trade to find old systems, including dowsing, and it is sensible to find them, because laying a new system over an old one can result in neither of them working, though the problem is lessened by going really deep. Dowsing does work, and I sometimes think my clients are more impressed by my water divining rather than my agronomic skills, but that is the way of the world!

To sum up, the most effective drainage is deep drainage. It is vital to go below the water table if surplus water is to be drained from soils above. Close spaced, shallow drains are a waste of money; most merely drain a foot each side of the drain line. Prevention by intercept drainage is often better than a cure. Subsidiary drainage can be installed with the mains, or, at a later date, on suitable soils by using mole drains pulled across the stone covered mains.

Finally, the first rule of drainage is to find an outfall, otherwise the only solution is pumping. The second rule is just as important; employ a skilled and experienced drainer. You are installing a system which may last a century and more, so planning is never wasted.

Chapter Fourteen

. . . . .

GOLF COURSE CONSTRUCTION

Few would dispute the claim that the two main areas of growth in the golf scene in the last decade of the twentieth century were litigation and soil analyses. Both are avoidable, rarely satisfy any client and are vastly over-rated as safeguards, equally against bad practices and poor results.

Certainly there is no other part of the agronomic aspects of golf than in course construction, or re-construction, which gives more opportunities for both these facets to cause maximum loss and maximum sorrow. However poor the result, the best advice is never go to law. This chapter may help to avoid the poor end-product which causes so much grief.

Litigation, an unwanted import from America, has a very negative effect on construction, destroying the old principle of trust and truth on which earlier constructions were based. Over thirty years of my supervising the construction of new courses and the improvement of old ones over most of Europe, I have seen some enormous changes. The main change, and probably an irreversible one, is in specifications. By this I do not mean the actual methods of building greens, tees and fairways, but the paperwork trying to define the precise methods. It cannot be over-emphasised that course construction is not an exact science and that guide lines are just that, not inflexible rules cut into tablets of stone.

SPECIFICATIONS NEEDLESSLY COMPLEX

Specifications in the 1960s, when the first major post-war boom started, were written by me on perhaps ten sheets of A4 paper. They were essentially programmes of work. Today some exceed ten times that number, with meaningless bills of quantities, favouring only the contractors in pricing and submitting claims for extras, and demanding the employment of resident engineers or clerks of work to enforce and measure them. We get no better courses, but it keeps the soil analysts busy and sends costs higher.

Of course, we made mistakes thirty and more years ago, but contracts were invariably fixed price and variations were met out of modest contingency sums. What is more significant is that those few specialist contractors involved would willingly put things right if the errors were down to them, or would be paid modest extras, if outside unexpected factors, or the architect, were to blame.

My first enlightenment on the darker side came in the early 1970s, when a contract for a public golf course was won, hands down, by a newcomer to the construction industry, whose expertise was solely in civil engineering. Later, I was to learn that they had taken one look at my simple specification and boasted that they could drive a coach and horse through it, undercutting shamelessly and relying on later submission of enormous claims for extras. They made only one mistake. I was supervising, and I had written the contract. It took some time before they admitted defeat. It would be pleasing to report that the course was a success, but lack of experience creates problems that no amount of subsequent correction can repair. In another contract, in one of those trying sessions laying down what was to be done with no extras, as it was their fault, their head man sarcastically referred to me as God. He was not suited when I pointed out that as far as he and the contract were concerned, I *was* God!

Today, we get complex documents attempting to cover every possible contingency. No one is so clever as to be able to foresee every possibility and, if it is not covered, then it is an extra. Far better to have a broad outline, with the proviso that work shall be to the full satisfaction of the architect and/or employer.

Of course, this implies team work and trust by all parties working together, based on past experience and mutual respect and understanding.

LITIGATION

So much litigation is avoidable. It must always be remembered that the only people who benefit from law suits are lawyers. It is far better to settle out of court. This means that employers should satisfy themselves that architects (who alone carry the ultimate responsibility) have generous professional indemnity, but most importantly are prepared to consult rather than confront their contractor, so as to achieve the best results for their client. I keep saying, to anyone whose professional advice is governed and qualified by excessive fears of the threat of being sued, that the easiest way to prevent that eventuality is to do it right first time. This sounds easier said than done, but if one uses a sensible, practical, proven specification; selects the correct materials; chooses an experienced contractor; and supervises him efficiently and intensively, with staff who know what to look for, very little can go wrong, except the weather!

Examination of the background to cases where litigation is threatened or has occurred, whether successful or not, reveals first and foremost a disappointed employer who claims, often with justice, that he was promised the best, paid for the best, but did not get the best.

It is remarkably easy to pinpoint the culprit or culprits in all such cases. Often it is a combination of problems, on the old principle of Murphy's Law, that if things start to go wrong, they get worse and worse.

Inexperienced architects may be excused, if not exonerated from the costs of correction, if they produce bad specifications, and by bad I mean including clauses, methods and materials which have been long and widely condemned in the past. We were all young once, but all of us should endeavour to learn from the expensively acquired experience of others. As a for instance, in green construction a potent cause of disaster has been the use of geotextile membranes in lieu of a blinding layer over stone drainage carpets. These inevitably silt up and impede drainage. Punching holes through them with a Verti-Drain is no answer. The real answer is to use a suitable gravel blinding layer, but of that, more later. Yet such mistakes are still being advised by so-called agronomists, who are being sued as a result.

Even if any architect produces a copy-book specification, if he or his agronomist picks the wrong materials, or compromises, as sometimes happens, by choosing "the best of a bad lot" to meet straitened budgets, then disaster looms. This is where detailed knowledge of sources of approved and tested materials is invaluable. We simply have no time in the average contract to be able to wait weeks for all materials to be analysed.

SUPERVISION

Equally, the best materials will not ensure success if constructors are unsupervised. I am not suggesting that there is any truth in the old adage that there are supervised contractors and bad contractors, but intensive inspection, checking and over-seeing can eliminate avoidable errors and leave less scope for cutting corners or burying mistakes merely to cut costs.

The contractors, in fact, have done much in the past decade or so to put their own house in order. The British Association of Golf Course Constructors (BAGCC) was set up in 1980–81 and has done much to eradicate the cowboy element and to set standards for its members, both commercially and technically.

Contractors, especially good, conscientious ones, welcome as well as need the fullest information on methods and materials to be employed, both in contract documents and in the field. The secret of a successful construction lies, as always, in team work and communication, with mutual trust and recognition of the varied specialist skills of each section. Needless to say, the missing element is experience, for which there is no substitute.

However, it is an imperfect world. There is an old farming adage to the effect that the farmer's foot is the best fertiliser. By walking his land or kicking a furrow-slice he knows instinctively when field conditions are optimum for each operation. Similarly, there is no substitute for the experience which permits accurate assessments to be made on work in progress. This, for example, can approve or reject truckloads of raw materials by the old method of looking at it or rubbing it between finger and thumb—so derided by our laboratory-imprisoned soil physicists. Supervision is the secret of success, but it must be intensive, knowledgeable and experienced. There is no point in looking in on work being carried out only at infrequent intervals or at prearranged times. We can all get caught that way. I once had to supervise a crooked contractor—in fact he went into liquidation at the end of that contract—and even by dint of calling in unexpectedly several times a week, sometimes twice on the same day, I could not prevent him cutting corners, but I could spot the deficiencies and make sure he corrected them. However, he had the last laugh. At a late stage in construction we were trenching round the backs of cut out (chair) greens, laying flexible drains and covering them with shingle to act as intercepts for surface flow. I watched every operation, and saw the pipe line in and covered. The next winter we had drainage problems and dug up the intercepts. Only two had flexible pipes. What he had done, as soon as I moved to the next green, was to rip out the pipe from the first and use it on the third green, with that from the second being whipped out and put round the fourth!

One architect I worked with for years, long deceased but never forgotten, solved one problem by saying to the constructor that he would, at the end of the contract, give him eighteen numbered slips to draw from and whichever green the contractor picked the architect would dig up and check! Whether it was a coincidence or not I do not know, but we never had anything but success with that constructor. I prefer to think that it was his conscientious adherence to a sound specification that was the real reason.

However, while there are countless experts, not all have either experience or expertise. This is where the soil physicists seize their chance to demand that everything used must be analysed. Even the stone in the stone carpet is analysed, at quite considerable cost, and with potentially costly delays of course, to see that they comply with the fairly wide parameters related to set criteria—particle size and performance levels included.

There are problems which may, hopefully, be fewer in the future when analysis techniques are standardised. There never was a more likely case for a successful law suit if, as has often happened in the past, one laboratory produces results which indicate unsuitability in a particular aspect, chiefly in related drainage and moisture/nutrient retention balance and another gives approval, especially if identical samples are sent to more than one laboratory. This especially applies when materials approved for 30 years are rejected, while dubious materials are approved.

Another problem, again more often confined to less experienced architects or designers, is that contractors and/or suppliers are asked to provide materials which will meet not just physical criteria, but performance standards. This is clearly not the responsibility of contractors, but that of the architect to specify exactly what he wants, and the contractor is to supply, in order to produce the desired performance figures.

Golf course construction is not an exact science. In practice, mixing, say, the materials for root zones is done by tipping a digger bucket full of an approved source of "humus" with three of approved sand, onto hard standing and thoroughly mixing them. If it needs a bit more of one or the other, someone puts in a little more or less and then it is turned and turned. Yet we see pedantic agronomists specifying 84% of sand and 16% of peat to achieve hydraulic conductivity figures for which tests in the field are rough and ready and in the laboratory contradictory. What a load of rubbish. There are broad rules which must be obeyed—of which more anon—but the best results follow good constructional techniques with consistent, tried and tested raw materials.

As for testing stone, you can easily get different results from the front and back of a load, let alone individual loads. Inexperienced operators demand analyses as a protection, but it is a dubious shield if things go wrong.

EARLY HISTORY

However, this seems an appropriate place to go back in history. This will help to explain how modern construction techniques evolved, partly to meet the relatively newly changed need towards all-year-round performance and partly to provide better wearing surfaces, with golf having developed massively since those, not so far off, days when it was more of an élitist sport, a game, as Bernard Darwin observed, played in England by a few gentlemen and by most Scotsmen.

Early history lacks documentation, but there is enough evidence to be fairly sure that the earliest greens (on links) were merely scythed out of a reasonably level and well grassed area of dune land. In fact this is still the system adopted for modern cheap and cheerful projects, on naturally well-drained sandy land.

However, as the increasing popularity of the game created a demand which could be met only on less suitable heavier land—near cities for example—clearly building courses on such heavy soil created problems, notably in drainage in winter.

The local soil was still used for greens, but was ameliorated with sand. Some of our early architects clearly understood drainage. Braid's trademarks were his swales, grass hollows, or rather shallow valleys, behind greens cut out of slopes. These were designed to collect and divert surface run-off, preventing it from finishing on more level putting surfaces and thus creating poor conditions, if not actual flooding.

Attempts were made to build courses and greens on very wet environments, either heavy clays or naturally badly drained land. Field drainage was, of course, nothing new, with early agricultural developments, stimulated by the need to grow more cereals after the Napoleonic wars, made feasible by the invention and use of clay pipes. These were originally "horse-shoes", flat clay tiles laid over poles before baking. Later they were laid on flat tiles in the base of deep slits, but field drainage really took off when the process of making tubular clay pipes reduced costs. Many of these old piped drains—some of only 2 in. diameter—were still working a century later because they had been laid deep, which is the secret of efficient long-lasting drainage (see chapter 13).

Unfortunately, golf course builders of the day (and greenkeepers), forgot this when trying to drain greens, by running a herring bone pattern of tile drains in shallow fashion under greens. Lacking depth and often topped with gravel or ash over the tile, they may have worked reasonably in winter, but every drain line showed itself in summer, especially with the inefficient irrigation systems of the day, if indeed any existed. Drain lines also sank and, even with generous top dressing to build up subsidences, such greens were always a pain to putt upon.

PERCHED WATER TABLE SYSTEMS

Clearly, some better form of under-drainage was required. The two independently developed aspects of the same principle, namely the perched water table system, evolved from assessments of field drainage, and especially the in-filling over deep field drains with porous materials. This was designed to improve the collecting powers of drains, while stabilising, i.e. preventing the collapse of the narrow slits, (made possible with narrow slit trenchers), and acting as intercepts. If the shingle in-fill was brought to within 6 in. of the surface and then topped with soil to hide the drain, and if one did not take precautions, the soil migrated into the shingle. Long before perched water table greens, we had learned to blind the larger shingle with pea gravel before topping up with a fairly coarse sandy root zone mix.

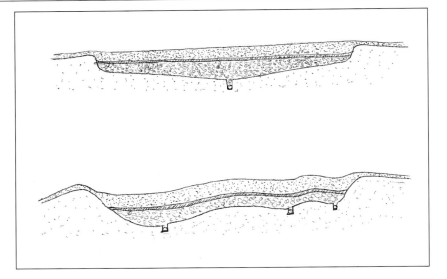

Cross sections of suspended water table greens. Note: all vertical scales are exaggerated. The top layer is rootzone material; the middle a blinding layer; the bottom a stone carpet.

Top: *Fairly gently sloped green site. Note valleyed base to assist lateral drainage on a 'flat' site.*

Bottom: *Severely contoured putting surface. Note base and all strata follow final contour of putting surface.*

In 1960 the USGA Green Section published details for the construction of golf greens on a drained sub-base, over which was laid a gravel carpet blinded with smaller grit, under a tightly specified sandy root zone. The principle has remained unaltered, though the details and criteria appear subject to some changes every year, in the light of current findings.

In essence, this principle is that moisture will be retained by a root zone in relation to the fineness of the particles, but drainage relates to the coarseness. What we must define is the relationship between particle size and drainage, versus moisture retention. Coarse mixes drain faster but retain less water. Mixes that are too fine may drain very badly but retain moisture. We need to strike a balance for each site, but on the whole, in northern Europe, free drainage is more important than moisture retention. We do, however, need a sensible level of the latter.

The striking of the balance between moisture and nutrient retention and drainage is important, but it is not necessarily the same balance for every situation. In hot arid climes, with the need for much more intensive irrigation, drainage is more important, just to cope with the vastly greater levels of water applied to the green. Where irrigation is limited by budgetary restraints or shortage of water, in temperate climes, moisture retention is just as important as drainage.

Of course, it is necessary to stop the relatively fine-particled root zone migrating into the drainage layers. After some experimentation, it was found that if the ratio between average particle sizes in the successive root zone blinding and stone carpet layers did not exceed 1:10, migration could be ignored. The principle is as simple as this, yet soil physicists produce complex formulae, often not understood by constructors or even architects, and demand that they be regarded as sacrosanct. This would matter less if they did not keep modifying them, self-admittedly, on occasions, on a purely arbitrary or pragmatic basis, to meet perceived changes. It is even worse when no modifications are made and the criteria are pedantically regarded as being unchangeable—thus incapable of modification.

Way back in 1966, knowing, I admit, nothing of the USGA or its work, I devised a similar system by trial and error, but based fortuitously on much larger stone than the $1/4$ in. pea gravel laid down by the USGA Green Section. This was a purely pragmatic selection. We wanted something which was large enough to give a stable base onto which we could run a 360° swing excavator and use it sited centrally—though stationary—to import and spread successive layers. Even with golf courses costing in those days not much in excess of £100,000 for 18 holes, and often less, we could not afford the luxury of hand work.

My first greens had no herring bone system under them, but a domed base shed water to a perimeter drain. Clearly this was prone to problems, if only because drainage was least efficient in the more widely used centre of greens. Quickly I reverted to a herring bone or grid system, whose effect on

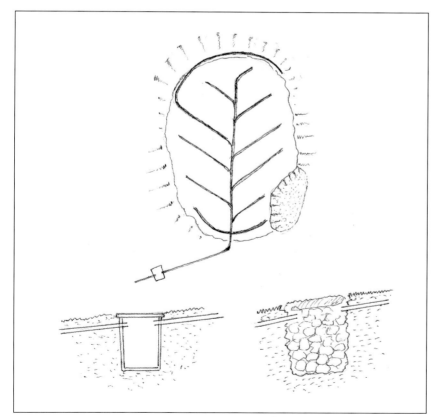

Top: *Sketch plan of the under-drainage of a new P.W.T. green.*
Note especially:-
(i) *Intercept drain at back of green connected to the main spine drain.*
(ii) *Alternate and opposite pattern of spurs.*
(iii) *"Smile" drain at front, collecting water from lowest part of stone carpet.*
(iv) *Outfall via inspection chamber well away from entire approach.*

Bottom left: *Inspection chamber. Note trap for sediment.*

Bottom right: *Sump in porous soil. Note drained on the overflow principle.*

the surface was masked by a stone carpet but, since our greens are usually less sloping and only slightly contoured compared with American ones, I constructed them with valleyed bases so that lateral movement to the drains, once the water had gone through the stone carpet, was facilitated. Of course, with more steeply rolling greens, such valleying was unnecessary, but as a result we did get deeper stone carpets in the centre of greens, where the need for drainage was greatest.

With larger stone (then available but no longer so), as a fairly uniform 3–4 in. (75–100 mm) grade, one had to opt for a deeper layer than the 4 in. of $1/4$ in. pea gravel stipulated in the USGA specification. Even on concrete, let alone a soft base, 4 in. of pea gravel is notoriously unstable—try walking on it.

Double blinding was only rarely needed, because it was possible to keep within the 1:10 ratio by using a larger grit for blinding and a coarser root zone. Today we tend to standardise on a 25–40 mm stone, blinded with 3–5 mm grit and with a root zone with 75–80% of the mix over 0.25 mm, up to 1 mm.

MOST ANALYSES WASTE TIME AND MONEY

My protestations that golf course construction is more of an art form than an exact science are scorned by theoretical physicists. Of course there are criteria to consider, but if one uses tried and tested materials, constant analyses are time and money wasting. One hears, as one example, constant and repeated emphasis on the level of hydraulic conductivity for root zones. Often the parameters are so wide that the stipulation is meaningless, but this is surely putting the cart before the horse and is loved by lawyers. Even minor shortfalls in laid-down standards are seized on as a reason to sue.

One reason for sample rejection is the use of different analytic techniques. Constructors are being asked to quote for and supply materials which will produce stated performance standards. What nonsense! Analysis results can vary, depending on when and where the sample is taken, for example from bulk deliveries, bulk mixings on site, as-laid root zones, and root zones after establishment.

Clearly we need to describe the right sources of materials. For example, sands must be lime-free, semi-rounded in shape, with a narrow profile of particle size, ideally, if not always achievable, 80% between 0.25 and 0.75 mm. Organic additives must have very low (as stipulated) clay and silt fractions and the organic source should be easy to turn into an homogenous uniform mix with sand.

But given all that, all that we really have to watch is the ratio of 1:8 or 1:10 between overlying strata. Why make such a song and dance about it? Why not use a perched water table specification, specifically designed for northern European, temperate conditions, rather than blindly sticking to the USGA Green Section Specification, which varies throughout that continent and also it seems, in certain aspects, year by year. There is even talk of abandoning specific criteria, with advisory rather than mandatory recommendations—in other words a guide rather than dogmatic instructions.

This change is not surprising, for large uniform "hard" stone is not freely available in parts of the United States and they are short of organic soils. They have no peat deposits equivalent to the fen peat being extracted from drained East Anglian fens. When visiting USGA agronomists and others are shown what we have, they say they would use it too, if only they had it!

CONSTITUENTS — GOOD OR BAD

There is no dispute about principles, but only about materials. Certainly, there is no divergence about root zones. The main difference is in relation to the size of stone in the stone carpet. The USGA itself has stated that they see no problem in having an increased depth of larger sized stone; it in no way prejudices the perched water table principle. There are points on which we all agree about vetoes. One is certainly in the use of geotextile membranes in place of a grit/coarse sand blinding layer. They cost more, silt up easily, impede drainage, get caught up in machinery during construction and afterwards and one ends up having to Verti-Drain through the membrane. Too much or too little of any constituent is equally a bad thing. Pure sand greens were a heresy introduced in the desert states of America to cope with enormously high levels of irrigation. They have been comprehensively condemned for use in other zones by all recognised agronomists. In my case, I had condemned them even before they were used here by inexperienced designers, partly because we do not need such exaggerated drainage, but especially because such greens must be heavily and regularly fed (hydroponically) with complete fertilisers (NPK) and lime if the grass is not to die. If that grass is US creeping bent, that demise comes fairly quickly. The resultant and predictable dominance of *Poa annua* produces most unsatisfactory conditions for many months of the year and well publicised disasters for televised tournaments!

Too much clay and silt is just as bad, as is excessive humus source, which drains badly and produces soft greens.

To reiterate, apart from these relatively minor strictures, the only basic principles that must not be varied are retention of the 1:8 to 1:10 ratio in particle size between the three layers; the root zone must be coarse-particled, not fine; and the depth of each layer should be uniform (this is essential with root zone and blinding). Variations in depth of stone carpet, e.g. by

A blinding layer being spread by stationary long jibbed excavator.

building up levels with stone instead of adjusting the bases, while not affecting the principle can be expensive. The base therefore must conform, within reason, to the contours of the final putting surface.

Obviously, selection of the correct stone, gravel or grit, and root zone constituents is vital, but that would be true of any specification.

A note on such construction materials is pertinent. The stone must naturally not be potentially decomposable. Attempts in the past to use lump chalk or limestone, especially on acid soils, were disastrous. The chalk fizzed away quietly to itself and decomposed into an impermeable "plastic" layer. When greens were lifted, when re-construction was unavoidable, the chalk layer curled and peeled off like a breaking wave under the digger blade. Similarly, soft sandstones are best avoided, but apart from that almost anything goes; from flint, granite, hard sandstone even, to broken brick in areas where stone would have had to be imported for hundreds of miles in the absence (e.g. in the Netherlands) of stone quarries, or of large enough shingle from riverside sand pits. Shape too is important, with very angular particles locking together, causing greatly reduced drainage capacity.

Blinding material can similarly come from a wide range, from fine gravel or grit to any suitable clean hard material of correct uniform size, the emphasis, as with screened ash, being on clean and uniform.

Root zone materials need to be more precisely specified. Certainly, local soils are almost always unsuitable, ruled out by excessive silt plus clay content. In practice we mix a sand, with a narrow particle-size profile, clean, lime-free, washed, and of the correct semi-rounded shape, with a source of humus. The sand is fairly easy to define and can be obtained in consistent quality

Golf Course Construction

and quantity. It is the humus source which creates arguments.

The choice is limited in practice to peats, peat-derived soils, and organic wastes. Dealing first with peat, the choice lies between sphagnum, sedge and fen peats—each formed by a different geological process. Sphagnum peat is formed under acid anaerobic conditions, typically but not exclusively as found in central Ireland. When it is first purchased, thus dry, it is brown and fibrous, very light and bulky and difficult to screen through a fine mesh. Indeed, one definition of sphagnum peat is that it must be possible to see the fibres, and it is the fibres that cause the problems. It is also very difficult to moisten once dried, even with the help of wetting agents. Those who remembered the west of Ireland before it was altered by prosperity (I will not say improved) will recollect the peat bogs. Cutting peat was as much the recognised pastime of courting couples as going to the cinema was elsewhere. The peat turf was cut in long strips, stacked and dried by "exposing it to rain!" When dry, it was carted to the shieling and stacked. Rarely was it protected from the

Mixing root zone of fen soil and sand, centrally, off site.

Mixing on site is a definite NO. Don't do it!

211

PRACTICAL GREENKEEPING

elements, for the ubiquitous plastic sheeting and bags had not arrived then. It did not need to be. Once dry, it took an enormous amount of rain to get it wet again, and could be put on the fire to slow burn, as good at the end of the winter as at the start. Later an industry grew up baling the peat in 1 cwt bales. Anyone who ever had cause to use these bales remembers two things. First, what man-killers they were to handle, and second, how impossible it was to get them wet. It was quite usual to toss the bales into the nearest pond, and they were still half floating a week later. This peat can absorb at least ten times its weight of water, given time, so the old 1 cwt bale could absorb in excess of 100 gallons, a lot of water.

This is the essential problem with sphagnum peat and the reason why I have consistently condemned its use, especially as top dressing, but also in root zones. The top dressing should always be as nearly the same physically as the root zone, and a mix of sphagnum peat and sand soon separates out, with the peat being lost in the mowing box or drag matted off.

Sedge peat is less acid, being formed, again in waterlogged situations, which prevent decomposition. This causes the build up of undecomposed humus, several metres deep, in low-lying, badly drained areas, characteristically poorly drained levels or flood plains with extensive winter flooding. Such ground would be used agriculturally only around the less flooded areas, as summer grazing. Sedge peat is better to handle and easier to get wet again once dried. It makes a better homogenous mix with other materials, including sand.

Fen peat occurs in extensive deposits which relate to the slow drying up of glacial lakes, mainly in the flat parts of eastern England. Often these deposits lay upon gravel and chalk, in other cases the basal formation is clay. Thus the first type is alkaline pH 6.5–7.0, while over clay the pH is 4.5–5.0.

Many of these deposits are being extracted, partly to get at the gravel, but also as part of an approved scheme to restore wetlands in nature conservation work.

It is, of course, ecologically indefensible to strip huge areas of their peat cover, to leave derelict land behind, just to satisfy the need for an organic source. The combination of protest movements and the finite nature of supplies makes the search for an acceptable alternative urgent. Even fen peat, although not subject to criticism by "greens", is not in unlimited supply, although enough remains for the next decade or two. It is far more physically satisfactory, does not dry out extensively, and can be wetted easily.

Unlike the other peat deposits, where only the surface vegetation, such as heather, needs stripping, there is often quite a reasonable depth of very organically-rich soil overlying the fen peat. Such soils have been cultivated in past years, growing vegetables and other crops, and in consequence have

GOLF COURSE CONSTRUCTION

been limed and fertilised for this purpose. This material is physically ideal for use in root zones, but analysis will indicate whether levels of lime and phosphates are unacceptably high for use as top dressings. In most cases, there having been no cropping for years, levels cause no concern.

Other sources of humus, used in the past, range from dried digested sewage sludge, fine screened materials like cocoa waste, screened leaf mould and various composted wastes. All, save the last, suffer from being too rich in plant foods, unavailable in quantity of a consistent quality, or have other faults and can be ignored.

The future must lie in composting recycled garden and horticultural waste, in that it is available in quantity and ecologically correct. At the moment some materials have nutritional levels that are too high and too alkaline, but doubtless this could be corrected by pre-selection of the basic material. High temperatures are generated in the composting process, so there is at least partial sterilisation. Indeed, because such composts are soil-less, the possibility of soil-borne fungi (such as take-all patch) attacking turf is less likely.

BUILDING A GREEN

A short stage-by-stage description of building a green to a standard perched water table system may form a helpful guide, rather than a rigid specification. First the site should be stripped of vegetation or turf, conserving it if feasible. Then remove and preserve the top soil for use on surrounds. Strip an area of at least 2000 m^2 to give adequate working space.

Shaping the base can be done with earth-moving equipment. Consolidation is not a problem because the base need not be permeable. Indeed it is an advantage for it not to be, if subsequent subsidence is to be avoided. The base should conform roughly to the final contours of the finished green. If greens are fairly flat, it is an advantage to valley the base to improve lateral movement of drainage water over the base to the inserted drain. If greens are reasonably sloping this is not necessary. The valley should not be more than 20 cm deep, less if practicable. No hollows or low places must be left or, if they are, then they should be picked up by a spur drain.

Into this firm base are cut narrow (20 cm wide) slits, just deep enough to carry the perforated, flexible plastic drains, i.e. 20–25 cm deep. The pattern will depend on the contours, either a herring bone or grid pattern, but with a drain on

Stripping of site and conservation of top soil

213

PRACTICAL GREENKEEPING

the perimeter at the foot of the slope, known descriptively as a smile drain. Additionally, in the case of green sites cut out of slopes, a similar drain can act as an intercept on the high side and be tapped into the green system. Such narrow and shallow trenches are far less liable to be damaged by the subsequent passage over them of machines. Broad and especially "V" shaped sections are emphatically condemned, as they collapse.

The subsidiaries will be connected to the main drain by pre-formed junction units, not butt-joined. The size of perforated drains will be 60 mm, the only exception being in the case of very large greens, where the spine drain could be 100 mm. These plastic drains must be laid directly onto the soil at the base of the slits and not on shingle, but once installed they may be shingled (3–5 mm grit) before bringing in the same stone as that used for the carpet.

Below: *The installation of a proper and effective herring bone drainage system is all important.*

Below: *The two examples illustrated here show deep "V" shaped slits, which collapse and are wrong.*

Right: *Perforated flexible pipes being laid on a herring bone pattern.*

The outfall from this main spine drain will be led, via an inspection trap, to existing drainage or at worst an effective sump. A stone-filled, metre cube hole in clay is not an effective sump.

Over this base is imported the stone carpet, using a 360° swing excavator, centrally sited, but not moving about. The depth should ideally be 20 cm, but with valleyed bases this becomes 10 cm at the perimeter and up to 40 cm in the centre. It is possible to reduce these depths on grounds of economy, but with shallower depths mechanisation of spreading is difficult and may rut the base, so it is often false economy.

The stone is carefully levelled with the excavator bucket, before introducing the 5 cm depth of blinding grit, again spread mechanically.

Over this is spread, in the same way, a minimum of 22 cm (if turfing) or 25 cm (if seeding) of the root zone material, measured in terms of final consolidation. Introducing it in two stages is no longer thought necessary.

No seed or turf bed fertiliser is needed with the right humus source, namely fen soil or recycled compost. In adverse conditions one might consider a little nitrogen only.

The horse-shoe main of the irrigation system should then be cut in, before building the surrounds, with upright tubing placed to help find it when inserting the pop up heads much later, when everything has settled.

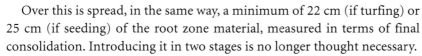

Cutting a narrow but deep drain line to an outfall

A stone carpet installed, following properly the contours of the finished putting green surface.

A long-jibbed excavator spreading root zone over a blinding layer of Cornish grit. The author, Jim Arthur, is in the foreground, right.

Surrounds and greenside bunkers will be finished then and the whole area prepared for seeding or turfing according to the season, the need for speed, or other factors.

All traffic must be kept off approaches, with machinery introduced from the rear of greens if possible. Approaches must be deeply cultivated and worked up, with the addition of a humus source worked thoroughly into the surface, to facilitate preparing a good root zone. Irrigation should be installed, preferably before seeding, to avoid damaging surfaces by pulling in pipework on established turf. It is not essential to fit pop-ups before seeding. Problems can arise, because pop-ups may be left proud by subsidence after seeding, or they may sink. A hose watering point to one side, supplying a hose pipe and sprinkler is sufficient. If the pipe work and wiring are installed during the construction stage, the end of the pipe run (where the pop-ups will be sited) must be marked with a vertical pipe, and needless to say the pipe ends must be capped to avoid soil getting into the pipes.

This method refers only to greens of course, the question of tees and fairways will follow.

Meanwhile, it needs saying that it is not always necessary to use the perched water table system for greens, but this should never be omitted on heavier sites, since the extra cost is not enormous and is well worth it in terms of better all-the-year-round golf.

On very sandy sites a stone carpet is not needed, but remember that not all sands drain well, and, if there is a naturally high water table, under-drainage is necessary, even on sand. Never put in a herring bone system, however deep, unless its potential surface effect in dry weather is masked by a drainage carpet.

GOLF COURSE CONSTRUCTION

In these cases, keep off the greens in shaping them, working from the perimeters but not the approach so far as is possible. Any compaction of bases must be counteracted by deep tining or cultivation and then by re-establishing a firm, but well drained, base over which is brought in a 25 cm final depth of approved root zone, well firmed down but not compacted or sealed. The best way of achieving this is still the time-honoured method of heeling and raking.

TEES AND FAIRWAYS

Tees today are becoming more and more like greens in terms of size and shape. The use of triplex mowers creates turning problems unless both ends are rounded. It was Tom Simpson who said, "greens are not square" (well, they were once, as photographs of Sunningdale in the early 1900s revealed), "so why should tees be." He landscaped his tees into the contours of their surrounds.

On heavier soils, it pays to build tees on stone carpets. The depth of root zone need not be so great, as we are not sinking hole cups in tees. Otherwise, follow the method above. With better soil conditions, it may be necessary to cut off surface flow and subsurface seepage on the high side. Even with a stone carpet, elaborate pipe drainage is generally not needed, but if the stone

This generous tee at Ramside Golf Club provides rounded edges throughout to facilitate easy turning with a triplex mower. Note also the natural appearance of waterside banks; demonstrating clever marginal management.

217

PRACTICAL GREENKEEPING

A poor excuse for a tee. No golfer should have to endure this or any other type of rubberised "temporary tee" horror, even in the depths of winter.

carpet sheds water laterally, it must be collected by a drain along one side or the other, or both, over the length of the tee.

Fairways are a bigger problem. With many new courses, one begins at best with a fallow of ploughed land, starting from scratch. All too often, logic is lost overboard when it comes to preparing fairways—admittedly it is basically an agricultural operation—but never was the old adage "ask a farmer and then do the opposite" more true.

Cultivations are not all that different from farming, but ploughing must be in one direction only, to avoid leaving the land in ridge and furrow

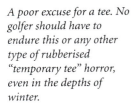

Stone burying is often necessary, as these before (left) and after pictures clearly illustrate.

218

Golf Course Construction

contours. We need no fertilisers or lime, and the poorer the soil chemically the better. What is usually needed is some soil improvement physically, by working in organic matter, such as fen peat, to improve soil structure.

Another variation from agricultural practices is in the case of stony land. While a certain level of stone left in the surface is acceptable in farming—in fact, some extremely heavy crops have been grown on deeply ploughed limestone brash, when the surface has been left with much more stone than soil—this is clearly unacceptable in preparing a golf fairway. In such cases, this stone can be buried by using a buryvator. This is, in effect, a heavy-duty rotavator throwing stones and soil backwards against a rigid grille, the soil going through but the stones dropping, to be quickly successively buried by the soil thrown through the grille as the machine travels forward. Stone-picking machines are less effective, while one is also left with the disposal problems of huge quantities of stone and a destructured, stone-free soil. The buried stone from buryvators acts as a stone carpet, but remember you cannot repeat the operation, so it has to be done correctly the first time. No second chances!

Most thinking architects, and indeed most golfers if they stop to consider, want bent or bent/fescue turf for fairways, not football pitches. Why then not start with bent and fescue seeds mixtures, never, never with perennial

PRACTICAL GREENKEEPING

Stone burying by machine is often the only sensible option. There are several sizes, with selection dependent upon the site conditions.

* *The BLEC stoneburier is available up to 2.5m.*

* *The Rotadairon 1 m stone, clod and debris burier.*

ryegrass. So-called dwarf strains are mis-named. Most land called upon for golf course use these days is ex-farmland and the last thing needed is a pre-seeding fertiliser—anathema to our native fine turf forming grasses.

Seeding ideally should be from late July to early September, but I am the first to agree that construction is often delayed by events outside the control of architect or contractor. Nevertheless, if the last date for seeding is missed, avoid the temptation to take a risk by sowing say in mid-October. I have even sometimes seen this done in November, just to try to achieve completion and so collect payment. Good architects should stop this—they have the power. Such late sowings are invariably thin and open, easily invaded by weeds and weed grasses. Over-seeding in spring might be something one can get away with in a favourable season, but, all too often, April is a winter month and May the start of droughts. There is no advantage in spring seeding, especially with all the risks involved. Waiting, if this is humanly or financially possible, until July is far better. Such seedings rapidly overtake those done three months earlier and a vigorous and dense sward results.

Talking of seeding, I never cease to be amazed at the prevalence of a custom which was roundly condemned by good greenkeepers sixty and more years ago, namely raking seed in. All this does is to draw the seed into lines with excessive competition in the drills so formed, while leaving bare ground between— an open invitation to unwanted species to invade. Worse still, this practice smothers the tiny seeds of *Agrostis*, and most die if they are covered by more than 2 mm or so. Then we get questioned why it is that a sowing of bents and fescues ends up as pure fescue or, worse still, fescue/annual meadow grass.

I was taught half a century ago to sow seed on a fine, firm, raked seedbed, never to rake it in, (though perhaps the back of a rake is permissible), but to drag a wet sack or piece of carpet over the sown area or even to lightly roll it in with a hand mower with the blades set well up. This way gives a strong, vigorous and dense turf which will keep out invaders, always presuming that seeding is carried out in good growing periods in late summer. We need a bit longer than the odd week of favourable conditions earlier and later, with ideally a minimum of six weeks from sowing, for safe establishment.

All too often sowing success is prejudiced by trying to get courses into play too soon. The problems of getting a return on expenditure are fully acknowledged, but a little patience at the start will pay handsome dividends in future years.

BUNKERS

Finally, a word on bunker construction. Fairway bunkers must of course be in keeping with the character of the course and in any case there is normally plenty of space to give full choice. On long established golf courses, many bunkers have to be rebuilt to get them further from the tee, so that they might catch the long hitter. Certainly, the bunkers should make him plan his tee shot, or be penalised if he ignores them. Alternatively, tees can be moved back if space permits. The high handicap players, especially those lacking in length off the tee, have enough problems of their own, for "they carry their own bunkers with them." They should not be able to reach the hazards in the first place, but to carry them with their second shots.

It is with greenside bunkers we are more concerned. Constant trimming of faces over the years results in the face being cut back, to such an extent that surrounds are unacceptably narrow, or even non-existent. The only answer is to rebuild them completely, moving the face well back. In this operation, the bunker floor has also to be moved back.

If there is unlimited space, one has a choice of styles, but all too often steep slopes or restricted areas mean that bunkers have to be steep-faced. This means revetting (turf walling) faces, to retain the soil packed behind in order to fill the space between the old and the new faces. Sand can still be swept right up the face to the turf rim. The slope is important; 10–15° off the vertical.

PRACTICAL GREENKEEPING

Many greenkeepers dislike bunker faces of turf rolled over, especially if the faces are grassed down to the sand floor. They create difficult mowing problems if the faces are steep, while if they are more gently sloping, players tend to climb up them, or balls get lodged in the grass.

Mowing of steep faces means a two-man operation with a hover mower on a rope, while shallow slopes take up a considerable area, which may not always be available.

When turf is taken to the absolute base then the lowest margin is laborious to present properly, while balls can finish up against the turf of a flat based bunker. Cleaning up the sand after mowing is tedious. If sand is raked up the face, then it will get blasted out onto the turf slope, which will eventually die.

It is far better in my view to construct, in the case of new courses, earth walled faces, up which sand can be raked, or where bunkers have to be reconstructed (as, for example, where constant

Above: *Revetting a bunker. The tried and tested method and so very handsome when done properly.*

Right: *A revetted bunker nearing completion*

222

Golf Course Construction

Difficulty in keeping sand in windswept shallow bunkers at Seaford has encouraged facing with turf as an alternative. The solution is neat enough, though grass tempts the player to clamber over, rather than exit rearwards. Furthermore, grassed banking makes a bunker difficult to discern from afar, with sand below the sight line.

cutting back edges to trim and tidy them means the bunkers cut into the surrounds and almost into the putting surface), then the only answer is revetting, building walls of turf laid upon turf (upside down), to retain the soil behind.

Revetted turf must lie back at an angle of 10°–15° from the vertical and the turves must be full width to give a longer period of years for cutting back and trimming. Each course of full width turves must be laid flat and

Revetting as an art form. This bunker revetting is about two years old.

223

Practical Greenkeeping

This old bunker is way past its best. Time to call in the repair team!

the desired slope back achieved by setting each course slightly back—stepped—from the one below.

Sand blasted from bunkers onto greens can soon produce sand-only mounds, with a build up of as much as 50 cm, demanding removal and lowering, both for maintenance and drought resistance problems. The smothering induces disease, which can spread from the edge across the green.

Personally, I deplore the Saharan-like expanses of flat sand, masquerading as sand traps, on some of our new courses. They are expensive to construct and more so to maintain, while presenting no problems for the better player, who can often play out of them with a wood. What is more, they are grotesquely unnatural. Only water features earn my wrath more. Golf is not a water sport, nor is it played in a glorified child's play-pit. Well-designed courses need no more than a dozen fairway bunkers, yet some of our newer monstrosities produce holes looking like a high rise lock system in a canal climbing a steep rise, with serried ranks of bunkers on both sides of the fairway.

CONCLUSION

There are many lessons to learn on construction, many starting with architecture, which is not in the brief of this book. "Use the land you are given" is a sound architectural tenet, going back all of a century. Keep it simple, work with rather than against nature. Obey a few simple constructional rules, forget the soil analysts and the lawyers whom they attract like flies to carrion, and do it right first time, using proven standards and methods and time-tested materials. Few golfers can resist the temptation, given the opportunity, of designing and building their own course, yet ignorance combined with optimism makes this the most expensive present they could ever give themselves. Perhaps nowhere more than in construction does it pay to learn from the expensively acquired experience of others, be it a multi-million extravaganza or a cheap and cheerful farmers' glory. Furthermore, if you do consult an expert, check that he really is one. What is his track record, what is said by satisfied (or dissatisfied) clients, and even if he is a brilliant designer, has he equally brilliant back-up in all the specialist aspects of construction, drainage, irrigation and ecology?

Above all else, remember that golf course construction is more of an art than a science, and that analyses can do nothing to ensure success, only to measure failure. Use common sense, time proven methods and materials, avoid gimmicks and short-lived fads and fancies and, above all else, seek the advice of those who have done it all before. They may not have seen absolutely everything, but very little will come as a complete surprise to them. We built excellent courses in the past, with specifications written on one side of a piece of paper, and the reasons were two-fold. The architect supervised personally and intensively, often living on the site, and they knew not only their golf but their grasses.

It is an unbeatable recipe, but commercial pressures make such intimate hour-by-hour supervision, seven days a week, financially impossible—and too many of those designing courses today lack basic agronomic training and education in grasses. Ability to hit a golf ball out of sight and with reasonable accuracy is no substitute for an in-built flair for good design, coupled with a willingness to learn from the experience of others and proper respect for the traditions of this Royal and Ancient game.

Chapter Fifteen

HEALTH AND SAFETY IN GOLF COURSE MANAGEMENT

With the introduction in recent years of so many new health and safety regulations, it is easy to form the impression that we are the bad boys of Europe and have a great deal to do to catch up. This could not be further from the truth. Greenkeepers have enjoyed a long tradition of safe working practices, coupled with good common sense, borne out by the fact that when compared with, say, agriculture, fatalities and serious injuries are a rare occurrence.

In terms of the law, we have had the Health and Safety at Work Act since 1974, together with its many regulations targeting specific work areas. This Act for the first time places legal duties on both employer and employee to take care of themselves and others. Other Acts before 1974 dealt with specific work areas where there were many serious hazards and records of deaths and serious injuries, for example in mines, quarries or factories.

However, that is not to say that golf club employers are blameless and need not be concerned. Clearly there are many employers who have not embraced the principles and practices of health and safety at work, while some golf clubs still cling to incorrect and traditional views. Good examples of this are "We are a private club so the law does not affect us," or, "We employ a small group of staff, some of whom are part-time, the law does not apply to us." Health and safety laws apply to all those who work, regardless of whether they are full-time, part-time, or self-employed. The requirement to prepare a written Statement of Safety Policy, and to make a record of the "significant findings" of risk assessments, applies to all employers who have five or more staff employed on the site as a whole. When counting heads, remember to include clubhouse staff and greenkeepers, whether full- or part-time, and do not neglect to add volunteers—such as artisans—who usually have some work-related duties.

Sad to relate, there are many sites with very poor facilities, with little or no arrangements for health and safety, and with no idea of what main workplace hazards there might be. Furthermore, there is no discernible trend whereby it could be said that only older, private members' clubs have neglected this important area. In reality, many new private and proprietary developments seem to have forgotten that greenkeepers need large sheds in which to store and maintain equipment securely, along with somewhere to wash and a room in which to take their break periods.

SOME GENERAL PRINCIPLES

It is not unusual to find some golf clubs confused about the identity of the employer. In private members' clubs it is the members themselves collectively who hold that title. These members elect committees to oversee the running and well-being of the club; with such committees making policies and decisions that directly affect the lives of the staff. The decisions of such committees are passed down to the relevant manager, whose job it is to implement them. Clearly, therefore, it is the elected officers of the day who are the employer and, on behalf of members, they are responsible—and liable—for ensuring that health and safety arrangements within the club are "suitable and sufficient."

Situations have arisen where the distinction between employer and employee has become muddled. In a few cases there are owners who work also at maintaining the course and manning the clubhouse, exacerbated by sometimes including members of the same family—thus we have poacher and gamekeeper!

A situation encountered far too frequently is one where an honorary secretary serves also as a member of a committee. This is far from ideal, for the individual concerned must implement and live with his own decisions, and those of his colleagues, which could lead to a conflict of interests. Where a golf club employs a secretary/manager, that person is an employee, probably the senior manager responsible for the effective administration of the club's business. Such a person therefore is not the one who signs the Statement of Safety Policy, but is nevertheless responsible for implementing such a policy, with the help of the rest of the management team.

Proprietary owners and clubs owned by large businesses will usually employ salaried directors who carry such responsibility.

COMMUNICATIONS — A MAJOR PROBLEM

In a world of satellites and cellular telephones, where we can communicate across the world in seconds, we seem to have lost the art of communicating within the workplace. Employees at work are especially at risk when they fail to receive or understand the requirements of an employer. Reports of accident investigations frequently refer to misunderstandings concerning that which was actually required. A recurring link reveals how failure to communicate an instruction clearly is often the root cause of an accident.

An employer has a duty to consult with his employees regarding health and safety matters and must have a formal means of doing so. A golf course policy document, stating in detail the club's requirements for its management, presentation, future development and standards of maintenance, will be the starting point. The choice of equipment, staffing, methods and work programmes, can then follow.

During a club's operating year there will of necessity be an annual programme of events, listing competitions, visiting golf societies and all other planned activities. This programme must be communicated to staff in sufficient time to allow for preparation.

It will come as no surprise to learn that accidents have occurred as a result of last minute instructions, resulting in the rushing of a job and the taking of risks in an attempt to meet requirements. In one case a chairman of green, instructed a greenkeeper on weekend duty to prepare for a last-minute event. The greenkeeper attempted to use equipment for which he had not been trained, and an accident occurred. The chairman had no authority to direct staff, had no knowledge of the work required, and was unaware of the risks involved. Fortunately, the greenkeeper's injuries were not serious and he was not obliged to spend more than three days away from work, so it was not a "reportable injury." Had this been the case, the accident could have resulted in an investigation conducted by the health and safety inspector. The matter was resolved at the next green committee, with clearer guidelines established for future chain of command. Had the greenkeeper been more seriously injured, and the matter had been investigated by an inspector, it is possible that enforcement action could have been taken against the committee and possibly against the chairman.

The employer also has a duty to prepare and operate a plan which will deal with foreseeable emergencies, both in the clubhouse and on the golf course. Such a plan should indicate methods of dealing with accidents, outbreaks of fire on the course, storm, flooding, or lightning strikes; even the sudden illness of a greenkeeper or player. A vital part of this plan is the formal means of communicating rapidly with key staff, and organising and directing the emergency services to remote parts of the golf course without delay. This means that for many golf courses it is necessary for greenkeeping management and field staff to be equipped with radio transmitters, pagers or cellular phones, and be trained in their use. Such equipment will also greatly improve normal operating efficiency.

Frequently there are disputes between golfers and staff as to who holds the right of way or priority on the course. Green staff and their equipment are frequently to be found in the firing line, with reports of hits and near misses being recorded, though often somewhat sketchily. Most disputes arise out of misunderstandings concerning who has priority. A golfer will assume he has priority unless he is directed otherwise by the club. A general club policy, declaring priority for the greenkeeper, can allow essential maintenance and also enhance safety on the course. Further guidance on preparing policies on priority will be found elsewhere in this chapter.

There is little doubt that improving communications throughout the club will enhance all aspects of health and safety, while making a significant contribution toward operating efficiency.

DEALING WITH PAPERWORK

The Statement of Safety Policy—reporting and investigating accidents and incidents—Risk Assessments

At a site meeting to discuss health and safety for a new golf course development, the Health and Safety Executive inspector made the following plea regarding documentation: "Please keep it directly relevant to the work activity, keep it brief and to the point, and remember, your documentation is a working brief for the employer, managers and staff." It is the club's responsibility to prepare, and keep up to date, a Statement of Safety Policy; the policy should contain the following key features:

1. A clear statement of intent:
   Our policy is to provide and maintain safe and healthy working conditions, equipment, and systems of work for all our employees, and to provide such information, training and supervision as they may need for this purpose. We also accept our responsibility for the health and safety of other people who may be affected by our activities.

   The allocation of duties for safety matters and the particular arrangements which we will make to implement the policy are set out in the following sections.

   The policy will be kept up to date, particularly as our business changes in nature and size. To ensure this, the policy and the way in which it has operated will be reviewed annually.

   Signed: _____ (Director/Chairman).

   Date: _____

2. The arrangements referred to in this sample text should name the person responsible for health and safety in each separate area of work, and the person or persons responsible for carrying out the essential safety checks on fire exits, fire alarms, emergency lighting and the like.

3. Any particular hazards identified should also be itemised and, where necessary, reference should be made concerning the detailed risk assessments that have been carried out.

3. Particular mention should be made concerning the arrangements for recording and reporting accidents, particularly, but not exclusively, those involving injury. Dangerous incidents (an incident is a non-injury accident that had the potential to cause injury) should also be recorded and, where necessary, investigated to see if a re-occurrence might be prevented.

MAKING SENSE OF RISK ASSESSMENTS

The duty to record the "significant findings" of a risk assessment may be found in several regulations. The structure and wording of these regulations would seem to suggest that the risk assessment process is a new concept requiring new skills, and in some cases special training. This is not necessarily true.

Experienced and competent craftsmen in any trade carry out risk assessments as an integral part of the planning and execution of their tasks. This was never a formal process, thus it was not identified as a separate part of their work. Where mistakes occurred and accidents happened they were frequently the result of an unforeseen situation arising, often suddenly, to an unsuspecting and unprepared operator. The principle objective of risk assessment is to reduce the likelihood of this happening, by identifying foreseeable hazards and taking some action to reduce, or eliminate, those risks. Hazard spotting, therefore, becomes a more formal process involving those actually at work.

Recording the "significant findings" is a very straightforward matter and thus should be brief and to the point. It is important not to fall into the trap of filling a document with risk assessments that common sense would dismiss in a minute. Remember, the idea is to spot hazards that have the potential to cause harm to green staff or golfers and are foreseeable. The test of whether the risk assessment is valid would be to pass the document to an experienced member of the team and ask him "does this make sense, and is it workable?" In most cases, an effective and reasonable risk assessment can increase operational efficiency, as well as safety. A good example of this concerns

Health and Safety in Golf Course Management

grass slopes that are unnecessarily steep and must therefore be mown by hand. If it is possible to reduce the angle of the slope, without significantly changing the way the course plays, the slope can then be mown safely using a ride-on machine. Slopes, raised greens and tees will need to be inspected at different times of the year, to ensure the assessment includes operational safety under all ground conditions. This may result in decisions to use different equipment, such as hand mowing in poor ground conditions where smoothly shod machines become unsafe.

Some golf courses have ditches and streams within the property and contain a variety of crossing points, often constructed with wooden sleepers, plus steps to elevated tees and towers for observation on blind shot holes. There is often an assumption (by the club), that their green staff are responsible for inspecting and maintaining such features. Meanwhile, the course manager may not be aware of this, and so nobody take responsibility until an accident occurs. Such features can be hazardous to all users and should be formally inspected annually.

Where a golf course is divided by a road, one that is crossed by staff, equipment and golfers, it will be necessary to ensure openings are directly opposite, with a broad and clear view provided for approaching players. If necessary, warning signs should be posted to alert oncoming motorists. It may also be necessary to ask the local authority to lower any raised kerbs, thus preventing additional delay while the greenkeeper and his machinery negotiate the road and obstruction. Crossing with equipment on dark winter mornings can be especially hazardous and the risk assessment should include the fitting of lights and flashing beacons to provide additional warning to

Full protection is afforded the operator within this enclosed cab (windows shut) using a state-of-the-art Hardi spraying unit.

231

PRACTICAL GREENKEEPING

any unwary motorists. Mature parkland courses with tree-lined fairways can also be a hazard, especially to tractors fitted with roll-over bars above the operators head. This is a good example of a safety feature which becomes a hazard in itself.

THE GOLF BALL PROBLEM

Greenkeepers often say that working on golf courses would be a lot better if there were no golfers. They have a point!

The risk of being struck by a golf ball is, to a certain extent, a hazard of the job. However, it is not acceptable for staff to be used as a practice target, or otherwise to be put at risk from such missiles. Records will indicate that on some golf courses, for a player or greenkeeper to be hit by a golf ball is a very rare thing. Good design, good standards of play, and some good old-fashioned etiquette combine to make these courses as safe as can be expected. Unfortunately, there also are some very bad designs; layouts that leave both greenkeepers and golfers hopelessly exposed to attack, and from any number of different directions. There is no doubt that where such a course is open to members of the public, many of whom will be non-golfers, the number of recorded hits rises sharply,

In addition to identifying hot spots—those places on the course where monitoring has indicated a high risk of being struck by golf balls—it is also necessary to have clear guidance for golfer and staff regarding the general matter of priority on the course. One effective way, delaying the opening of the course until essential morning maintenance work is completed, ensures the work is done quickly and without interruption. Some golf course managers have devised patterns of work that avoid direct contact with early morning players, a prime example of practical risk assessment being carried out as part of work planning. That stated, on some courses it does not seem to matter how early the greenkeeper begins his work, he never gets ahead of the early golfer.

Having a policy on priority will greatly enhance safety for both player and greenkeeper. Here is a suggested format.

PRIORITY ON THE COURSE

Players—guidance

In order that essential maintenance on the course is carried out to schedule, staff will, wherever possible, prepare the course ahead of play. However, there are essential operations that must continue during play and these can present a hazard to staff by the possibility of being struck by golf balls. In order that such work can proceed as safely as possible, it is the policy of this club that *GREEN STAFF HAVE PRIORITY ON THE COURSE.*

Health and Safety in Golf Course Management

In order that play is not interrupted, green staff have been briefed to be aware of play and to give way at all times where it is safe to do so. On observing players approaching, green staff will stop work and face towards the players. However, if it is not safe to do so, or the work must be completed before players arrive, for example by changing holes or applying top dressing, staff will complete the job and then indicate to players that they may play through. In this case, players are requested to wait. If staff are working on a green and the flag is removed, the green is not in play. Players will wait until the flag is replaced, use any temporary green that has been provided, or move on to the next tee.

Staff who use machinery on the course will always try to be aware of play and will stop work when it is safe to do so, remaining stationary and allowing players to play through. However, in cases when staff are unaware of play approaching, a cry of "Fore" may not always be heard, especially above machinery noise. In such situations, players must wait until their presence is acknowledged; seen by the member of staff stopping work and facing the direction of play.

Green staff—instructions

When working on the course you will at all times be aware of play, giving way whenever it is safe to do so. Your objective will be to complete the task in hand while trying also to minimise interruption of play. When operations require that you are unable to give way, or it is unsafe to do so, you have priority and players will wait.

When giving way to play, you will stand to one side and face oncoming players. When using ride-on machinery, you will stop work and remain stationary. It is unnecessary to signal to the players, for in stopping work and standing to one side, your actions will be interpreted as offering them priority. They will judge whether it is safe for them to play their shot.

If you or your vehicle is struck by a golf ball, or a near miss occurs, try to find out who played the ball. If, in your view, the shot was played deliberately—and you were in the line of fire—this is a dangerous occurrence. The matter should be reported without delay, so that it can be investigated. Do not dispute the matter with the player, but simply confine your comments to establishing his or her identity.

Priority on the course—a scorecard notice
Green staff have priority on this course, though they will give way whenever practicable. The ball will not be played where green staff are within range. Please wait until the way is clear, or you are called through.

STAFF TRAINING

Where qualified and well motivated greenkeepers are employed, a great deal of valuable training is carried out on the job. A craftsman should automatically accept responsibility for passing on his skills to others. Safe working practices taught on the job become second nature, and this is perhaps the main reason why records of serious injuries to greenkeepers are very low. That stated, there is always concern that poor, or indeed non-existent, arrangements for reporting accidents within some clubs might well be a contributory factor in keeping these figures artificially low.

However, to satisfy that working duties are performed safely and with competence, it is necessary to record the way in which such training has been achieved, for example by using training cards. Where training manuals, such as those provided by the Greenkeepers Training Committee, are available, they also should become an integral part of the greenkeeping staff training programme.

The passing on of job-related skills (the how) should not become confused with providing the background knowledge (the why), or, to use modern jargon, the "underpinning knowledge." To achieve a full understanding of the reasons why we carry out tasks, it is necessary to acquire both knowledge and skills. Colleges of education cannot by definition be places where practical skills are passed on; they are better suited to providing the underpinning knowledge. There is no doubt that some colleges have managed to make the transition from pure education, in order also to encompass practical skills training. It cannot, however, be assumed that this dual role exists in all cases, thus employers should closely examine what is on offer before committing staff and fees to any seat of learning.

When considering the training of a greenkeeper, it is necessary to prepare a programme of training that includes the aforementioned essential elements. Remember also that when considering the employment of an apprentice, or in taking a young person from school for work experience, there is an additional duty for a training plan to be prepared—stating who will be responsible for supervising the training—*before* the young person commences work.

PREMISES

Modern health and safety legislation sets minimum standards, both for premises and staff welfare facilities. Buildings should have a safe means of entry and exit, while being well lit and heated and having sufficient space to permit equipment to be stored and maintained. These facilities must be provided without putting staff at risk by exposing them to substances, harmful fumes, or by being trapped in the case of fire.

Health and Safety in Golf Course Management

A modern maintenance facility, traditionally called the greenkeepers' "shed". Indeed, some ancient buildings used were little more than sheds and many lacked even the most basic facilities for man and machine.

The staff facilities should be adequate for the numbers employed, while taking account of the needs arising out of any risk assessments. These include the need to take showers, with the provision of hot and cold water for washing and decontamination purposes.

Many staff facilities in golf are woefully inadequate. This unsatisfactory situation is not confined to older established golf clubs, for many new courses have been constructed with zero provision of staff facilities. Inspectors

The clubhouse gets another facelift, while moving toward the new millennium this sort of archaic horror apparently is quite acceptable. Priorities, it seems, are often misplaced.

visiting are given some vague reference to the availability of facilities "in the clubhouse."

When considering any new design, or the alteration of existing facilities, it is important to arrange rooms and doors in such a way that staff entering will be obliged to move through the changing/drying/washing/toilet area, before going into the rest room. The changing/drying area should contain personal lockers, and a room that is sufficiently heated and ventilated to ensure that work clothes can be dried rapidly. A shower is an essential item not only for washing, but also for decontamination following working in hot dusty conditions or after using pesticides.

The rest room must be used only for the purposes of taking breaks and must not contain protective clothing, dirty footwear or any work equipment. It should also contain facilities for preparing food and the washing of crockery and cutlery. An adequate area should be provided whereupon notices may be exhibited, in particular copies of safety policies, risk assessments and the Health and Safety Information to Employees notices.

Outside, the new facility will provide adequate scraping/washing equipment, in order that staff will not carry excess amounts of mud into the building. Flooring and wall surfaces will be durable and washable, with floor drains installed where necessary.

If space availability and budget allows, the rest area, or perhaps an additional room, should be large enough to serve as a training room, providing seating for up to twelve persons, with a white board (2 3 1.5 m) at one end. Such a room allows staff training programmes to take place without putting undue pressure on other facilities.

NEW SHEDS — DESIGN CONSIDERATIONS

Door openings and heights, smooth floors and adequate room sizes, together with proper shelving, all these are important factors where mechanical handling (the use of pallet handling and pedestrian-operated fork lift trucks) takes preference over traditional methods.

Adequate lighting, suitable ventilation (including local exhaust ventilation or LEV), heating, and clearly marked fire escape paths; all of these provisions are important, as are safe locations for pesticides, flammables and combustible fuels. The location of these must be carefully considered, essentially to ensure that staff are not placed at risk in the event of an emergency.

Security is another important consideration, for it must be assumed that attempts will be made to break in and steal equipment. Perimeter steel fencing and gates, steel shutters to windows, secure construction cladding materials, the use of automatic lights and adequate alarms—all are essential features in the war against theft and villainy.

The new maintenance sheds at St. Andrews follow the land contours and are nicely camouflaged.

Where yards and buildings are in a remote location, there is an additional risk of daylight theft, especially where work patterns are predictable and the yard area is left unmanned for long periods. In this situation it will be necessary to have securely locking perimeter gates and doors—and for them to be used.

MACHINERY AND EQUIPMENT
Suitability — Maintenance — Training — Competence

Factors which come into play when selecting machinery and equipment so often centre around price, personal preference and versatility, rather than suitability and safety. Yet failure to provide a supplier with information regarding the intended use of the equipment may result in the wrong specification being delivered. A good example of this may be found where a site is undulating, yet a conventional tractor is in use, or at least its use is attempted, under poor ground conditions. The purchasing of maintenance equipment can be seen as an opportunity to advance the process of reducing risks as well as increasing efficiency.

Machinery that is not maintained to the specification provided by the manufacturer will soon become unreliable and unsafe. Thus any daily or weekly checks demanded to be carried out by operators should be strictly observed. Tyre pressures, couplings, safety guards and switches, wear and tear on hydraulic pipework, plus the maintaining of a clean cab and

PRACTICAL GREENKEEPING

Suitable personal protection is vital, whatever the job. Here the operator is wearing a hard hat, ear protectors, a clear visor and steel capped footwear.

windscreen, all these can contribute to safe use. Conversely, abuses are known contributory factors in many accidents and breakdowns.

Any accident investigations that take place will seek to establish if the equipment has been maintained correctly, to the manufacturer's specification. Maintenance records are therefore essential for each machine, while providing valuable information concerning running costs.

Operator competence in the use of maintenance equipment is a further factor in safe use, while also reducing undue wear and tear. When interviewing prospective new employees it is important to carry out a check test on the equipment they may be asked to use, in order to establish levels of competence. Check testing can also be used as part of any on-going staff training programme, while also being a very good way of sharpening operator skills.

HEALTH AND SAFETY IN GOLF COURSE MANAGEMENT

USING PESTICIDES
Products — Equipment — Operator Competence

Pesticides are perceived to be hazardous to operators and the environment. There is no doubt that in the past this was true, although good common sense and care in use has ensured that very few short or longer term problems exist. Nevertheless, good greenkeeping practice should be aimed at reducing the use of fungicides and herbicides to a minimum.

When using a pesticide there are some key steps to take that will ensure the operation will be effective and trouble free.

- Check with the manufacturer or distributor to ensure that the product to be used is still approved for use. Product review and commercial decisions can result in products being withdrawn. It is wrong to assume that a product in store will always be approved.

- Do the spray records contain comments on the effectiveness of previous treatments? Spray records that merely record the use, while excluding the results, are worthless. The effectiveness of treatments can be influenced by weather conditions and/or calibration of the equipment. Avoid the temptation to always blame the product, for often it is the operator who causes the treatment to fail.

This type of lightweight golf trolley (model by Allmann) may be used for applying chemicals using either a tractor mounted sprayer or turf vehicle. Note the full protection worn by the operator, including special suit, full face mask and gloves.

- Do not assume that past calibration details still hold good. Wear in machinery and nozzles can significantly alter the output of a sprayer. This applies particularly when spraying has not been carried out for some time. On each occasion, before using a sprayer, at the very least carry out a flow test to check the output of the chosen nozzles. If the results are significantly different from previous tests—and the manufacturer's data—conduct a full calibration of the whole unit.

- Plan the disposal of washings before starting to spray. This will ensure that any work undertaken complies with the requirements of the Regulations and Codes of Practice.

- On completion, be sure to wash the unit fully, both inside and out. Even small amounts of pesticide residue can adversely affect the future efficacy of a different product. Small amounts of dried pesticide, lodged inside pipework and the spray tank, may well be dislodged when next used, and be mashed in the pump, blocking filters and nozzles.

Sensible and workable health and safety arrangements will reduce accidents, while increasing overall efficiency and helping to establish a better working relationship with the club.

The health and safety inspector has wide powers to enforce health and safety law, with the ultimate power to institute prosecution proceedings where necessary. A golf club that has made a start on improving arrangements for health and safety—one that is able to show some commitment in terms of allocating resources—will be able to call in the inspector and ask if he considers the proposals to be "suitable and sufficient." In such cases, the inspector will almost certainly give very valuable advice while being much less inclined to take enforcement action, even though it may take a year or two for the club to finalise the exercise.

Improving health and safety is a continuous process, rather than a special exercise. It should become an integral part of the working life of any golf club.

Chapter Sixteen
.....
Golf Course
Conservation

At first sight, golf courses and motorway verges appear to have little in common save in one respect, they are largely undisturbed by man, by wheels and feet alike. They also share another common factor in that even areas of deep rough or steep motorway embankments have to be managed. This is the essence of conservation: a combination of minimum disturbance to the habitat with a sensible management programme.

Conservation is not preservation! If matters are left to nature there is an unpreventable, predictable and inevitable sequence—in ecological terms, succession—as when open grassland changes successively to scrub, young woodland, full maturity, followed by ageing and decay. Unless this sequence is halted by external factors, usually man's interference, the cycle repeats itself, admittedly over a very long term. If one wishes to stop the sequence and to stabilise a given environment, whether for reasons of appearance, playing conditions or even safety, then management must be planned and executed with knowledge and enthusiasm and to a laid-down plan. It is always well worth initiating a soundly based conservation management plan, advised by a qualified ecologist.

Conservation is the term given to this type of land management, designed to stop the inexorable progression of habitat type at that stage which is required or defined by the demand put on that land, for example playing conditions or scenery as well as wild-life. It is not, of course, confined to golf courses or nature reserves, though the same principles apply. With golf especially, seemingly opposed interests must learn to live together. Golfers will tolerate conservation as long as it does not interfere with their game, and clever conservationists will amend their management plans to give golf the priority it quite properly demands.

GOLF IS A LEGITIMATE LAND USE

Conservationists must accept that golf is a legitimate land use in its own right and not necessarily an open opportunity for nature conservation. There is a great need still for mutual awareness and understanding. Multiple recreational use of land and water features is a concept that is here to stay, but amiable co-existence demands acceptance of the other man's point of view. In the past, there have been too many manic preservationists and too many aggressive golfers with no patience with conservation principles.

Before covering the special needs of the various and varied environments over which golf is played, we need to describe something of the background. Golf courses in Britain and Ireland, though numbering approximately 2500, occupy in fact a tiny proportion of the total land area—a fraction of one per cent—and the relative figure for the rest of Europe is far less. Nevertheless they have a disproportionate effect on the environment, partly because many mature courses are long established ecologies, maintained positively to stabilise their surroundings, and thus providing a relatively constant habitat which causes less stress to fauna and flora than an environment which is constantly progressing and unmanaged. Other golf courses, though relatively small, provide oases in deserts of intensively farmed arable land or suburbia from which the resident fauna can sally forth to forage, returning to safe havens in a protected area of natural vegetation. Urban foxes often excavate their earths in part of busy urban golf courses, for example under tees, as well as in suburban gardens, under sheds.

Others have a disproportionate effect in relation to their size, because an increasing number of golf courses adopt conservation as a facet of their overall management plan. Conservationists, especially the more extreme and blinkered variety, forget that they have no monopoly in the care of, and interest in, our native wild life that shares our environment. Many dedicated head men, some no longer with us, were true conservationists long before "greens" meant anything more than cabbages. Golf course management, and indeed many golfers, now accept that conservation is to their benefit, as well as to the resident fauna and flora.

GREATER MUTUAL UNDERSTANDING

What is encouraging is the greater mutual understanding of the views and needs of opposing interests and parties. So often their interests are seen to be parallel and can be merged. The earlier mutual antipathy of "greens" for golf and of golfers for "greens" is becoming less evident, though one has to admit that there are still manic extremes on both sides and no doubt this will remain for many years.

There is greater appreciation at all levels that sound golf greenkeeping

Golf Course Conservation

does not imply or involve the gross over-use and misuse of inorganic fertilisers, toxic pesticides, herbicides and fungicides, or indeed the over-use of water (affecting both over-extraction and use of limited supplies and leaching through drains to water courses). Elaborate preventative measures to stop the effluent from fertilisers and other materials previously applied to putting greens reaching the drains, have been proven to be quite unnecessary. So little should be applied, while that which is used is largely organic nitrogen, with virtually no soluble phosphatic nor potassic fertilisers, so that nothing goes to the drains. Furthermore, irrigation, if correctly limited, will or should be substantially taken up by the root zone, and thus the turf, so that little or nothing finds its way to the drainage outfalls via the stone carpet. On older courses, with no such under-drainage, the problem is even less, because such greens cannot take excessive irrigation without becoming unplayable.

Over-watering and over-feeding are still the two worst sins of golf greenkeeping. The concept that "if it isn't green it must be dead" pervades golf at all levels. Consequently, those preparing courses, and even greenkeepers with one eye on their members, always have in mind the television cameras, hence lakes dyed blue and greens dyed green. The end result of such mistaken short-term procedures is all too often a spectacular disaster. Such tarted-up

Bluebells and gorse just a few yards off the fairway. A public footpath meanders through the downland course at Seaford, East Sussex.

Foxgloves flourish in the rough on the Carnegie links at Skibo Castle. Much of this course is designated SSSI.

presentation is totally anti-conservationist, as what succumbs to these unnatural policies is the wide variety of species, resulting in an ecology dominated by a single species. This is artificial, and is as bad for golf as it is for conservation, especially if that species is *Poa annua*.

It bears repetition that the best golf courses are found on the poorest soils, and that the poorest clubs have the best courses. Why? Because they do not have the financial resources to spend wrongly to mess up a natural environment. It follows that their courses are maintained against change or succession by positive, sensible management, run on natural traditional lines.

It is worth considering the impact of the late Professor Woolhouse's thesis that "the best scenery in Europe owes its existence to metal toxicity" but it is a fact that much of our remaining unspoilt heather moorland exists on soils where the concentration of free aluminium would be toxic to crop plants. In consequence, such land was never ploughed, even in times of food production crises, and thus became available for other non-agricultural pursuits, from grouse moors to golf.

One could indeed argue that golf was a potent source of protection for our fauna and flora long before conservation became a byword, or ecology a political pressure point. Even today, with nearly 90 official Sites of Special Scientific Interest (SSSIs) on English golf courses and approximately 30 in Scotland, there are far more "unofficial" nature reserves on courses, initiated and administered quite independently, by course managers or by their clubs. So many greenkeepers are enthusiastic and knowledgeable naturalists that their work should be much more widely acknowledged and appreciated by conservationist bodies. Too many of the latter are convinced that they, and only they, have the correct answers. Part of the problem is slowly being overcome, namely that we must get our priorities right. The multiple recreational use of land is not a new idea. Sacrosanct reservoirs, from which all human activity was banned not all that long ago, are now actively used for sailing, angling, and bird-watching. Certainly, industry and golf alike are facing up to their environmental responsibilities, while golf is now realising that what benefits wild life can equally enhance their courses and benefit the game.

Golf courses exist so that golf may be played. No animal, plant or insect is more important than *Homo sapiens*. Nevertheless, there is increasing acceptance that there is room for all, given some degree of tolerance and understanding of others interests. Those interests do not extend to the right of unlimited trespass, whether we are talking of golf courses or grouse moors. The biggest protection for wild life is this absence of pedestrian trespass. Contrary to some belief, the deep rough of any golf course sees less traffic than almost any other grassland, but it still has to be managed, although that management is periodic and infrequent, and wild life adapts remarkably quickly to sudden short-lived disturbance. A small bird having narrowly escaped being clutched by a hungry sparrow hawk does not need counselling; it shakes its feathers and gets on with feeding or whatever!

The worst curse of extreme conservation by ardent "greens" is anthropomorphism—assuming that animals think like humans. Actually nature is a tough old bird with enormous resilience and powers of recovery. Man may impose his influence on the scenery, but animals often ignore his efforts provided they have a food source. Urban foxes are now almost as common, and certainly more often seen, than their rural cousins. Prairie dogs still frequent the Colorado mountain valleys, as they did before man arrived over a century ago in establishing a mining industry and associated railway, even though the derelict mining scene has been replaced today by tourism. To the prairie dogs, man's interference was on a minute scale timewise. Life progressed as it always had, and man's artefacts were just part of the scenery as far as they were concerned. However, it is clearly better for management to emulate nature, rather than for nature to have to adapt itself to man's management.

POLLUTION

Pollution may be a problem, though it is infinitely worse in the undeveloped world. No one would wish to tolerate it, but sensible precautions and swift remedial action can deal with most of the long term effects. Even emptying half Kuwait's oil reservoirs into the Gulf, disastrous as that was short term, has had little significant long term effect. Significantly, the worst pollution of our water courses is not from toxic substances, but is organic, namely silage effluent!

Certainly, well-managed golf courses cannot be accused of being polluters. In fact the conservationists have a far weaker case. Their influence has banned the use of relatively harmless (except to the proposed victims, which are pests) materials, leaving us with no easy cures. This inevitably will lead to the abuse of permitted products, employed at excessive rates, with all the problems of over-kill and pollution. Traditional austere greenkeeping minimises the need for both pesticides and fungicides and ensures that no pollution occurs because of excessive use of fertilisers. However, not all golf courses, sad to relate, are managed on such sensible policies, so we have to ensure that over-feeding and over-watering are discouraged and the dangers spelled out to the culprits.

I remember in the 1980s being horrified at the common practice on some south western golf courses in America, where massive doses of a permitted fungicide with associated secondary insecticidal powers were regularly used to deal with a pest problem, when the sensible insecticides were banned on conservation grounds. On enquiring about the side effects, the operators agreed that this killed everything, including the grass, but they merely resowed. Unfortunately, it is not so easy to reintroduce the soil micro-life on which the health of a soil so depends.

Thus we need moderation in all things, with acceptance that the main function of a golf course is to provide an arena on which to play golf, and that other activities and conservation should be not merely tolerated but encouraged, provided that they do not severely affect the game. The most important animal on a golf course is the golfer, though he is hardly a threatened species! This does not mean that other animals, let alone plants and insects, should not be actively encouraged, but not if this means a clash. Compromise nearly always works, especially when, on discussion, so much common ground is discovered between erstwhile warring interests, who may well be pleasantly surprised to discover, in non-acrimonious dialogue, how much they all want the same thing. One example springs to mind, with some rare plant threatened by fairway mowing. If such plants are penalised in the fairways, but protected and managed in the semi-rough or rough, then in no way can conservation interests demand that fairways are not mown.

Golf Course Conservation

Conservation is just a fancy name for management, which of course means management in the interests of all the users of land, be they human, other animals, plants or insects. Without such management, there would inevitably be a change, and not necessarily for the better for present users. Conservation is not about preservation nor does it imply automatic resistance to any change, whether that change is part of succession—e.g. trees overgrowing available space and interfering with both management and play; or positive—e.g. to improve drainage for better winter play. At the same time it is designed to perpetuate by positive means those standards which are optimum for the users, be they golfers or other fauna, plants or insects.

The 15th at West Sussex Golf Club. This delightful short hole is second to none, while proving that the best is also the most natural.

MANAGEMENT SURVEYS AND PLANS

In proposing a new conservation scheme for any golf course it is sensible to produce a management plan, with guidance from a qualified ecologist.

A survey showing vegetation patterns across the whole course, plus the incidence of other than run of the mill fauna and flora, which it is desired should be protected, is a first stage.

The emphasis is on practicality. Each scheme has to take into account not just local conditions, but so far as the golf club is concerned, the four Ms, men, machinery, materials and money. Only if the project is affordable will it go ahead, and even more important, will it be sustained. Setting up a scheme and abandoning it is akin to feeding birds so that they abandon their normal feeding grounds, which of course are promptly taken over by competitors, and then stopping, so they have nowhere else to turn and may well die. Any management plan must be realistic, achievable and attainable.

It is essential that any scheme is not only long term but its continuity is ensured by constitutional rule, so that it is not at the mercy of changing committees.

Many management plans fail because they are too ambitious, because their objectives have not been clearly defined, or because they are too complicated and full of only partly-understood technicalities. Plain speaking is essential, to ensure comprehension and agreement before the plan is started.

Such management plans must always be based around the concept that sensible course management will normally be paramount. Management which may temporarily affect wild life may have to be undertaken, for example in the desilting of ponds and clearing of water courses, but this can be done sympathetically. It certainly should not be prohibited. In fairness, sound ecologists accept these limitations. It is always sensible to seek specialist advice so that correct decisions are made.

Progress needs monitoring, not necessarily at set intervals, especially to measure progress in the elimination of unsatisfactory species; invasive birch in heather, rhododendrons in moorland or Himalayan balsam on invaded water courses.

It helps to achieve understanding and co-operation with golfers if the aims of a conservation scheme are clearly spelt out and that in any conflict of interest, that of the golfer should normally be paramount. This is no problem where sensible austere greenkeeping practices are employed. A clash is unlikely if the management plan is sensibly drawn up in the first place, dispelling the fears of both members and management alike that their course is not being taken over by a special interest group, but cared for, with the benefit of all living organisms in mind, including themselves.

Golf courses, as with any other semi-natural (i.e. managed) habitat, should not be regarded in isolation. Certain species have always been near their northern limit, and/or may be threatened minorities. Such species may be common elsewhere. Where is the sense in penalising majority users, i.e. golfers, to preserve (I use the term advisedly) some threatened colony vulnerable to so many external factors, if that species is common elsewhere. A balanced view is necessary. Good conservationists and ardent golfers are not contradictory terms, but the latter do resent frequently inexperienced representatives of the first school imposing their ideas and vetoes on quite sensible management practices. An extreme, but by no means unusual, case is where essential routine drainage work such as silt clearance from water courses is banned, thus flooding fairways for long periods in winter just to preserve a few amphibians, even if they are rare in that area. Some compromise can nearly always be found.

It is not a question of threatening the world survival of any imperilled rare species, but of joint recreational use of land with all sides being considered and a balanced compromise achieved. However, this stand-off confrontational situation need never arise if those concerned start amicable discussions to determine areas of common, or indeed specialised, interests. It is surprising how often there is no real clash, once each side takes on board the others problems. Furthermore there are often benefits to the golf club, not just in cash terms of grants in aid, but also in them being accorded greater respect and recognition.

So much for the generalised approach. What of the particular? Golf courses have been established on a remarkably diverse range of soil types and natural environments. In addition, with far too many modern golf courses the first law of golf architecture has been disobeyed, namely, use the land with which you are presented and do not try to make contours conform to preconceived, identikit reproductions of famous courses in other countries. In so doing, whole ecologies are destroyed and some species may not recolonise the established course. This is quite apart from the destructuring of soils and the destruction of natural drainage, which may even be permanent, or at least very costly to restore.

There is much talk of the importance of facilitating movement of fauna by providing, or rather not destroying, corridors between conserved area. This is fine in practice, but two things need to be considered. First, animals are remarkably unaffected by the normal sensible land use of traditional greenkeeping, as with the best management practices on golf courses. Second, such corridors or bridges must not interfere with the movement of golfers or their game or they will not long survive. Clearly, design must take fully into account natural features so that they are not harmed ecologically.

Sensible course management, conflicting with a rigid refusal to understand that fine turf demands light and air, as well as water, and that trees grow and often outgrow their sites and start to interfere with both play and maintenance, leads inevitably to confrontation. One would think trees were sacrosanct, to hear some of our tree lovers, who fail to understand that trees are living organisms, even if they are not deliberately harvested. One despairs of those who moan about clear-felling of planted (coniferous) woodland in preparation for rotational replanting. Not only do they fail to accept that such plantings are as much of a crop as a field of wheat but, if they did but know it, the period of re-establishment after felling creates an environment which is much more friendly to a vast range of species,

Tradition heathland at Sunningdale, though mature conifers must be carefully managed, or they could take control.

compared with the sterile, dull, gloomy shades of semi-mature conifers.

Where such short sighted objections prevail, all too often sensible environmentalists take the law into their own hands. Then conflict starts and the fury of some defenders of a tree or trees on their course has to be heard to be believed. If sensibly planned replanting for replacement is carried out, where is the problem? Those who complain about tree surgery are often those who, when quizzed, cannot remember where the tree was, before it was felled. One is reminded of a course superintendent in the United States faced with usual outcry against felling trees which had outgrown their sites, who had two chain-saws, one called "Thunder" and the other "Lightning". Invariably the cleared tree had been struck by one or the other and had to be tidied up! Far better, however, to enlist professional support for dealing with trees which have outgrown their sites.

It may be helpful to specify management problems and solutions in relation to their type. Golf courses are found on an enormous range of soil types and environments, though most have something in common in good drainage (natural or imposed), and low soil fertility. The last thing golfers or conservationists require is lush turf. Over-feeding and over-watering create conditions inimical to a wide range of grasses (and other flora), which leads directly to a reduction in the variety of species on the site. A typical example of such monocultures is the dominance of *Poa annua* in response to over-watering and over-feeding, even on fairways, with all the resultant problems with drought, disease and wear.

With so many and so varied environments on which golf courses have been established in the past 600 years, it is permissible to think that each has its own special problems, but this in fact is not true. Perhaps they do in detail, but in principle the whole aim of sound golf course management is based on establishing well aerated, free-draining soils with low nutrient status. Whether that environment is dune or down, marsh or moor, heathland or parkland, or just some farmer's field, the principles of management are the same. It is only partly coincidental that those same conditions and standards at which we aim for better golfing conditions are those which favour the widest range of fauna and flora in a natural as opposed to artificially maintained ecology. In other words, traditional greenkeeping practices aim to copy nature and encourage the fine wiry turf so characteristic of our native bent and fescue turf, uninvaded by more fertility-demanding coarser grasses. This shows that true conservationists should concentrate on encouraging aeration and discouraging over-feeding and over-watering rather than worrying about pollution and pesticides, which are non-starters in traditionally managed golf courses.

Yet conservationists have criticised aeration "as likely to damage root structures" of links fairways, little realising that compaction, uncorrected by aeration, will have a far more serious effect on the flora by penalising deep-rooting, drought-resistant species. However, some guidelines on specific types of courses in relation to correct conservation measures may concentrate minds and opinions.

TYPES OF COURSES

Links

Conservation must be based on maintaining the native flora and especially grass type. Alien practices of unrestricted fairway watering will change the grass species to *Poa annua*, inhibiting the native grasses, of which there are at least a score more than just bents *(Agrostis)* and fine fescues.

The rough must be managed to avoid the invasive spread of such smothering species as sea buckthorn *(Hippophae rhamnoides)*, itself an alien introduced species in so many our western links, and, like rabbits in Australia, uncontrolled and uncontrollable. Originally brought in many years ago from the east coast, where it is native, it was hoped it would stabilise mobile dunes in the conservation of new courses. Now it is almost out of control.

Few of our links have tree problems, but white poplars *(Populus alba)* and sycamores *(Acer psuedo-platanus)* need to be ruthlessly eliminated.

These, too, are introduced aliens and combine the two characteristics which lead to any species becoming a pest—vigorous invasive growth and an enormous capacity for regeneration by seedlings or roots.

Not many new links courses have been constructed in recent years, but any planting plans need to be very carefully vetted. This especially applies to tree planting schemes, for trees are just out of place on sandy links. Gorse, however, is very much in place, while its management is labour-intensive. Just as with heather, we cannot afford to let it grow tall and leggy. Constant topping is vital to encourage new young growth and constant flowering.

We also need to conserve dune-stabilising grasses—marram and sea lyme—to reduce the risk of wind or tide erosion of dunes. The essence is to prevent trespass and to ensure these grasses are regularly smothered with wind-blown sand. If starved of sand-blow, they decline. Fighting coastal erosion is a complex subject which would fill a book; often the problem starts so far up the coast that prevention is impossible.

Mother Nature at her best—sea buckthorn, though invasive, provides the backdrop to this green at Portstewart Golf Club, Northern Ireland.

Golf Course Conservation

Natural links land in Sutherland, Scotland. The Carnegie course at Skibo Castle boasts acres upon acres of similarly glorious country. Many wonderful golf courses have been carved from similar settings. Note the absence of trees.

Rabbits need to be controlled, though they may do some good away from those parts of the course in play by eliminating seedlings of undesirable shrubs and trees. Their unrestricted activities, with scrapes and nibbling on greens, not to mention burrows, cannot be tolerated.

Heathland

As the name implies, such land is dominated by heather, but will not long so remain unless the heather is managed. Heather hates three things, alkalinity, traffic and grass invasion.

In these enlightened days we feel sure no one would dream of liming any course, but many materials are alkaline, including some fen peats. Take care that one is not liming accidentally.

Traffic is always a problem. One sees areas of mown-heather approaches looking like the Mississippi delta; a ramification of converging tracks, grass or bare ground, inexorably spreading laterally until the heather gives up the struggle. All too often, erosion follows, since the impoverished soil does not readily support healthy fine turf to provide stability and reduce wash-out.

The answer is to divert the traffic, with specific trolley paths and the roping off of damaged areas to encourage natural recovery, with a free lift and drop for any shot landing in the protected area.

By far the worst problem is the invasion of grass which prevents natural

regeneration from shed heather seed. This must be killed by selective grass herbicides, sprayed on when the heather is dormant in late winter. There is rarely any need to apply positive remedial action, save for raking and cutting. Topping heather is a vital part of its management in order to stop it growing long, leggy and weak. Such topping must be done when the seed is set, so that the shed seed can help regeneration, aided by scarification of thin areas to help seedlings establish. Scarification of this nature may leave ground bare for a season, but heather will quickly recolonise such "cultivated" areas and produce excellent new young stands.

The biggest conservation headache on heathland is the invasion of seedling birch and pines which, if not cleared, will soon transform the appearance of the course from open heathland to woodland. The solution is to ruthlessly clear every seedling, using a mattock (flat-bladed pick-axe) to cut them off below ground. Nothing is more difficult to deal with than a cut stump which has produced masses of shoots from the old bole. Unless tree clearance is ruthless, the end result is a wood—a change of environment as undesirable for wild life as it is for golfers.

Bracken is another invasive and smothering weed but can be sprayed and controlled, again very much to the advantage of a varied fauna and flora. Such spraying, with the approved herbicide, must be done at a critical stage when the fronds are opening up, never when bracken is more mature.

Heather abounds and flourishes at Hankley Common, while scrub presence demands a keen appreciation of nature's encroachment. Ruthless eradication of invasive seedling birch and pine is absolutely essential to retain heathland character.

Golf Course Conservation

Heather hugs the banking of this greenside bunker at Hankley Common, while helping to defend it. Not surprisingly, golfers seem loath to trample across such attractive foliage.

Parkland

The main problem is that of tree management. Trees live and grow, but trees also die. Where majestic mature specimens determine the line of play, their demise creates major problems. Sensible management—tree surgery—can prolong life, but eventually plans must be made to replace them. This means planting perhaps three specimens and looking after them. Plan their sites so that they are not damaged when the old tree has to be felled, and then be bold enough to move two when the best one has established itself, if this is necessary.

Parkland courses often suffer from the shading of greens by trees which have outgrown their space, not to mention roots seeking water below irrigated greens. Plan ahead and plant replacements further back from vulnerable greens and tees, and fell the offenders when the replacements are established.

We also have to consider the undergrowth below trees. All too often this consists of dense brambles and scrub. This may well harbour some birds and beasts, but one should weigh up the advantages of emulating the old husbandry of "coppice with standards," which gave us our sheets of wild flowers in bygone springs. Clearance of hazel poles on a rotational pattern let in light and air. No one suggests the whole course should be so managed, though the resultant display in spring is worth all the effort. Certainly such

PRACTICAL GREENKEEPING

management of margins of woodland results in a very attractive appearance, while helping play and being very good for conservation.

On the subject of unwanted shrubs, that pernicious weed *Rhododendron ponticum* must be ruthlessly cleared; easier said than done, but it is extremely invasive and produces a sterile ecological state.

While hardly parkland, many courses have suffered from the thoughtless planting of single-species stands of conifers, especially spruce. Few areas are so sterile of all life than the centre of such gloomy plantations. Shade and pine needles combine to smother even the hardiest of shrubs. There is no food and therefore no life, except on the perimeters. The answer, surely, is to plan felling and leave clearings. Nothing is worse than unrelieved banks of dark and dismal conifers in terms of either appearance or play. When one looks at photographs of such courses taken perhaps 50 to 80 years ago, compared with their appearance today, one cannot but wonder if those who were responsible for such planting realised what they were doing. Any attempt at rectifying the position rarely escapes severe criticism. Had there been more forethought many years ago, or had thinning and brashing been practised with planning and energy, we would suffer less from the syndrome of playing down sombre avenues of ever encroaching conifers.

Leylandii planted as a "ball stop" barrier behind the first green at Royal Eastbourne.

Golf Course Conservation

On the subject of trees, if any species are to be planted, on either new or existing courses, the first rule is to visualise how they will look, and affect their environment, in say 50 years. Is there space? Will they affect greens and tees by shade or roots? Are they like flowering cherries, out of place?

Then consider species. There may be a case for some conifers, but never, never for rapid growing Leyland cypress (*Cupressocyparis leylandii*), which are so out of place and so harmful to the playing of the game. We need clean stems to about 2 metres if trees in play are not to be a grossly unfair hazard if a shot lands under them. These very fast growing conifers are also shallow rooting and, as individuals, are prone to be blown over in gales.

Avoid fast growing sycamores, and of course such species as poplars, alders and willows, where their water-seeking roots could block drains. Even horse chestnuts can cause problems, with small boys seeking conkers!

In planting, especially new courses, it is a sound rule to look around and see what trees grow naturally in the area and to select those which suit both golf and the appearance of the course. Furthermore, trees need careful management, especially in early stages, if they are to mature. Larger trees, properly managed, are a better bet than whips, which are extremely vulnerable to pruning—by gang mowers and golfers alike.

Leylandii, though not indigenous to Sussex downland, have been planted at Royal Eastbourne to define internal lines and act as barriers.

The banks of this pond on Minchinhampton Golf Course have been allowed to mature and develop naturally, with no clinical edging.

Water features

Let me repeat it: golf is not a water sport. Nevertheless more and more courses of all types are designed with water features, perhaps as a result of aping the trend in Florida, where to make fairways they had to be built up with excavated materials, and the resultant holes in such marshland areas became lakes.

If these water features were sited where they looked natural, one could tolerate them, but so many are constructed half-way up hills. Others are built under trees and suffer contamination from fallen leaves. The worst fault however, is where the water feature doubles as an irrigation reservoir. Towards the end of a dry summer, with demand exceeding replenishment, the water level falls alarmingly, exposing vulnerable liners or, worse still, the clay banks which crack and leak. They have all the charm of an African watering hole at the end of the dry season.

The main problem with water features is, of course, algal growth. There is no need to debate this point. Anyone who has had to deal with the smothering, slimy, evil-smelling blankets of filamentous algal growth will

Golf Course Conservation

unhesitatingly agree. It chokes irrigation pick-ups and filters and can play havoc with pumps if it succeeds in getting through into the system. It mops up oxygen, thus killing aquatic life. If left, it creates toxic conditions in the water, but if it is removed (with great difficulty) the heaps of dredged weed smother and kill any grass on which it is dumped. Heavy algae growth will increase the alkalinity of water, which could have repercussions with irrigation.

Algal growth is connected with excessive sunlight, stagnant water and high soil nutrient levels, as in run-off or seepage from adjacent fairways unwisely fed with NPK fertilisers. Fairways do not need complete fertilisers, only in extreme cases a little organic nitrogen.

The cures are therefore easy to define but harder to implement. Some shade is beneficial. Depth of water is important to reduce light. In passing, deep water features should have shallow marginal shelves, both for the safety of players trying to dredge out balls, and for planting. Marginal growth is both attractive and a conservation bonus, but do not overdo it. Reedmace *(Typha angustifolia),* and bulrush *(Scirpus lacustris),* along with water lilies, are luxuries no one can afford and soon take over completely, a negation of true conservation.

If the water can be fed from a running water source this helps, but of course it is illegal to divert an existing water course or extract from it, save in winter, and then only with permission from the Water Authority.

Limestone heaths and downland

Despite the very alkaline subsoil, the surface turf is often acid, especially in the absence of earthworms or other cultivation. This is because rain is invariably slightly acid, though not to be confused with the vastly exaggerated

Above: *Sycamore. A close-up of these over-shadowing trees, hard by the fourth green.*

Left: *Downland at Royal Eastbourne. Note sycamore encroachment upon the downs. When sheep grazed these hills some 80 years ago, sycamore was absent, now its growth is rampant.*

acid rain problem. Water goes down, usually, though there is an exception with excessively heavy irrigation needed in very hot climates. Here the resultant evaporation, which can also draw water back to the surface, leads to deposition of toxic levels of salts. Thus downland and especially limestone heaths are best treated on the same lines as sandy heathland.

The main problem on downland is heavy tree invasion from sycamores, ash and scrub. This in the absence of grazing animals— sheep and rabbits— which, before, trimmed off the seedling trees. Ruthless felling is essential, if we are not to be left with a sterile monoculture of rather unattractive scrub, smothering the native, alkaline-loving flora.

CONCLUSION

To sum up, one must stress the need to live together for the mutual benefit of golfers and the wild life on their course. Extremes of opinion on either side are very harmful to that which must be the way ahead; namely mutual understanding and trust that we all really want the same thing. Golfers, or most of them, understand this, but will not tolerate proper management being interfered with, especially if that affects course conditions. Conservationists must not lose a sense of proportion or overstate their case. Golfers must not resent these contributions as interference. The main aim must be to avoid any product or treatment which could be potentially harmful, trying to find alternative ways by avoidance rather than remedial measures.

What all must accept is that sound traditional greenkeeping, based on essentially minimal fertiliser treatment and no phosphates, along with controlled, low level irrigation, will not pose a threat to any conservation-based management. It really is a conservation measure itself, the conservation of those fine grasses which make the best golf courses. Sound agronomic advice must be respected and sought. Perhaps the worst feature of the last decade of this century has been a senseless chase after colour just for the sake of it.

To achieve results we need an overall long term management plan agreed by all and not subject to the whims of changing committees. Conservation is neither difficult nor expensive and it does not have to interfere in any way with golf, but it is dependent on agreement and compromise if it is to be both effective and welcomed.

Such management plans are best drawn up under the guidance of professional conservationist bodies, since only rarely is the necessary expertise available "in house."

Chapter Seventeen

ALL LIFE GOES IN CIRCLES...

A SOUND MAXIM in preparing a lecture, or even in writing an article, is to first say what you are going to say, then say it and then say what you have said! Equally, busy people tend to read the summary at the end of a published paper to see if it relates to their special interests and may then decide whether or not to delve more deeply.

My theme, and that of the specialist contributors and invigilators, throughout the writing of this book, has been to emphasise principles which have not changed in a century or more, rather than detail, which changes frighteningly quickly. It has also been to write in terms that can be understood by all, not just the élite few who are conversant with highly technical terms and descriptions.

Finally, the aim has been to avoid extremes. This is nowhere better exemplified than in conservation, where the common-sense of the middle ground is endangered by the manic opposite minorities of those who rate animals and plants above the human race, and at the other extreme by selfish golfers. The latter care not a jot about the effect on others, including other humans, so long as they can play their chosen sport every day and in every condition, even when a small compromise would meet half-way the recognisable, legitimate and understandable concerns of others.

Greenkeeping is more of an art than a science. That old-fashioned computer sited between the ears of most of the human race will tell us more, if we give it half a chance, than all the scientific aids which make such good sales plugs for commercial interests. Not that we should ignore the huge advances made possible by such firms, be they machinery manufacturers, producers of herbicides, fungicides and insecticides, or indeed any of that wide range of suppliers trying to meet the demands of a perceived market.

Our aim must be to see that new developments do actually help rather

PRACTICAL GREENKEEPING

than hinder the production of all-the-year-round, playable golfing conditions to meet the clear demand of today's golfers.

Never shoot the bearers of tidings, however harmful the message they bring. This book tries to explain what is needed—and it certainly is not lush green grass. Television producers who show golf at Augusta on that lush quilt of under-played and astronomically expensive sward, along with those who praise beautifully green courses, have much to answer for.

We must never prostitute the art of greenkeeping to the interests of commerce, but harness that sales drive to aid the production of traditional standards. In this aspect we need to state those standards, summarised as fast, firm greens and tight lies, as distinct from verdant meadows. If we do not resist such siren voices, our traditional game will be lost, possibly for ever. The pitch and run—so essential to real golf—is being replaced by the target golf school, played on the other side of the Atlantic and a very unwanted import (as with litigation), from America. Even there, some are arguing for tradition and a reversion to the old game, played along the ground and not in the air, which they describe as "bump and run."

The principles of greenkeeping have never altered, for the simple reason that the needs and management of the desired grasses (bents and fine fescues) which still make the best playing conditions, as they have for more than 500 years, have not altered.

It is no accident that the best courses are found on the poorest land, and not solely because that poor land was available for golf—by being totally uneconomic to farm. Ask a farmer what to do, then carefully go and do the exact opposite, is a saying which goes back to the turn of the century. Farming and golf greenkeeping are diametrically opposed in methods, simply because the two sides have diametrically opposite ideals and aims and are therefore pointed in opposite directions.

Greenkeeping is not an exact science. If we want poverty or, put another way, a very low soil nutrient status, why waste time analysing soil to prove it is too rich. No amount of laboratory analyses will replace experience, for analyses do not ensure better construction techniques, better maintenance or better playing conditions.

Measuring or identifying excesses is pointless, for we can do little about reducing them. We welcome so-called deficiencies, as greenkeeping is based on low levels of soil nutrients, and in fact true deficiencies by greenkeeping standards are virtually unknown. There is no commercial benefit—to analyst or client—in carrying out chemical analyses showing the levels of a range of nutrients, when all that is needed is a little nitrogen, for which there is no easy test. Tissue testing is a technique better suited to intensive agriculture, especially as there are no records of trace elements causing problems in fine turf by so-called deficiencies. Technically, experience is based on making mistakes and then correcting their effects, but more particularly on the avoidance of repeating the same errors. Learning from the expensively acquired experiences and mistakes of others can save great expense, not least in having to pay for the correction of problems caused by errors in the first place.

However, if greenkeeping principles have not changed, golf greenkeepers' professionalism most certainly has. Today we have vastly more qualified practical men, and clubs should, if they are so lucky as to employ such men, listen to them and give them responsibility. The greenkeeping fraternity, and to a lesser extent those in agronomy, have put their houses in better order, though there are still too many in both camps firmly pointed in the wrong direction.

There has been no such benevolent change in the way most clubs are managed. A few—far too few—have seen the light, and by virtue of written management plans and policies have achieved the all-important element of continuity. Regrettably, we still have far too many regularly changing green committees, manned by those whose qualifications for the post are certainly not based on greenkeeping, agronomic experience or expertise.

One can but condense the old saw—

A committee of one gets things done . . .

A committee of three will wait and see . . .

A committee of nine wastes endless time . . .

A committee of more is an endless bore!

The best committees consist of an uneven number, and three is too many. With an agreed written management policy, debate is unnecessary, and a skilled head man can produce the desired results far quicker and better if he has not to answer to well meaning, but all too often ignorant, committee members. Chairmanship of the green committee is seen by some not as a devoted, thankless, if self-rewarding duty, but as a direct route to their devout ambition to be captain.

Perhaps the one shining light in the past 50 years in greenkeeping is the vast increase in scope and quality of greenkeeping education, but we are still way off covering all the management team. One has to accept that whatever the problem is, there will be opposed schools of thought.

The feed and water school maintain they are producing only what their members, or the professional tour, require. They should consider that such policies are costly, that they bring with them all manner of problems, and that it becomes increasingly difficult to maintain a totally artificial ecology, so that the end result is far too often an all-too-public disaster, as seen on television.

All life goes in circles—if one stays with one policy long enough one comes back into favour, but equally stay too long and you go out again! What one must hope is that with better education and understanding in all aspects of course maintenance and club management, we learn from the expensively acquired experience of others and stop repeating all the same old mistakes on a depressingly regular pattern. Those who value our Royal and Ancient game must increasingly stand up and be counted if they are not to fall into the same old traps.

However, all is not doom and gloom, though we have still much to do. When I look back on 50 years of advisory work and on the educational scene then and now, I cannot fail to be impressed by the changes for the better, even if some have been forced on club management by the pressures of ever-increasing play.

It is all too easy to be depressed by the stupidity of the feed and water brigade, but when I remember, too, all those many friends, some no longer with us, but others finding time to get in touch with exhortations to "hang on in there," I am more assured about the future. These friends, from all walks of life and ages, have one thing in common; a love for the old game and an appreciation of standards set by time and tradition.

My last words must be to thank them all, greenkeepers, course managers and students, chairmen and convenors of green committees, club secretaries, specialists in drainage, engineering and irrigation, golf course architects and constructors, fellow advisers, a few of the gentlemen of the press, some trade firms, and fellow enthusiasts. Their support has kept me from giving up the struggle over the years and my reward is to see younger generations of keepers of the green so much better educated, better rewarded and better regarded by their employers and their peers. They will keep the banner flying and will ensure that traditional greenkeeping, producing traditional conditions, will not die out beneath the weight of commercialism under which golf is labouring today.

Bibliography and Further Reading

The greater part of this book is based upon the practical experiences of the author, culled over some fifty or more years of work as an expert turfgrass agronomist, a career in the field which culminated in official advisory representation for the R. & A.; guiding the ruling body on long-term preparation and eventual fine-tuning of the many courses upon which the Open Championship has been staged. Guidance and inspiration comes in many guises and Mr Arthur freely acknowledges the understanding that has come his way from study of the works of others. The following list is by no means complete, though it is representative of additional information which the reader might find worthwhile. It should be understood, however, that many of these titles are long out-of-print and will probably be difficult to obtain.

Practical Drainage by Turner Cooper. Published by Grampion Press 1965.

The Mole by Kenneth Mellanby. Published by Collins 1971.

The Land of Britain, its Use and Misuse by L. Dudley Stamp. Published by Longmans Green & Co. Ltd 1947.

British Grasses by S F Armstrong. Published by Cambridge University Press 1917.

Britain's Structure and Scenery by L. Dudley Stamp. Published by Collins 1947.

The World of the Soil by Sir E. John Russell. Published by Collins 1957.

The Soil by B. Davis, N. Walker, D. Ball & A. Fitter. Published by Collins 1992.

Grasses, Ferns, Mosses and Lichens of Great Britain by Roger Phillips. Published by Pan Books 1980.

Rocks Minerals & Fossils of the World by Chris Pellant. Published by Pan Books 1990.

Field Guide to the Insects of Britain by Michael Chinnery. Published by Collins 1972.

Grasses Sedges Rushes and Ferns by R. & A. Fitter. Published by Collins 1984.

Grasses by Dr Jaromir Stolfa. Published by Hamlyn 1978.

Grasses by C. E. Hubbard. Published by Penguin 1954.

An Insect Book for the Pocket by Edmund Sandars. Published by Oxford University Press 1946.

A History of Golf in Britain by many authorities. Published by Cassell & Co. 1952.

Real Golf by Eddie Park. Published by A. Quick & Co. 1990.

Golf Course Management & Construction by James C. Balogh & Wm. Walker. Published by Lewis Publishers 1992.

Golf Course Turf and Design by Claude Crockford. Published by Thos. Wolveridge & Assoc. 1993.

A History of Golf by Robert Browning Published by J. M. Dent & Son 1955.

A Practical Guide to the Ecological Management of a Golf Course by R. S. Taylor. Published by BIGGA/STRI 1995.

Sands for Golf Course Construction & Maintenance by S. W. Baker. Published by STRI 1990.

Health and Safety on Golf Courses, Management and Maintenance. Anon. Published by Health and Safety Executive Books 1994.

Management of Turfgrass Diseases by J. M. Vargas Jnr. Published by CRC Press 1994.

Fungal Diseases of Turf Grass by J. Drew Smith. Published by STRI 1959/1965.

Turf Grass Pests and Diseases by Neil A. Baldwin. Published by STRI 1990.

Practical Lawncraft by R. B. Dawson. Published by Crosby Lockwood 1939/revised 1959.

Pests Diseases and Disorders by Stefan Bucjacki and Keith Harris. Published by Collins 1981.

Weed Control Handbook by J. Fryer & R. Makepeace. Published by Blackwell Scientific Publications 1958 (regularly updated).

Living Together by Dr Anne-Maria Brennan. Published by the English Golf Union 1996.

An Environmental Strategy for Golf in Britain by David Stubbs. Published by the European Golf Association 1996.

USGA Green Section Specification for a Method of Putting Green Construction. Published by the USGA 1960 (regularly updated).

A Moment on the Earth by Gregg Easterbrook. Published by Penguin Books 1996.

The Grass Crop by Dr William Davies. Published by Thanet Press 1952.

Lawns for Sports by Reginald Beale. Published by Simpkin, Marshall, Hamilton, Kent & Co., Ltd 1924.

Compendium of Turfgrass Diseases, Published by the American Phytopathological Society.

Golf Architecture by Alister Mackenzie. First published 1932, republished Grant Books 1982.

Golf Has Never Failed Me by Donald Ross. Published by Sleeping Bear Press 1996.

Classic Golf Links of Great Britain and Ireland by Donald Steel. Published by Chapmans Publishers Ltd. 1992.

Book of the Links by Martin Sutton. Published by W. H. Smith & Son 1912.

Early Golf by Steven J. H. van Hengel. Published by the author 1982.

Index

aeration 76, 102
   depth of 103, 108
   how often 102
   opponents of 89
   shallow 93
Agrostis 147
Agrostics canina 151
Agrostics castellana 150
Agrostics palustris x 151
Agrostics stolonifera 151
Agrostics tenuis 150
Aira praecox 148
alders 257
algal growth 258
Alison, Hugh 23
ameliorating materials 91
ammonia 36, 72
analysis techniques 208
annual dressings 79
anthracnose 160, 164, 165
anthropomorphism 245
approaches, irrigation coverage 133
arc of spray 132
ash 260
authority to direct 228
Auto Certes 114
Auto-Turfman 98
Autocrat 101, 104, 105

bad specifications 202
badgers 181
bills of quantities 200
biological control products 176
birch 248
blinding material 210
blood, application of 36, 72
Board of Greenkeeping Research 40
bore holes 137
bracken 254
Braid, James 23

Braid's trademarks 205
brushing of greens 121
Buckner 128
Budding, Edwin 112
bulrush 259
bunker faces
   earth walled 222
   of turf 222
buryvator 219

casting earthworm, the worst pest 186
Certes 113
chafers 183, 184
changing/drying/washing/toilet area 236
chemical analyses 62, 65, 66, 262
chemical criteria 65
Chlordane 186
claims for extras, submission of 201
clays 57
co-existence 242
cocoa waste 213
Cocksfoot 155
colour 41, 43, 124, 134, 141, 145
Colt, Harry 23
communicating with key staff 228
compaction 103
competitive quotations, importance of 131
compost, mushroom 82
conifers 256
conservation is not preservation 241
consistent policy 86
contour drainage 196
contoured greens 130
controlled irrigation 158
Corticium 145
course closure, decision 181
courses, number of in Britain 13
Crenshaw, Ben 27
Culbin Sands 81
Cynosurus cristatus 148

Dactylis glomerata 149
dangerous incidents 230
Darwin, Bernard 17
Dawson, B. R. 40, 78, 79
decontamination 236
dew ponding 126
dew ponds 93
disease, diagnosis of 160
divert the traffic 253
drag mats 88
drains
　early history of 190
　perforated, size of 214
　tile 191
dried blood 71
drought 42, 69
dry patch 160, 172
Dunn, Old Willie 19
Dursban 184

early hair grass 155
earth walled bunker faces 222
earthworms 55, 57, 58, 75
　casting 186
　most promising line of attack 187
education of members 134
extermination, a balanced view 185

Fairways, irrigation of 133
fairy rings 169
falls 193, 194
Farrar, Guy 98
felling of planted (coniferous) woodland 249
fen peats 211, 212
Ferguson, Harry 104
Fernie, Willie 19
ferreting 178
fertilisers
　nitrogen 64, 66, 69, 76
　nitrogen only 38, 39
　phosphatic 38, 39, 42
　slow release nitrogen 71
Festuca 147

Festuca species 152
F. ovina 152
F. pratensis 152
F. rubra 152
fever fly grubs 183, 185
Field woodrush 156
floor drains 236
Flymo 113
four M's 247
Fowler, Herbert 23
foxes 181
　urban 242
fungicides 239
　systemic 164
fusarium patch 145, 159, 160, 161, 162,

gear-driven heads 132
geotextile membranes 202, 209
golf course is divided by a road 231
golf, number of courses in Britain 13
good greenkeeping practice 239
gorse 252
grass,
　desirable species of 146
　five major diseases of 160
　identification of 143, 147
　undesirable species of 146
grasses
　number of 143
　other 155
"Green is not great" 44, 124
Greenkeepers Training Committee 234
Greenkeeping Station 40
greens, brushing of 121
grid system 207
grooming 118
grooming reels 119
growth herbicides 157

Hackett, Norman 39, 67
hand-pushed machines 117
Hawtree, Fred 23
hazard spotting 230
Health and Safety at Work Act 226

Index

heavy sanding 77
heeling and raking 217
herbicides 239
herring bone system 207
Himalayan balsam 248
hit by a golf ball 232
Holcus lanatus 148
hollow tining, problems with 95
honorary secretary 227
hoof and horn 36, 71, 72
horticultural waste 213
hot spots, identifying 232
hover mower 113
humus 88
hydraulic conductivity 208

IBDU 72
identifying hot spots 232
identity of employer 227
Integrated disease management 161
iron 36, 39, 72, 157
iron sulphate 163
irrigation performance specifications 131

Jones, Bobby 24

lakes dyed 243
land, unstable 60
lawyers 201
lead arsenate 186
leatherjackets 183
Lehman, Tom 29
levelling
    by top dressing 81
    laser beam 193
Leyland cypress 257
Libbey, Richard 40
lime 74, 75, 77
limestone 210
liming 42, 74, 75
liquid iron 163
litigation 200, 201, 202
Lloyds of Letchworth 117
Lloyds Paladin 114

loam soils 56
local soils 210
Locke, Bobby 125
Lolium perenne 147
Lolium species 154
Low, John 30
lump chalk 210

Mackenzie, Dr Alister 23, 25, 67
main line PVC 131
maintenance records 238
Man, most important animal 246
management plan 247
marram and sea lyme 252
materials, right sources of 208
Micklem, Gerald 30
moisture retention 206
mole ploughs 195
Moles 182
montmorillonite clays 83, 91
mower
    first 19" roller mounted 112
    first mains electricity mower 113
    hover 113
    triplex 115
mowing
    frequency of 122
    height 120
Murphy's Law 202
Murray, Dr C. M. 39
mushroom compost 82
mycelium 162

Netherlands 11, 12, 210
notices 236
NPK 40, 68, 73, 76, 127, 178, 209, 259

open ditch, the best drain 189
outfall, find an 199
over-watering 44, 125
"Over-watering is the cardinal sin of greenkeeping" 124
Overgreen 114

Park, Willie, Jnr. 19
particle shape 56, 85, 87
particle size 56, 86, 206
Paul Fork 95
peaty land, the draining of 198
Pencross 151
performance standards 204
pest, definition of 177
pH 75, 167
pH values 52
Phleum pratense 148
phosphates 72
pink snow mould 162
pipework 131
Poa 147
P. annua 154
P. bulbosa 154
P. nemoralis 154
Poa species 153
P. pratensis 153
P. trivialis 154
pollution, worst 246
pop-ups
   abused 129
   automatic 127
   positioning 129
   prone to abuse 126
   system design 130
   the choice 128
poplars 257
priority 232
pure sand greens 70, 75, 209
putting greens, watering 127
PVC 192

qualified ecologist 247

rabbits 38, 177-8, 253
   fencing 179
   scalds 36
   urine 177
Radko, Al 44, 124
raking seed in 220
Ransomes of Ipswich 112, 113

recycled garden and horticultural waste 213
Reedmace 259
reservoirs 135
responsible for inspecting 231
rest room 236
revetting 221, 223
Rhododendron ponticum 256
rhododendrons 248
rig and furrow land 189
right of way, golfer or greenkeeper? 229
risk assessments 230
rolling 120
root zone materials 210, 215
Ross, Donald 23, 25
Ross, Mackenzie 23
Royal North Devon Golf Club 14
running sand 198
rushes and sedges 156

S.T.R.I. 40, 63, 68
safe working practices 234
Safety Policy, Statement of 226, 227
samples 204
sands, fine and very fine 55
sandstones 210
scarification 118
sea meadow grass 38
sea sands, use of 55
sea lyme 252
sea weed 70, 77
security 236
sedge 211
sedge peat 87
seedling birch and pines 254
sewage sludge 82, 213
shading of greens by trees 255
Shinnecock Hills 29
silage effluent 246
silts and clays 55
Simpson, Tom 23, 68, 155, 217
Stapledon, Professor George, Sir 44, 47
Sisis 97, 101
siting the club house 59
slitting 95, 109

Index

smile drain 214
smothering 163, 224
soils
    loam 56
    local 210
soot 39, 71
specifications 200
speed of putting surface 120
sphagnum peat 79, 87, 88, 211, 212
spruce 256
squidge 82, 174
SSSI 245
St. Andrews 127, 134
St. Andrews, secret of greens 81
Stimpmeter 121
stone-picking machines 219
succession 241
Sulphate of ammonia 70, 157
Sulphate of iron 70, 82
sulphates of ammonia 71, 72
supervision, importance of 203
surface alkalinity 163
susceptible 168
Sutton, Martin 31
swales 196
sycamores 251, 257, 260

take-all patch disease 160, 166
Taylor, Bob 29
tees, irrigation coverage 133
thatch 91, 92
    as a food source 171
    effect on the playing qualities 171
    formation 92
    three choices for control 172
thatch fungi 160, 170
Thomson, Peter 28, 33
Timothy 155
tines
    types of 94
    solid, the problem with 94
Toadrush 156

top dressing 39, 43, 44, 76
    ideal material 84
    quality of 86
    reasons for 80
    shape and size of the particles 84
topping heather 254
trace elements 51
track record, importance of checking 225
travelling sprinklers 139
tree roots 198
tree surgery 255
trenchers, narrow slit 205
trenching 132
Trevino, Lee 29
triplex mowers 115

underpinning knowledge 234
United States Department of Agriculture 54
unsatisfactory species 248
unstable land 60
urea 72

USGA Green Section 44, 54, 124, 206, 207, 209
Verti-Drains 39, 83, 91, 94, 101, 105, 202, 209
verticut reels 119

waste, recycled garden and horticultural 213
water lilies 259
water
    function of 140
    injecting 106
    quality 134
weeds 146, 156
well points 198
wetting agents 170, 173
white poplars 251
willows 257
woodland, felling of 249
Woolhouse, Professor H.W. 244
worm casts 157
worst pollution 246